Contents

Trail Highlights

West Coast Crayfish Trail   2–3
Cederberg Heritage Route   4–5
Postberg Wild Flower Trail   6–7
Hoerikwaggo Tented Classic   8–9
Boland Hiking Trail   10–11
Whale Trail (De Hoop)   12–13
Swellendam Hiking Trail   14–15
Oystercatcher Trail   16–17
Swartberg Hiking Trail   18–19
Otter & Tsitsikamma Trails   20–21

Atlas Section, Western Cape

Keyplan & legend   22–23
Atlas pages   24–31

Trail information & maps

Trail 1   **West Coast Crayfish Trail**   32
Trail 2   **Cederberg Heritage Route**   46
Trail 3   **Postberg Wild Flower Trail**   68
Trail 4   **Hoerikwaggo Tented Classic**   78
Trail 5   **Boland Hiking Trail**   96
Trail 6   **Whale Trail (De Hoop)**   108
Trail 7   **Swellendam Hiking Trail**   120
Trail 8   **Oystercatcher Trail**   136
Trail 9   **Swartberg Hiking Trail**   152
Trail 10   **Donkey Trail**   166
Trail 11   **Otter Trail**   174
Trail 12   **Tsitsikamma Trail**   174
Green Flag Trails Information   197
General Kit List   202
Outdoor Gear Retailers   204

Local kids

DAY 3 We popped in to peep at the Muisbosskerm

Muisbosskerm

DAY 3 We could of this walk witho shoes!

DAY 1 Children of the white mussel gatherers

DAY 2 Tannie Burger's farm breakfast

Die Plaaskombuis at Steenbokfontein

STADIG

DIE PLAASKOMBUIS

TRAIL HIGHLIGHTS

DAY 3 Swimming in the tidal pool, Lambert's Bay

DAY 4 Long, white beaches

Lambert's Bay fishing

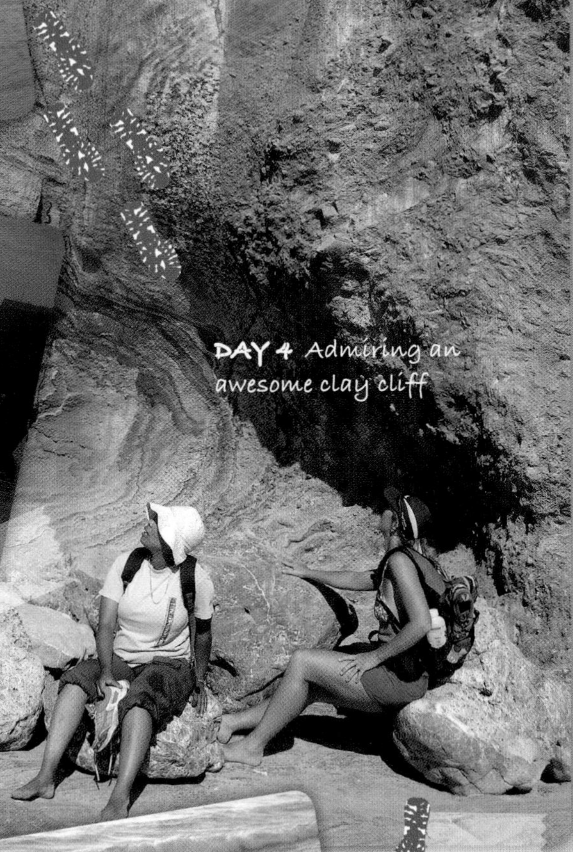

DAY 4 Admiring an awesome clay cliff

DAY 4 Clay on my face!

Gannet

Tossed our shoes

DAY 1 First night's stop in Clanwilliam

DAY 2 Ochre-coloured rock paintings

Weathered formations on Forr

Living landscape project

On top of Krakadouw

DAY 3

Mind-blowing view from Krakadouw

Krakadouw

Krakadouw sunri

TRAIL HIGHLIGHTS

DAY 4 Cool Cave

Boulder-hopping the Grasvlei River

Weathered cedar tree

Brugkraal

DAY 5 Lunch at Boontjieskloof hut

Klein Krakadouw Trail

Wuppertal shoes

DAY 2 Hold on tight!

TRAIL 2 CEDERBERG HERITAGE ROUTE

DAY 2 16 Mile Beach

DAY 2 Wreckage of the Pantelis A Lemos that sank in 1978

Deserted ostrich egg nest in dunes near 16 Mile Beach

Coastal vegetation near the Pantelis A Lemos shipwreck

Washed up bits of the wreck

DAY 1 Plankies

Loos at Plankies Bay

TRAIL HIGHLIGHTS

Turn off 16 Mile Beach onto the dunes

DAY 1 Room with a view – camping at Plankies Bay

Before 16 Mile Beach

Carpet of flowers at Konstabelkop

Coastal scenery

Houseboats on the Langebaan Lagoon

Do's and Don'ts

West Coast National Park

South African NATIONAL PARKS

Gate times:
April - August: 07:00 to 19:00
September - March: 07:00 to 19:00

Marine protected area: Tsaarsbank & 16 Mile beach

TOILET

Sundowner at Plankies Bay

Angulate tortoise

TRAIL 3   POSTBERG WILD FLOWER TRAIL

8

DAY 1 Exploring the entrance to the Woodhead Tunnel

Watsonia

DAY 4 Disa Gorge

DAY 1 Between Slangkop and Signal Schools

DAY 4 Woodhead Dam wall

DAY 1 View from the Blockhouse at Kommetjie

Blockhouse

DAY 1 Slangkop camp

TRAIL HIGHLIGHTS

DAY 3 Orange Kloof ablutions made of recycled wood

DAY 3 Orange Kloof tented camp

DAY 2 Silvermine tented camp

DAY 3 Indigenous forest Orange Kloof

Slangkop Lighthouse at dusk

DAY 2 Hout Bay seen from Chapman's Peak

DAY 2 Climbing wall at Silvermine

TRAIL 4 HOERIKWAGGO TENTED CLASSIC

DAY 2 Hikers near Boesmanskloof

Breathtaking views between Landdroskop and Jonkershoek

DAY 1 Clear signage a blessing

DAY 1 Space

LANDDROSKOP
SHAMROCK
SPHINX

Scenery between Landdroskop an Jonkershoek – to

Pro

Bedroom at Boesmanskloof Hut

Lichen

Optional walk from Landdroskop to Jonkershoek

DAY 3 Bridge Boesmanskloof to Nuweberg

DAY 3 Typical fynbos

TRAIL HIGHLIGHTS

HIKING TRAIL
PALMIET
VOETSLAANPAD

DAY 1 Leaving Nuweberg

DAY 2 Above the suspension bridge

BOEGOEKLOOF
SUICIDE START 2km
BOEGOEKLOOF 1km
ALOE RIDGE

After the suspension bridge crossing

...egoekloof

Waterfall and pool
on Boegoekloof section

SUICIDE GORGE

DAY 2 Kloofing
on canyon trip for
adrenalin junkies

Crystal pool
to refresh the soul

TRAIL 5   BOLAND HIKING TRAIL

DAY 1 Views from the big hill after leaving Potberg

DAY 5

DE HOOP NATURE RESERVE

SCATTER YOUR MEMORIES

NOT YOUR LITTER

DAY 3 Soon after leaving Noetsie

DAY 1 The summit

DAY 3 Stilgat cave

Cupidoskraal hut

DAY 2 Crossing near dam

DAY 2 Noetsie Camp

Fynbos

TRAIL HIGHLIGHTS

DAY 3 Sand dunes at Hamerkop

DAY 5 Ruin past Vaalkrans

DAY 4 Cliffs and shelves at low tide

DAY 4 Rock pools

DAY 4 Chilling at Vaalkrans

DAY 4 Early start

Bontebok

DAY 4 Rugged rocks and awesome rock pools

TRAIL 6 WHALE TRAIL (DE HOOP)

DAY 1 Arangieskop Trail – looking up to 1850 m beacon

Arangieskop Trail hut

DAY 2 Goedgeloof huts

Glenstream hut

DAY 3 Soaking up the sun

DAY 3 Protea Valley hut

DAY 1 Indigenous forest shortly after leaving reserve camp

DAY 4 Ventersbank view

DAY 1 Rivers after rain – treacherous crossing

TRAIL HIGHLIGHTS

DAY 2 Trail above Goedgeloof huts

DAY 5 Stream in forest

DAY 2 Leaving Boskloof

DAY 3 Protea Valley hut

DAY 5 Erica in bloom

DAY 4 Between Protea Valley hut and Nooitgedacht

DAY 6 Indigenous forest early on trail

DAY 5 Wolfkloof hut

DAY 6 River crossing between Wolfkloof and reserve camp

TRAIL 7 SWELLENDAM HIKING TRAIL

Optional day hike:
Summit of Cradock Peak

Garden Route Trail

Hunter Gatherer Trail

Drive from Gouritz
River Mouth to
Sandpiper cottages
at Sunset

DAY 2 Cape St Blaize Cave

DAY 2 Passing the
Pinnacle Point golf course

DAY 2 Aloes on St Blaize Trail

DAY 3
Washed up
hippo sculpture

TRAIL HIGHLIGHTS

DAY 1 Sandpiper cottages
Boggoms Bay

Hand tool

Fossilised trees
near midden

Dolphin fossil

DAY 3 Kanon Dunes

DAY 2 St Blaize Trail

DAY 4 Optional accommodation
Dune House

Oystercatchers

TRAIL 8   OYSTERCATCHER TRAIL

BOTHASHOEK -12.8 KM>
DE HOEK 21.2 >
GOUEKRANS - 27.9 KM>

View from Gouekrans back to De Hoek

DAY 3 The Neck (Nek) Swartberg Pass

DAY 3 Ou Tol

DAY 2 Peaks crossed heading from Bothashoek to Ou Tol

DAY 1 View out of Bothashoek hut

DAY 3 Ou Tol

DAY 1 Up valley from De Hoek

Proteas

Donkey Trail aloes

DAY 4

TRAIL HIGHLIGHTS

DAY 1 Donkey Trail – Living Waters Mountain estate farmhouse

DAY 1 Donkey Trail

AY 4 Gouekrans hut th rock

chashoek hut

DAY 1 Donkey Trail – Wyenek camp

DAY 2 Donkey Trail – Skull-like rock

Mountain biking Swartberg Pass

DAY 1 Otter Trail – Storms River chalets in sea mist

Otter Trail – Bloukrans River mouth

Otter Trail – crossing Bloukrans River

Otter Trail

Otter Trail

Evening on Otter Trail

DAY 1 Storms River Mouth – start of Otter Trail

Otter Trail

Otter Trail hut

TRAIL HIGHLIGHTS

Tsitsikamma Trail – view from Bloukrans

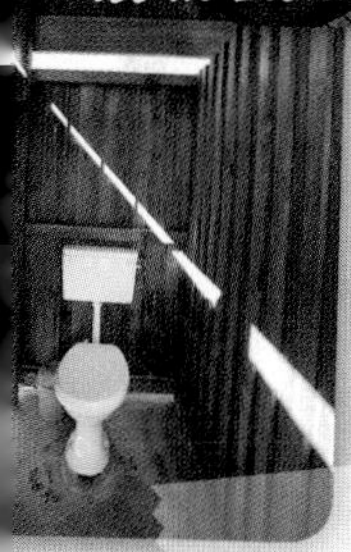

DAY 3 Tsitsikamma Trail – tree ferns near Keurbos

DAY 2 Tsitsikamma Trail – loo at Bloukrans hut

DAY 5 Tsitsikamma Trail – between Heuningbos and Sleepkloof

Awesome spider's nest

DAY 4 Tsitsikamma Trail – flowers lining stream near Heuningbos

DAY 4 Tsitsikamma Trail – waterfall below Heuningbos

DAY 2 Tsitsikamma Trail – inviting pool

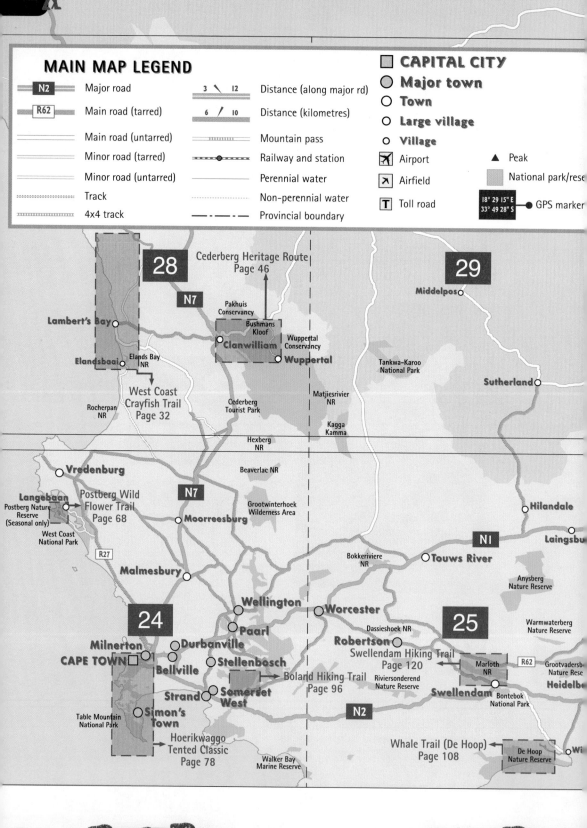

MAIN MAP LEGEND

N2	Major road	
R62	Main road (tarred)	
	Main road (untarred)	
	Minor road (tarred)	
	Minor road (untarred)	
	Track	
	4x4 track	

3 \ 12	Distance (along major rd)
6 / 10	Distance (kilometres)
	Mountain pass
	Railway and station
	Perennial water
	Non-perennial water
	Provincial boundary

- ⬛ **CAPITAL CITY**
- ⬤ **Major town**
- ◯ **Town**
- ◦ **Large village**
- ∘ **Village**
- ✈ Airport
- ⇗ Airfield
- T Toll road

- ▲ Peak
- National park/rese
- 18° 29 15" E / 33° 49 28" S ● GPS marker

28 Cederberg Heritage Route Page 46

N7

Pakhuis Conservancy

Bushmans Kloof

Clanwilliam

Wuppertal Conservancy

Lambert's Bay

Elandsbaai

Elands Bay NR

West Coast Crayfish Trail Page 32

Rocherpan NR

Cederberg Tourist Park

Wuppertal

Matjiesrivier NR

Kagga Kamma

Hexberg NR

29 Middelpos

Tankwa-Karoo National Park

Sutherland

Beaverlac NR

Vredenburg

Langebaan

Postberg Nature Reserve (Seasonal only)

Postberg Wild Flower Trail Page 68

N7

Moorreesburg

Grootwinterhoek Wilderness Area

West Coast National Park

R27

Malmesbury

Bokkeriviere NR

Touws River

N1 Laingsbu

Hilandale

Anysberg Nature Reserve

Wellington

Paarl

Worcester

Dassieshoek NR

25

Warmwaterberg Nature Reserve

24

Milnerton

CAPE TOWN

Durbanville

Bellville

Stellenbosch

Robertson

Swellendam Hiking Trail Page 120

Marloth NR

R62 Grootvadersb Nature Rese

Strand

Somerset West

Boland Hiking Trail Page 96

Riviersonderend Nature Reserve

Swellendam

Heidelb

Bontebok National Park

Simon's Town

Table Mountain National Park

N2

Hoerikwaggo Tented Classic Page 78

Walker Bay Marine Reserve

Whale Trail (De Hoop) Page 108

De Hoop Nature Reserve

Wi

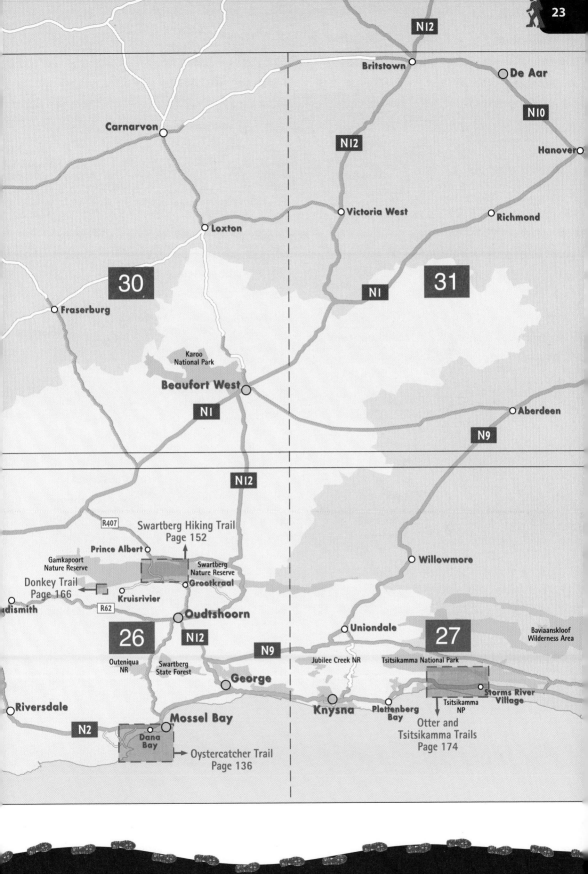

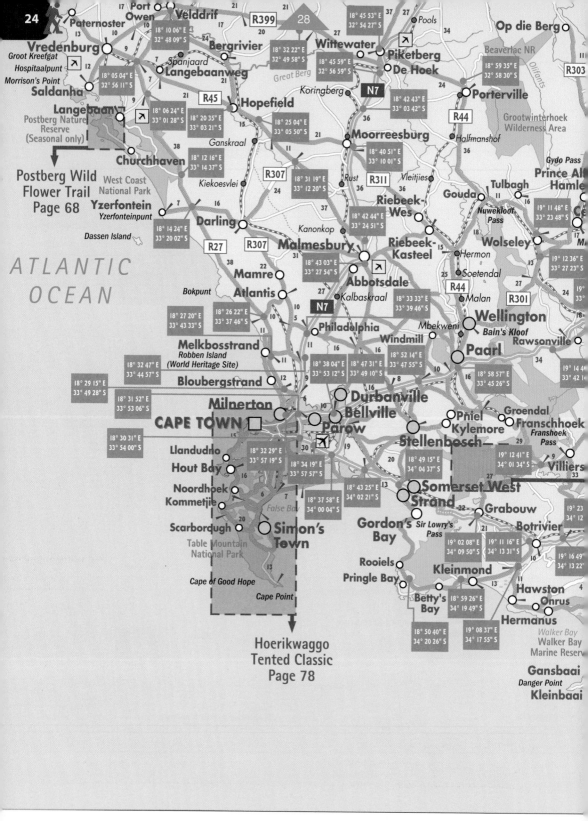

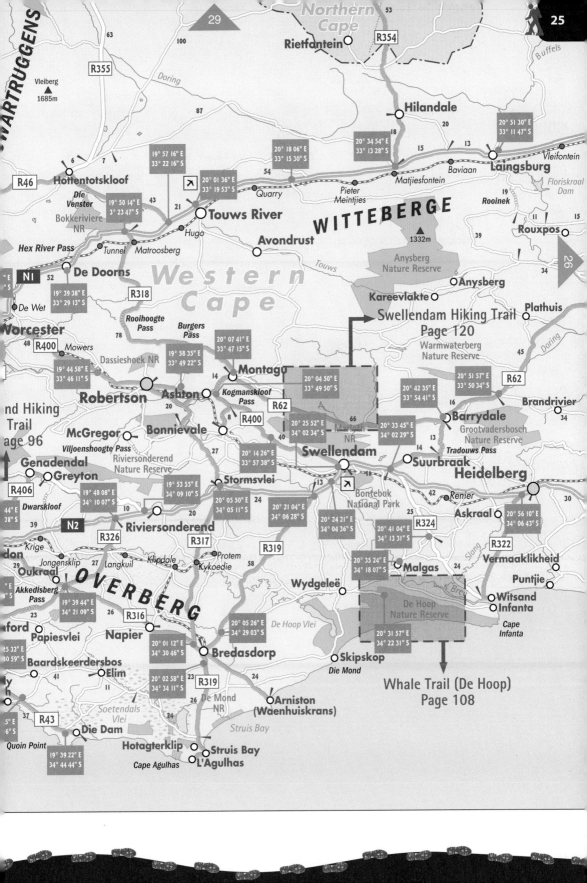

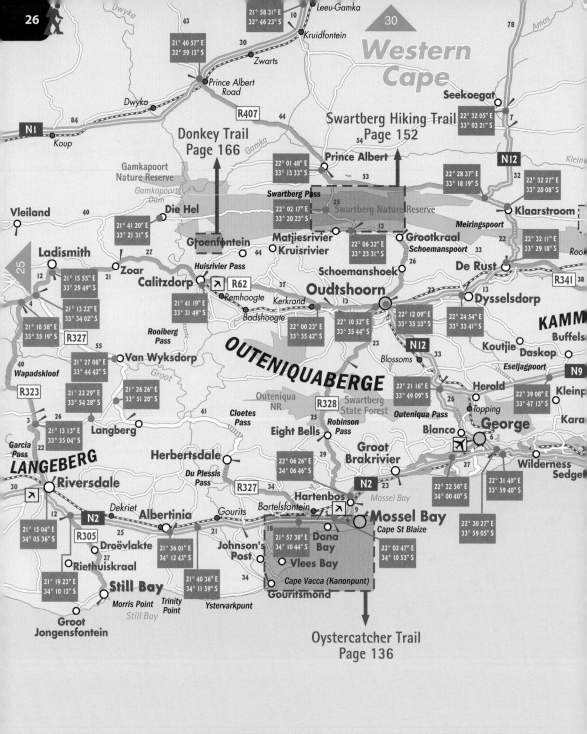

Western Cape

Donkey Trail
Page 166

Swartberg Hiking Trail
Page 152

Oystercatcher Trail
Page 136

Leeu-Gamka

21° 58 31" E
32° 46 23" S

Kruidfontein

21° 40 57" E
32° 59 13" S

Zwarts

Prince Albert Road

Dwyka

Koup

N1

Seekoegat

22° 32 05" E
33° 03 21" S

R407

Gamka

Gamkapoort Nature Reserve

Gamkapoort Dam

Die Hel

Vleiland

Ladismith

21° 41 20" E
33° 21 31" S

Groenfontein

Prince Albert

22° 01 48" E
33° 13 33" S

Swartberg Pass

22° 02 17" E
33° 20 23" S

Swartberg Nature Reserve

22° 28 37" E
33° 18 19" S

N12

Klaarstroom

22° 32 27" E
33° 20 08" S

Meiringspoort

Matjiesrivier

Kruisrivier

22° 06 32" E
33° 23 31" S

Schoemanshoek

Grootkraal

Schoemanspoort

De Rust

22° 32 11" E
33° 29 18" S

R341

Rool

Zoar

Calitzdorp

Huisrivier Pass

R62

Remhoogte

Kerkrand

Badshoogte

Oudtshoorn

22° 00 23" E
33° 35 42" S

22° 10 52" E
33° 35 44" S

Dysselsdorp

22° 24 54" E
33° 33 41" S

KAMM

Buffels

Daskop

N9

Koutjie

22° 12 09" E
33° 35 33" S

N12

Blossoms

Eseljagpoort

21° 15 55" E
33° 29 49" S

21° 13 22" E
33° 34 02" S

21° 10 58" E
33° 35 19" S

R327

Van Wyksdorp

21° 27 08" E
33° 44 42" S

Wapadskloof

R323

Groot

21° 22 29" E
33° 54 28" S

21° 26 26" E
33° 51 20" S

Rooiberg Pass

OUTENIQUABERGE

Outeniqua NR

Cloetes Pass

R328

Swartberg State Forest

Outeniqua Pass

22° 21 16" E
33° 49 09" S

Herold

Topping

22° 39 08" E
33° 47 15" S

Kleinp

Kara

George

22° 31 40" E
33° 59 40" S

Wilderness

Sedge

Blanco

Garcia Pass

LANGEBERG

Langberg

21° 13 13" E
33° 55 04" S

Herbertsdale

Du Plessis Pass

Eight Bells

Robinson Pass

Groot Brakrivier

22° 06 26" E
34° 06 46" S

22° 22 58" E
34° 00 40" S

22° 30 27" E
33° 59 05" S

Riversdale

Dekriet

Albertinia

Gourits

Bartelsfontein

Hartenbos

R327

Mossel Bay

Cape St Blaize

Mossel Bay

22° 02 47" E
34° 10 53" S

N2

21° 15 04" E
34° 05 36" S

R305

Droëvlakte

21° 36 01" E
34° 12 43" S

Johnson's Post

21° 57 38" E
34° 10 44" S

Dana Bay

Vlees Bay

Riethuiskraal

21° 19 23" E
34° 10 13" S

Still Bay

21° 40 36" E
34° 11 59" S

Morris Point

Trinity Point

Ystervarkpunt

Cape Vacca (Kanonpunt)

Gouritsmond

Groot Jongensfontein

Still Bay

Dwyka

Amos

Klein

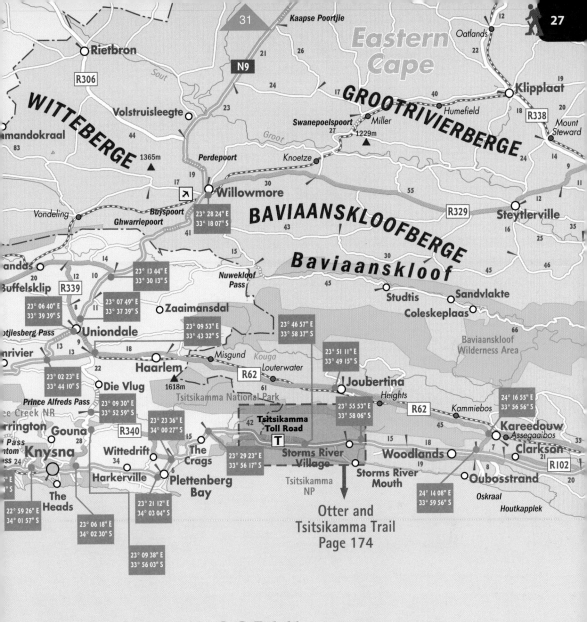

31

Kaapse Poortjie

Eastern Cape

Rietbron

Oatlands

12

22

19

Klipplaat

N9

R306

R338

Mount Steward

20

18

40

Humefield

Swanepoelspoort

Miller

27

1229m

GROOTRIVIERBERGE

17

24

14

9

11

Volstruisleegte

44

23

Groot

55

amandokraal

83

Sout

21

26

24

Perdepoort

Knoetze

30

Willowmore

12

Steytlerville

Vondeling

Buyspoort

Ghwarriepoort

17

19

R329

BAVIAANSKLOOFBERGE

23° 28 24" E
33° 18 07" S

41

43

16

35

35

45

Baviaanskloof

15

Nuwekloof
Pass

30

45

Studtis

Sandvlakte

46

Coleskeplaas

Baviaanskloof
Wilderness Area

66

andas

14

23° 13 44" E
33° 30 13" S

20

12

10

R339

8

23° 07 49" E
33° 37 39" S

Zaaimansdal

23° 46 57" E
33° 58 37" S

23° 51 11" E
33° 49 15" S

23° 06 40" E
33° 39 39" S

11

Buffelsklip

23° 09 53" E
33° 43 32" S

otjiesberg Pass

Uniondale

9

18

Misgund

Kouga

Louterwater

Joubertina

nrivier

13

22

Haarlem

R62

Heights

Kammiebos

23° 55 53" E
33° 58 06" S

24° 16 55" E
33° 56 56" S

23° 02 23" E
33° 44 10" S

23° 09 30" E
33° 52 59" S

1618m

Tsitsikamma National Park

61

R62

45

Prince Alfreds Pass

ee Creek NR

23° 23 36" E
34° 00 27" S

42

Tsitsikamma Toll Road

15

18

Kareedouw

24° 14 08" E
33° 59 56" S

rrington

Gouna

R340

T

Woodlands

19

Assegaaibos

Clarkson

21

Pass

28

Wittedrift

34

The
Crags

23° 29 23" E
33° 56 17" S

**Storms River
Village**

15

7

8

Knysna

Harkerville

Plettenberg
Bay

Tsitsikamma
NP

**Storms River
Mouth**

Oubosstrand

R102

20

The
Heads

6

22° 59 26" E
34° 01 57" S

23° 21 12" E
34° 03 04" S

**Otter and
Tsitsikamma Trail
Page 174**

24° 14 08" E
33° 59 56" S

Oskraal

Houtkapplek

23° 06 18" E
34° 02 30" S

23° 09 38" E
33° 56 03" S

INDIAN OCEAN

N7

Ottaspoort
18° 07 01" E
30° 48 32" S

Grootberg
1022m

BOKKEVELDBERGE

R355

5

Groen   Swart Doring
Rooiwalspoort
R358

Kotzesrus
Lepelsfontein

Rietpoort
Bitterfontein
18° 16 09" E
31° 02 27" S
Graafwater

Western
Cape

778m

R357

75

Komkans
Paddagat

17

Nuwerus
18° 21 39" E
31° 08 40" S

R363

18° 31 47" E
31° 13 47" S

Sout

Brandkop

Waterklip
46

Nieuwoudtvill

Landplaas
Landplaas

66

19° 06 30" E
31° 22 11" S

54
34
20

Kliphoek
Koekenaap
Lutzville

Skaapvlei

Blinkwater
Bay
Geustyn se Gat

N7

Vanrhyns
Pass

R27
49

18° 43 45" E
31° 36 28" S

Vanrhynsdorp
Urionskraal

58
24
R3

Lutzville
23

Lossand
Vredendal

25

Cederberg Heritage Trail
Page 46

35

Papendorp
Strandfontein
Doringbaai

R362
18° 20 40" E
31° 33 34" S

31

Spruitdrif

R362
22

Klawer
18° 38 11" E
31° 46 45" S

Doring

Botterk

1

18° 14 32" E
31° 49 16" S

Kanon Point
Rooidbinpunt
(Cape Donkin)

47

Vaalvlei
59 Kleipan

Trawal

18° 37 58" E
31° 53 12" S

Doringbos
R364
54

18° 25 48" E
31° 51 19" S

Heerenlogement

38

19° 07 38" E
32° 03 56" S

Bushmans
Kloof
Pakhuis Pass

Biedouwvalle

West Coast
Crayfish Trail
Page 32

Lambert's Bay
6

18° 34 00" E
32° 00 31" S

Ratelfontein

N7

Wupper
Conserva

18° 28 52" E
32° 13 13" S

16

Graafwater
R364
29

Clanwilliam
19° 12 56" E
32° 16 30" S

Kouberg Pass

Walfhuis
Kreefbaai

27
10

Leipoldtville

14

18° 52 06" E
32° 10 23" S

Nieuwoudt
Pass

Wuppertal

Cederberg
Wilderness Area

Elandsbaai
Baboon Point

Elands Bay
N R

Sandberg

R365

18° 56 21" E
32° 21 50" S

Uitkyk Pass

19° 03 22" E
32° 22 23" S

52

Cederberg
Tourist Park

Sneeuberg
2027m

Ceder

ATLANTIC
OCEAN

28

Noordkuil

27

26

Paleisheuwel

18

Het Kruis

Hex

Redelinghuys
Rocherpan
NR

Dwarskersbos

28

18° 44 58" E
32° 36 24" S

Droeryskloof

Piekeniers-
kloof

Citrusdal
19° 15 3
32° 30 1

Middelberg
Pass

The Baths

Stompneuspunt
Stompneus Bay

Dwarskersbos
St Helena Bay

18° 27 59" E
32° 43 15" S

Aurora

22

Eendekuil
18

18° 56 57" E
32° 37 36" S

R365

40

Riet
se Vloer

Brandboom

R357

Swartkolkvloer

Northern
Cape

R27   R353

Blomberg
se Vloer

8

Sakrivier

Tontelbos

R353

eriesfontein

44   Bodam

77

Oumuur

Sak

HANTAMSBERG

81

Vlakhoeksberg

1530m

36

Moordenaarspoort

Swawel

Stuurman

27

R27   Kootjieskolk

Koosdrif

Hoedjies

Blousyfer

Snykolk

Walkraal

Williston

Petrusville

R353

R63

68

51

Calvinia   Downes

36   16   7

Dorlogskloof

Keiskie se Poort

48

Quaggasfontein Poort

51

30

Bloukrans Pass

R354

Bloukrans

R355

Matjieskloof

15

Belgravia

Fish

34

Snyderspoort

22

Middelpos

23

30

pankraal

Die Bos
15   43

Oupoort

39

Danielskuil

R356

Van Wyksvlei

56

Oupoort

R354

Tankwa

669m

ROGGEVELDBERGE

1735m

Rooipoort

11

Sutherland

Bloupoort

20° 39 41" E
32° 23 39" S

weefontein

70

Tankwa–Karoo
National Park

Oudebaaskraal
Dam

Onder-
Wadrif

81

Bo-Wadrif

20° 48 01" E
32° 24 35" S

Rooikloof

39

Verlatekloof

Komsberg Pass

1721m

srivier

Amandelnek

24

R354

KOMSBERGE

53

Kagga
Kamma

Gansfontein

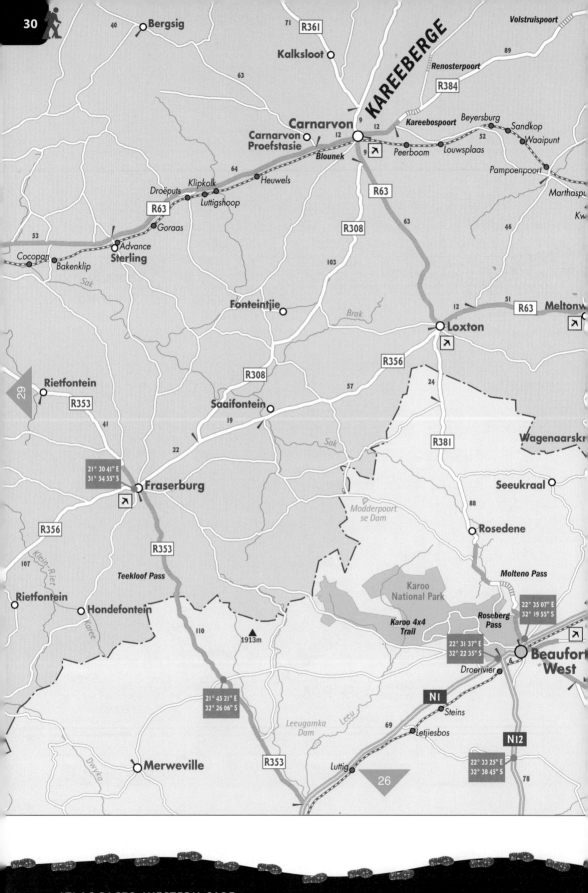

TRAIL 1

West Coast Crayfish Trail

West Coast Crayfish Trail

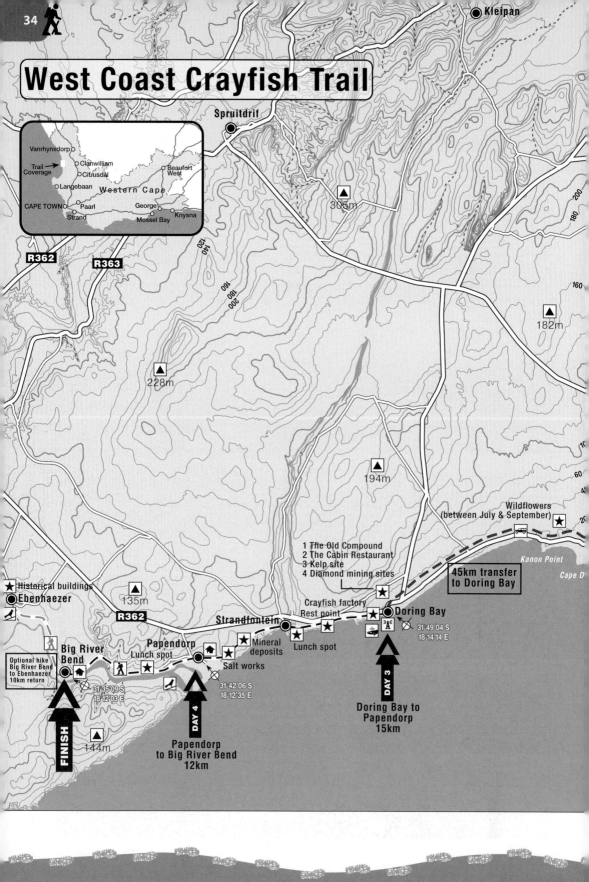

Kleipan

Spruitdrif

Vanrhynsdorp ○
Trail Coverage →
○ Clanwilliam
○ Citrusdal
○ Beaufort West
Western Cape
CAPE TOWN ○
○ Paarl
○ Langebaan
○ Strand
○ George
○ Mossel Bay
○ Knysna

R362
R363

305m

200
180
160

228m

182m

194m

Wildflowers
(between July & September) ★

Kanon Point

1 The Old Compound
2 The Cabin Restaurant
3 Kelp site
4 Diamond mining sites

45km transfer
to Doring Bay

Cape D

★ Historical buildings
Ebenhaezer ○

135m

Crayfish factory
Rest point

★ Doring Bay
31 49'04 S
18 14'14 E

R362

Strandfontein

Papendorp
Lunch spot

★ Mineral
deposits

Lunch spot

DAY 3
Doring Bay to
Papendorp
15km

Optional hike
Big River Bend
to Ebenhaezer
10km return

Big River Bend

31 35'09 S
18 12'03 E

Salt works

31 42'06 S
18 12'35 E

DAY 4
Papendorp
to Big River Bend
12km

144m

FINISH

TRAIL 1

To N7

R365

Leipoldtville

R364

200
180
160
140

Wolfhuis

402m

151m

336m

161m

120

100

80
60
40

32·09·17 S
18·18·56 E

Boesman
Cave

Kreefbaai

White mussel
harvesting

32·18·38 S
18·20·46 E

Elands Bay Guesthouse

Elands Bay

Vleihuis

Baboon Point

START

Mrs Burger's B&B

Steenbokfontein

Plaaskombuis

Bird Island

Waterfront
Eureka
Flats

White
mussel
harvesting

Lambert's Bay

32·05·39 S
18·18·20 E

DAY 2

Steenbokfontein
to Lambert's Bay
9km

Elands Bay to
Steenbokfontein
18km

1 Post Office
2 Bird Island Restaurant
3 Township lunch
4 Museum
5 Isabella's Restaurant
& Coffee Shop

Muisbosskerm
Open-Air Restaurant

Atlantic Ocean

LEGEND

Hiking	Point of Interest	Index Contour	
Optional Hike	Lighthouse	Contour	
Cycling	Whale Watching	Major Road	
Surf Spot	Post Office	Main Road	
Spot Height	Bird Watching	Other Road	
Accommodation	Homestay	Hiking Trail	
Boating	Fishing	Vehicle Transfer	
Shipwreck	Viewpoint		
Town Spot	4x4 Track / Transport	R777 Route Marker	
Waterfall	River	GPS Points	

WEST COAST CRAYFISH TRAIL

This community-run guided and portaged trail up the Cape's West Coast is both a superb coastal hike and a showcase for grass-roots tourism. The West Coast Crayfish Trail links the communities between the surfing mecca of Elands Bay, a three-hour drive north of Cape Town, and the old 17th-century mission station of Ebenhaezer on the Olifants River. This short stretch of the coast is remarkably diverse, and the trail meanders along empty beaches flanked by white dunes, along rivers, wetlands and saltpans, and takes in a tour of one of the West Coast's most famous sights – Bird Island at Lambert's Bay. The coastal fynbos is beautiful at any time of year but particularly in spring when the veld explodes into a blanket of colour, and, during spring and early summer, whales are often spotted out at sea (don't forget your binoculars). Equally fun is the interaction with the people of the West Coast that you enjoy along the way – the fishermen, white mussel harvesters and your hosts who welcome you into their homes and guesthouses. Although billed as a hiking trail, it's also intended to be a cultural experience – a fascinating insight into life in this remote section of the country.

The 55km five-night trail follows the beach for the first part of the way before heading onto the cliffs at Doring Bay, then heading inland along the Olifants River. Although you hike some 18km on the first day, it's along the beach and not unduly strenuous. In fact, since you can take it slowly and there's always the option of a back-up vehicle if you really struggle, the trail is quite within the capabilities of young, old and unfit hikers. There is also a tented trail option, and the opportunity, if you bring your own mountain bike, to ride the gravel road that runs parallel with the trail. To enjoy this trail to its fullest, go with realistic expectations. The accommodation, like that of the Cederberg Heritage Trail, is in comfortable, but fairly rustic, community guesthouses where your hosts, women from the communities, serve up vast portions of local fare. There are no pretences, so don't expect luxury or sophistication. Rather enjoy the magnificent scenery, the prolific bird life, the wonderful people, rock art and traditions of the West Coast.

DISTANCE 55km	
DAYS 4	
DIFFICULTY MODERATE	
MTB ONE ROUTE – AN ALTERNATIVE TO HIKING ON DAYS 3 AND 4	

66 South Africa's coast is a rich and diverse national asset, a treasure for all to enjoy, and provides a source of opportunity for many South Africans. Our coast is interlinked with tourism, with the coastline attracting thousands of foreign and local tourists to its beaches, which brings socio-economic growth and development to the coastal areas.' 99

Deputy Director-General of DEAT, Dr Monde Mayekiso, at the launch of the West Coast Crayfish Trail

TIDAL POOL NEAR LAMBERT'S BAY

DAY 1 Elands Bay to Steenbokfontein
18km, 5–6 hours

I'd recommend arriving early the day before the trail starts to explore Elands Bay, enjoy a chilly dip, or, if you like to play in the waves, to try a bit of surfing or body surfing at one of South Africa's best-known surfing playgrounds. The drive from Cape Town is delightful, particularly if you turn off the N7 at Piketberg along the picturesque Verlorenvlei, one of the Cape's best-known birding destinations. Most groups are put up in the quaint Vleihuis cottages just on the left as you come into Elands Bay, while larger groups are housed in the private Elands Bay Guesthouse. As you can guess from the name the cottages look out onto the vlei, so you're surrounded by bird life, particularly at dusk and dawn when you'll see all manner of waders as well as spoonbills, pelicans and flamingoes. It's a magical spot. If you have time that afternoon one of the guides will take you up to the nearby cave painting, Bobbejaanberg, high up in the cliffs with a great view out to sea. The cave, which shows evidence of human habitation for the last 15,000 years, is covered with handprints, and if you look closely you'll spot an eland and a large fat-tailed sheep. Dinner is served early

WHITE MUSSEL COLLECTORS' CHILDREN SEEN EN ROUTE

ROASTING CRAYS ON BEACH

The West Coast Crayfish Trail forms a key part of the South–North Tourism Route (SNTR) initiative, a community-based responsible and sustainable tourism route that stretches from Cape Town to Ganigobes in southern Namibia. The route is divided into a number of subroutes, including the Kamieskroon, Hardeveld, Diamond, Nama and Richtersveld routes, with the hiking trail an integral part of the southern Crayfish Route.

The trail, part of the Department of Environmental Affairs and Tourism's (DEAT) alternative sustainable livelihood programme, has been a success story, developed in response to the government's recognition of the growing pressure on the country's coastal and marine resources. Economic diversification, particularly the establishment of a self-regulated tourism industry that will ensure that benefits accrue to local people, has been seen as a key priority on the West Coast, where the decline in the fishing industry and increasing levels of poverty threaten the fragile balance. Unlike many of the other 'community' trails which have the support of booking and marketing agents, private enterprise outside the community, SANParks or CapeNature, the West Coast Crayfish Trail is entirely run by community members. It's a fabulous example of diversification that one can only hope will be modelled elsewhere.

RESPONSIBLE TOURISM

at the guesthouse and usually consists of a traditional feast of snoek, or, if it's available, crayfish, salad and potatoes; simple but tasty fare and the rooms too are homely and simply furnished.

A hearty breakfast sets you up for the day and the cheery chefs send you off with freshly made sandwiches for lunch. If you arrived too late to visit the cave the night before, that will be first up on the agenda before you park your car at the police station and set out on the trail. You'll be on the beach for the next two days so you can take off your shoes and tie them to your backpack – a wonderful sense of freedom. The sand is hard along this stretch and the going is fairly easy so you have time to look at the shells, explore the dunes and check out the birds. This area is rich in white mussels so if you're hiking anywhere near low tide you'll probably see several groups of figures shuffling in the shallows. It's a hard, but fascinating task.

SUNRISE IN LAMBERT'S BAY

OVERNIGHT ACCOMMODATION DETAIL

Each permit holder marks out his/her territory with stakes in the sand between the great gaggles of men and women with their pants and skirts rolled up, grinding their feet into the sand trying to feel for molluscs. If you've brought a mussel permit (you can get one in advance at any post office, including the one at Elands Bay) and can face the cold water, you can try the mussel shuffle. The mussels are only a few centimetres beneath the sand, so once you feel one with your toes you simply scoop it out. Well, I say simply, but judging by the rate at which the harvesters are hauling them out there is some skill involved – and if it's a big mussel it can be quite a tussle. Though the scenery doesn't change much, the hike passes quickly, even if you stop regularly to cool off in the freezing water. The big white dune fields form a natural barrier cutting off the beach from the rest of the world, so you really feel a sense of isolation and space.

WHITE MUSSEL HARVESTING LESSONS AND LAUGHTER

TRAIL 1

The bird life is fantastic; little plovers dart around, you see cormorants sunning themselves on the rocks and big flocks of gulls take flight as you approach, landing further down the beach. If you're on the trail between July and December there's a good chance of seeing southern right whales off the coast and hikers see dolphins and seals year round. The guides have amazing eyesight and once they've spotted a marine mammal you can scramble up the dunes for a better view.

Try to hike at low tide where possible, not only because the sand is harder and you're more likely to see the white mussel harvesters but also so that you can explore the rock pools. Squatting down to check out the colourful anemones, limpets, tiny crabs and little fish that inhabit the tidal pools is one of the delights of this section – you can poke around for hours. Many of the rocks are covered with black mussels so if you've brought a mussel permit you can gather a few to cook later. You leave the beach shortly after Kreefbaai (Crayfish Bay) and head over the soft sand of the dunes to Steenbokfontein, where the charming Mrs Burger will sit you down, offer you fresh lemonade, tea and cakes and welcome you to her homely B&B. Mrs Burger is a fount of information on the area and is clearly proud to be part of the trail. If you have collected white mussels she'll happily show you how to cook them as a pre-dinner snack, then you wander over to the adjacent Plaaskombuis (farm kitchen) to dine on local specialties such as mussel soup, chicken pie, vegetables and salad, with traditional koeksisters as dessert.

DAY 2 Steenbokfontein to Lambert's Bay
9km, 2–3 hours

In order to create as many jobs and involve as many people from each community as possible, trailists have a different guide each day, so you'll be greeted by a new face at the start of day two. But before you hit the trail, Mrs Burger will insist on you working your way through an enormous breakfast. You're almost embarrassed by the effort that she has gone to. Then it's back to the beach for a morning dip – another glorious day in Africa. The little bay is very picturesque but once you manage to drag yourself away, miles of empty deserted coastline stretch out

STEENBOKFONTEIN OVERNIGHT ACCOMMODATION

OVERNIGHT ACCOMMODATION – TANNIE BURGER'S HOME

Among the dolphin seen off the West Coast are the small, rare Heaviside's dolphin, with its distinctive triangular fin and white stripe down its sides, and the acrobatic dusky dolphin. Both species occur only up the South African West Coast and Namibian coast, so it's a treat to watch their playful acrobatics.

THE ORIGIN OF A NAME

Lambert's Bay takes its name from Admiral Lambert of the British Navy who surveyed the bay between 1826 and 1840. It was used as a harbour for British warships during the Anglo-Boer War. The first crayfish factory opened in 1918.

LOCAL MAN FIXING FISHING NET

STADIG

before you. (I always marvel at how incredible it is to find such beautiful areas of wilderness so close to Cape Town.) As on day one, most of day two is spent simply enjoying the space and the smell of the sea, strolling barefoot along the sand, lost in thought, scanning the sea for whales and dolphins or peering into colourful rock pools. The cold Benguela current brings nutrients from the southern oceans and you can see evidence of the richness of the marine life all along the coast. Again you'll probably come across local people harvesting molluscs. The rocks in this section are covered with limpets, which are collected for their flesh and cooked up into curries or put on the braai. Keep an eye out for the magnificent Cape Gannets, which frequent the coast. The distinctive beady-eyed golden birds are often seen diving into the water. If a big shoal of fish is close to the coast the display is incredible as the gannets drop out of the sky like falling snow before emerging with their catch.

If you're on the trail between July and September the coastal fringe just before Lambert's Bay is an absolute delight as you walk through a profusion of colourful spring flowers. But at any time of year the guides point out little flowers

and herbs, explain their uses and help you train your eyes to see detail that you can so easily walk by. Lunch is served at the home of a welcoming local lady, Tannie Jeanette, and she's clearly intent on fattening you up.

One of the highlights of day two is a visit to Bird Island, home to around 25,000 gannets, some 15% of the world population of these threatened sea birds. A short walk over the causeway from the town's harbour brings you to the big interpretive hide on the island, from where you're able to view the fascinating birds interacting with each

other as the guide explains the background to Bird Island, the reasons that the colony is protected, the threats to the habitats and the gannets' social behaviour. Seals and penguins also inhabit Bird Island and this can upset the delicate balance. In 2005 the community of Lambert's Bay was devastated when the gannets moved away after attacks by Cape fur seals, but after much brain racking the colony was cleverly lured back by bird decoys created by a local artist.

The rest of the afternoon is free, leaving you time to relax in the Waterfront Eureka Flats, where you'll be spending the night, or explore Lambert's Bay. The small museum, with

LOCAL WINE

its archaeological display, book and photographic collections and the propeller of the *HMS Sybille,* is well worth a visit.

Otherwise you can hit the beach or the big tidal pool on the south side of town or simply chill out around the picturesque harbour photographing the fishing boats and interacting with the local people – a friendly community, many of whom have the most incredible weather-beaten faces.

Dinner at Isabella's Restaurant and Coffee Shop

BETWEEN LAMBERT'S BAY AND PAPENDORP

is the gastronomic highlight of the trail. The unassuming wooden building is right on the waterfront with a great view onto the harbour and Bird Island. But it's the nautical décor that gives it real charm; fishnets hang on the walls while the floor is covered with black mussel. It's nothing fancy but the food is great. The outside walls are covered with paintings of whales and interpretive signboards and you'll sit out on plastic chairs eating the superb fresh fish and seafood off plastic tablecloths. Isabella's is special because it epitomises Lambert's Bay – a charming, simple fishing village.

DAY 3 Doring Bay to Papendorp
15km, 5 hours

After breakfast you hop into a vehicle for the 45km transfer to Doring Bay, where, you guessed it, you'll find a crayfish factory and an attractive lighthouse. According to the guides, before the town developed the bay was used as an anchorage on the sea-trading route up the West Coast. Goods that were off-loaded were then transported to Vanrhynsdorp by camel.

The scenery changes dramatically at this point; instead of beach walking you hike along the top of rugged, precipitous coastal cliffs. It's a beautiful place –

DUNES DAY 3

THE ISLAND OF BIRDS

Bird Island, managed by CapeNature, is one of only six places in the world where Cape Gannets breed and the only easily accessible site for visitors. The island, 3ha in size, is also an important breeding and roosting site for other sea birds, including cormorants and African Penguins, and for Cape fur seals. Between 1888 and 1990 guano collected on the island was an important source of revenue for the town and a section of the island was paved to facilitate collection.

During this time the number of African Penguins resident on Bird Island declined severely as their eggs were also collected as a delicacy. This is now illegal and the number of birds has increased, thanks in part to the artificial 'burrows' that have been built on the island to encourage the penguins to breed.

LEAVE NOTHING BUT FOOTPRINTS IN THE SAND

BETWEEN LAMBERT'S BAY AND PAPENDORP

the trail winds up and down the undulating clifftop, while below you can see deep tidal pools and crashing waves. The guides take time to point out the unique plants of the area, so it's a hard choice between studying the coastal fynbos or enjoying the views. You pass a few relatively unobtrusive works where minerals are still being extracted and, sadly, the ugly scars of past diamond workings. The areas were abandoned, without any attempt at restoration, once they were no longer viable, though there appear to have been some recent attempts at dune rehabilitation.

Roughly 8km along the trail an attractive coastal resort comes into view and the scenery changes again. Strandfontein is a holiday town with attractive sea-facing houses, a pretty beach and a green, terraced camp site seeming to dominate the centre of town. The guides change over here, with your guide of the morning returning to Doring Bay and a new guide taking you down to Papendorp.

This is one of the most interesting and varied sections of the trail. Initially the golden sands are stained with black ore, then littered with colourful round pink and orange pebbles. The guide has a surprise in store: behind a yellow rock face is a hidden band of bright clay that is soft and pliable to the touch. Nearby is an even more spectacular phenomenon. At first glance it seems as if there are rock paintings on the cliffs but in fact it's just coloured mineral seams forming a natural gallery. The bands of orange, red, pink and white are exposed only at this one spot it seems, so take some photos – it really is one of the most extraordinary features of the coast. Just beyond this is yet another geological treat. Suddenly the white dunes that flank the beach are replaced by high dunes of fine red sand such as you find in the Kalahari. Quite bizarre.

The geological adventure ends almost as quickly as it began and you soon leave the beach to head inland to Papendorp, crossing over a wide, muddy pan. In summer the pan dries up and salt is harvested from deep pits by local *soutrapers* (salt gatherers) in the traditional fashion. It's an eerie, empty place – a vast expanse encrusted with crystals. The day ends with a short walk through the wetland to Papendorp on the Olifants River.

Most of the inhabitants of the village derive their livelihood from fishing in the estuary – one of only four estuaries on the west coast of Southern Africa. Papendorp, named after the former governor Von Papen, is also known as Viswater (fish water).

It's a sleepy place with a great view of the wetlands and river estuary and an interesting history. If you arrive early enough you'll be shown the remnants of the old reed-and-mud houses where the fishermen dwelled in the past,

One of the delicacies of the West Coast is bokkom, or West Coast biltong, a dried, salted mullet that is generally served as shavings on top of buttered bread.

FISH BILTONG?

KELP COLLECTORS

KELP

and the shell middens, before settling into the attractive guesthouse. This elegant whitewashed building enjoys a superb setting on the river where you can sit out on the deck watching the birds fly home and the herons and egrets nesting in the trees. Some 183 species of bird have been identified in the

The original farmhouse at Big River Bend was built on a chert outcrop, which the SA Museum has identified as a Khoisan factory that manufactured arrowheads and stone implements. Keep scanning the ground as you walk through the farm – there are many interesting rocks, including flint stones, white quartz crystals and round stones of all descriptions lying around.

The 600ha farm has been in the same family for the last five generations dating back to the time of the original settlers, the Fryers, in 1820. The Fryers married into the Louws and then became the Dittmer family. Pam's great grandfather, Adolph Dittmer, a German accountant, married Jessie Fryer whose family exported horses and farmed sheep, ostriches and malt barley (which was sent to a brewery in Cape Town).

They had one son, Heindrich, who was an engineer and fought in the Anglo-Boer War. After the war, Heindrich went to study in Germany, then moved to England where he married Doris Burfield, Pam's grandmother. The first of their eight children was born in England before they moved back to South Africa in 1910 at the signing of the Vereeniging Agreement. In the Cape they divided their time between Rondebosch and Big River Bend Farm, on which they farmed karakul and merino sheep and barley.

Nowadays, sheep, ostriches, vegetables, bees and lucerne are farmed and tourism is increasingly important. In addition to those on the Crayfish Trail, visitors come to the farm to enjoy the outstanding seasonal bird life and the beautiful spring flowers.

feature in the otherwise flat valley. The Olifants then makes a big bend to the right and soon you leave the river bank and head up the gently sloping hill to the appropriately named Big River Bend Farm, historically known as Zoutpansklipheuvel.

Pam and David Brash will welcome you to their guesthouse, which has three twin rooms, a lounge/dining area and a fabulous view over the river from the verandah. There are additional double rooms for couples in their home where you have dinner and breakfast. In the afternoon there's a boat trip on the river and you can also

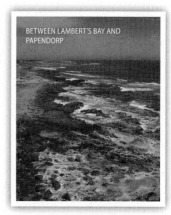

BETWEEN LAMBERT'S BAY AND PAPENDORP

wetland and river area and the Papendorp/Ebenhaezer region is an Important Bird Area, which is hoping for recognition as a Ramsar Site.

DAY 4 Papendorp to Big River Bend
12km, 4–5 hours

You will be woken by twittering birds, and it's worth rising early to enjoy dawn from the deck. Mist rises from the vlei – the perfect time to watch the bird life through your binoculars before tucking

into breakfast. The trail, along the Olifants River, is very different again on this last day, and you'll often encounter muddy patches as you follow the trail past solitary fishermen and countless water birds. Despite the somewhat soggy conditions it's an easy stroll along the flood plain, stopping to eat your packed lunch at a scenic rocky promontory roughly halfway, opposite a steep river cliff on the northern bank. This ridge of rock, known as Tierkrans and Langklip, is a marked

try your hand at angling or, if you're feeling energetic, hike a further 5km (each way) to Ebenhaezer before dinner, typically a delicious meal of home-baked bread and preserves, braaied snoek, salad, baked potatoes and dessert. After celebrating your last night on the trail you're transferred back to your cars in Elands Bay in the morning.

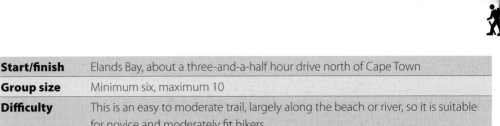

Start/finish	Elands Bay, about a three-and-a-half hour drive north of Cape Town
Group size	Minimum six, maximum 10
Difficulty	This is an easy to moderate trail, largely along the beach or river, so it is suitable for novice and moderately fit hikers.
Facilities	All accommodation is in shared rooms and bathrooms. Two nights on the trail are spent in simple, but beautifully located, community guesthouses, though large groups are put up in a luxury guesthouse in Elands Bay on the first night. The second night is in a private, homely B&B, the third night in three-star, self-catering flats on the beach at Lambert's Bay, and the final night is in a private guesthouse on a farm. Beer and wine are for sale at Plaaskombuis and at Isabella's but not in the community-run guesthouses and only on request at Big River Bend Farm, so if you're partial to a tipple, bring your own.
And the kids?	Children aged seven and upwards are welcome on the trails provided that they are reasonably fit.
When to go	The trail can be walked year round. Spring (August to October), when the wild flowers are at their best and when whales are often spotted from the coast, and autumn (March to May) are ideal times. Winters are cool and sometimes wet – though the morning fogs certainly add atmosphere – while it can be windy in summer.
Contact	West Coast Crayfish Trail, 027 432 2875/073 370 0782, coreenc@lantic.net, www.south-north.co.za
Kit list	See general kit list, page 202 **Specific** 🚶 Mussel permit if you want to collect mussels from the sand or rocks 🚶 Crocs or sandals tied onto your pack for negotiating rocky/shelly bits on the beach 🚶 Your own tipple for three nights 🚶 Cash for drinks at the restaurants or for shopping in Lambert's Bay 🚶 First-aid kit – including personal medications, throat lozenges, lipsalve, aspirins, antiseptic cream, insect repellent.
On your bike	If you prefer to cycle along the gravel roads that run parallel to the trail on days three and four then the trail organisers will be happy to provide you with bikes.

OPTIONAL HIKE to Ebenhaezer

10km (return), 3 hours

The historic mission station of Ebenhaezer was founded in 1854 by Sir and Lady Fryer, who, apparently, were reminded of the moors in Ireland. The centre of a farming and fishing community, the village has an old-world charm with many interesting historical old clay buildings. Some have been renovated; others, sadly, are rapidly deteriorating.

TRAIL 2

Cederberg Heritage Route

Cederberg Heritage Route

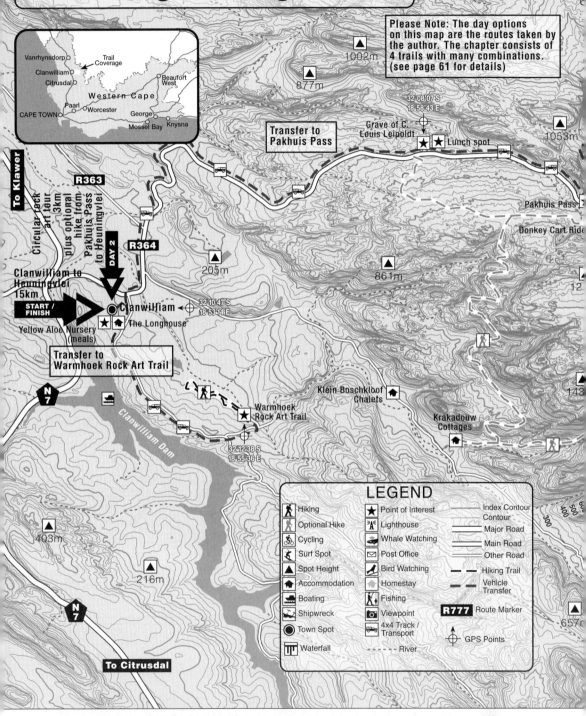

Please Note: The day options on this map are the routes taken by the author. The chapter consists of 4 trails with many combinations. (see page 61 for details)

Trail Coverage

Vanrhynsdorp
Clanwilliam
Citrusdal
Western Cape
CAPE TOWN
Paarl
Worcester
George
Mossel Bay
Knysna
Beaufort West

1002m
877m
1053m

32 08 07 S
18 58 43 E

Grave of C. Louis Leipoldt
Lunch spot

Transfer to Pakhuis Pass

Pakhuis Pass

Donkey Cart Ride

To Klawer

R363

Circular rock art tour 3km plus optional hike from Pakhuis Pass to Heuningvlei

R364

DAY 2

205m

861m

Clanwilliam to Heuningvlei 15km

START / FINISH

32 10 47 S
18 53 14 E

Clanwilliam

Yellow Aloe Nursery (meals)

The Longhouse

Transfer to Warmhoek Rock Art Trail

N7

Clanwilliam Dam

Warmhoek Rock Art Trail

Klein Boschkloof Chalets

Krakadouw Cottages

32 12 38 S
18 55 36 E

403m

216m

N7

657m

To Citrusdal

LEGEND

🚶 Hiking	⭐ Point of Interest	— Index Contour Contour
🚶 Optional Hike	🗼 Lighthouse	— Major Road
🚴 Cycling	🐋 Whale Watching	— Main Road
🏄 Surf Spot	✉ Post Office	— Other Road
▲ Spot Height	🐦 Bird Watching	– – – Hiking Trail
🏠 Accommodation	🏠 Homestay	·–·– Vehicle Transfer
🚣 Boating	🎣 Fishing	**R777** Route Marker
⚓ Shipwreck	📷 Viewpoint	⊕ GPS Points
● Town Spot	🚗 4x4 Track / Transport	
▦ Waterfall	– – – River	

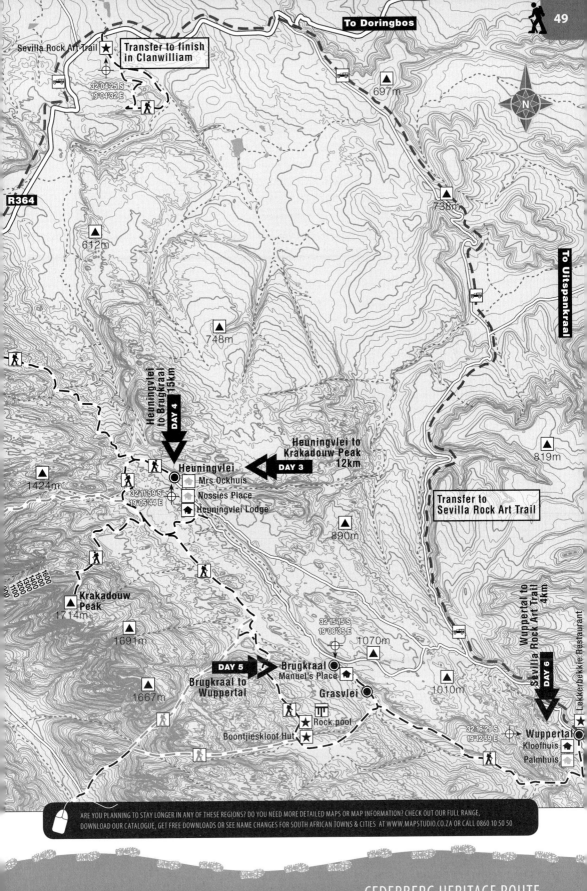

To Doringbos

To Uitspankraal

Sevilla Rock Art Trail ★

Transfer to finish in Clanwilliam

32·04'25 S
19·04'32 E

R364

697m

738m

612m

819m

748m

Heuningvlei to Brugkraal 15km
DAY 4

Heuningvlei to Krakadouw Peak 12km
DAY 3

Transfer to Sevilla Rock Art Trail

1424m

Heuningvlei
32·11'59 S
19·05'44 E
Mrs Ockhuis
Nossies Place
Heuningvlei Lodge

890m

1600
1500
1400
1300
1200
1100

Krakadouw Peak
1714m

1691m

32·15'15 S
19·08'35 E
1070m

1010m

Wuppertal to Sevilla Rock Art Trail 4km

Lekkerbekkie Restaurant

DAY 5
Brugkraal to Wuppertal

Brugkraal
Manuel's Place

1667m

Grasvlei

DAY 6

Rock pool

Boontjieskloof Hut

32·16'29 S
19·12'59 E
Wuppertal
Kloofhuis
Palmhuis

ARE YOU PLANNING TO STAY LONGER IN ANY OF THESE REGIONS? DO YOU NEED MORE DETAILED MAPS OR MAP INFORMATION? CHECK OUT OUR FULL RANGE, DOWNLOAD OUR CATALOGUE, GET FREE DOWNLOADS OR SEE NAME CHANGES FOR SOUTH AFRICAN TOWNS & CITIES AT WWW.MAPSTUDIO.CO.ZA OR CALL 0860 10 50 50

CEDERBERG HERITAGE ROUTE

HIGHLIGHTS

The Cederberg Heritage Route (CHR) comprises three guided hiking trails through one of South Africa's most spectacular and remote wilderness areas: the three-night Klein Krakadouw Trail, the four-night Groot Krakadouw Trail and the five-night Wuppertal Trail. All trails start and end in the historic centre of Clanwilliam, one of South Africa's oldest towns, and take hikers through one of the most beautiful and bio-diverse centres of the Cape Floral Region World Heritage Site and to some of the most important rock art sites in Southern Africa. In short, the CHR is a superb opportunity to really immerse yourself in this floral wonderland with its dramatic eroded peaks and deeply incised gorges and to interact with the people who live in this remote area as they lead you on the hikes and host you in their houses. The six-day Wuppertal Trail, the longest and most varied of the routes, is described below, but many of the elements are common to all and each trail is fascinating and rewarding. So choose according to the time that you have available to immerse yourself in this rugged wilderness.

- **DISTANCE** 46km
- **DAYS** 6
- **DIFFICULTY** MODERATE
- **MTB** 13 ROUTES (SEE PAGE 63)

> *viooltjies in die voorhuis –*
> *viooltjies blou en rooi:*
> *viooltjies oral op die veld*
> *en oral, ai, so mooi.*
> C Louis Leipoldt

DAY 1 Setting the scene

The drive north from Cape Town is an adventure in itself. You leave the city behind and, once over the steep Piekenierskloof Pass, descend into a dramatic landscape of lush citrus orchards and vineyards towered over by the high peaks and ravines of the Cederberg Mountains. The Cederberg is famous for its spectacular rock formations, such as the Wolfberg Arch and Maltese Cross, its fine examples of San rock paintings and its spectacular display of spring flowers (between early to mid-August and September). Most of the Cederberg is a designated Wilderness Area and thus remains one of the most undisturbed areas of the country. The hiking trails of the Cederberg Heritage Route aim to make this beautiful area accessible to walkers with the use of charming community guest cottages in the Moravian mission villages of Heuningvlei, Brugkraal and Wuppertal on the eastern side of the Wilderness Area and up-market guesthouses in or near Clanwilliam on the western side.

The schedule suggests that you arrive in Clanwilliam in the late afternoon and stay overnight at The Longhouse or Die Waenhuis. Both guesthouses are extremely comfortable and the food is excellent. Clanwilliam is one of South Africa's oldest towns, settled by 1725. In 1820 about 350 Irish settlers moved in and some of the attractive houses from that era still stand in Park Street. The town is now a centre for an agricultural community cultivating rooibos tea, citrus, table grapes and vegetables. Clanwilliam also has a thriving tourist centre, so it's worthwhile arriving earlier in the afternoon and taking a little tour of the Old Gaol Museum, the rooibos tea factory, the craft shop at the Living Landscape Project and the Strassberger Shoe Factory where the famous *veldskoene* (locally produced leather shoes) are made. Or, if you feel like stretching your legs, you can sign up for an hour-long Sederville Slinger walking tour of the community with one of the community guides.

In 2004 UNESCO inscribed the Cape Floral Region Protected Area as a World Heritage Site, a natural phenomenon that is recognised as being unique and irreplaceable and of such outstanding universal value to humanity that it needs to be conserved. The Cape Floral Region (CFR) is a vast area of shrubland, dominated by fynbos (fine bush) made up of protea, erica (heathers), restios (reeds) and geophyte (bulb) species which comprises most of the Western Cape, some of the Eastern Cape and a small part of the Northern Cape. Seventy percent of the plants found in the CFR occur nowhere else in the world, so if these populations are destroyed we lose these species forever. To understand how special a visit to the Cederberg Wilderness Area is, it's important to recognise that the WHS inscription does not refer to the *whole* Cape Floral Region – rather eight separate but representative sites have been chosen as the Cape Floral Region Protected Area, i.e. the World Heritage Site. These are the Cederberg Wilderness Area, Groot Winterhoek Wilderness Area, Boland Mountain Complex, Boosmansbos Wilderness Area, De Hoop Nature Reserve, Swartberg Complex and Baviaanskloof. Between them this makes up an area of 500,000ha, or about 6% of the total area of the Cape Floral Region. They're unique, special places that showcase the greater region with its highly distinctive flora, exceptional species richness and high degree of endemism. The thinking behind this? Well much of the region described is no longer in its natural state and is now farmed or urbanised rather than being pristine fynbos. Also, because the CFR is such a big area, stretching from the winter rainfall areas of the southwestern Cape through transitional areas to the arid Karoo, it's impossible to find one area where all the unique, precious floral species found in the CFR are concentrated. So, the solution was eight protected areas, each representing different habitats. The Cederberg is one of the chosen few. Quite special, right?

SCENERY NEAR HEUNINGVLEI

Every year during August and September visitors from around the world come to see the extraordinary wild flowers that carpet the Cederberg, the West Coast and the Northern Cape. The area around Clanwilliam is one of the top spots for natural floral displays, thanks to the fact that the area is the meeting place of three biomes: the Fynbos, Succulent Karoo and Nama Karoo. As a result there is an enormous diversity of plant species. It is said that Clanwilliam has the largest variety of wild flowers in one district in the world due to the variety in the topography. All I can say is that it is very pretty!

LIVING LANDSCAPE PROJECT – GUIDED TOUR

ROCK SHELTERS IN THE JAN DISSELS VALLEY

DAY 2 Circular rock art tour
3km, 3 hours

Plus optional hike from Pakhuis Pass to Heuningvlei
12km, 3–4 hours

After a hearty breakfast (remember this is farming country so you'll be fattened up at every meal) you're collected and driven the short distance out of Clanwilliam to the Jan Dissels Valley for a rock art walk with one of the local guides trained up as part of Clanwilliam's Living Landscape Project. The guides, who have been mentored by some of South Africa's top rock art specialists such as John Parkington and floral fundis such as Dr Penny Mustart, are absolutely passionate about the Cederberg and its heritage and their knowledge and enthusiasm for the paintings is inspiring. You'll find yourself squirming into low overhangs, squatting down to examine ochre-coloured eland, tiny outlines of fat-tailed sheep, the distinctive depictions of shamans and other features you barely noticed when you first looked at the rock faces. There are five sites, of which you'll probably visit two or three depending on your level of fitness and interest, and your guide will have plenty of opportunity to point out the techniques used, the likely ages of the paintings and the various interpretations of the scenes – particularly the trance scenes and the pressure points. The guides have a very interactive, questioning style and since the walk is not taxing it's an ideal way to introduce youngsters to the rock art of the area.

Lunch is usually taken at the grave of C. Louis Leipoldt, halfway up the Pakhuis Pass. Leipoldt, a local doctor, poet, botanist and cook, was one of the area's most famous sons, acclaimed for his poetry written about the Anglo-

Boer War. Less well known is that he acted as personal physician for Pulitzer (of the prize fame) while the latter was journeying on his yacht in the Caribbean. The packed lunches, like all the meals on the trail, are good: fresh whole-wheat sandwiches, eggs, perhaps a piece of chicken and some fruit. You say goodbye to your guide at the top of the pass where the donkey carts are waiting. Then the real fun begins! The journey along the Jeep track to Heuningvlei sounds innocuous enough, but don't go expecting a sedate transfer. While there are cushions and pillows to sit on, the wooden carts are rustic and you bounce along on the uneven, alternately rocky then sandy track. You have the choice of walking the 12km to Heuningvlei but to do so would be to miss out on one of the most exhilarating experiences you're likely to have in the Cederberg. The donkey cart, usually pulled by three or four pairs of donkeys, is still

the main form of transport in the area, so the animals, and drivers, know the ropes. But if you're of a nervous disposition be warned: the downhills are usually taken at speeds which can be quite unnerving, particularly when you realise that the only way the cart's momentum can be arrested is with a piece of old car tyre with which the driver applies friction, via a foot brake, to the back wheels.

At the bottom of each hill the pace slackens as the donkeys take the weight of the cart in their harnesses again, and your thumping heart can calm down before the next downhill charge. You get more confident as the journey continues, but chances are you'll arrive in Heuningvlei in need of a stiff drink!

From the Pakhuis Pass the Jeep track leads up through a spectacular stretch of the Cederberg known as Rocklands. It's one of South Africa's best-known sport climbing areas and you'll often see muscled young men and women bouldering

DONKEY CART TRAILS

The Donkey Cart Adventure is a collaboration between the Wuppertal and Northern Cederberg conservancies, CapeNature, the Greater Cederberg Biodiversity Corridor (GCBC) and the Heuningvlei community. It has been operating since 2007 and aims to improve the livelihood of all the inhabitants of Heuningvlei by promoting tourism. The donkey is the traditional means of transportation in the rugged Cederberg Mountains and the people of Heuningvlei used such carts to carry their produce to Clanwilliam.

HOLD TIGHT, HANG ON FOR DEAR LIFE!

(climbing on low boulders without ropes) or scaling the sheer sandstone walls of the higher cliffs as you ride or hike past. After the initial climb the track contours round, affording magnificent views over towards the Brandewyn River Valley (where you'll be doing the Sevilla Trail on the final day) and past wonderful rock formations and floral displays. The dominant flora is fynbos vegetation and

JEEP TRACK BETWEEN PAKHUIS PASS AND HEUNINGVLEI

Pakhuis Pass was built by the famous Cape pass builder, Thomas Bain. Thomas learned his skill from his equally famous father, Andrew Geddes Bain, when he helped him to build Bain's Kloof Pass near Wellington. In the 1860s the Cape authorities were petitioned by the residents and farmers of Calvinia to construct a proper road to Clanwilliam. Bain started work on the Pakhuis Pass in 1874 and the pass was opened in April 1877. Bain also built a short route from the top of the pass to the settlement at Heuningvlei.

Various explanations have been offered for the name 'Pakhuis'. The name literally translates as 'warehouse'. One school has it that the piles of rocks that are a feature of the mountain slopes resemble the piles of goods stacked in a warehouse. Another explanation holds that the 'stacked' rocks resemble the dry-packed stone walls of many Karoo buildings, 'kliphuis' or 'pakhuis' being a common local term for such buildings. Finally, there is an interpretation that holds that 'pakhuis' is a corruption from Khoekhoe, meaning 'dassie's rocky place'. Whichever explanation may be correct, all certainly refer to the extraordinary rocks and formations encountered on the pass – pillars, stacks, arches and towers that have resulted from powerful geological and climatic forces.

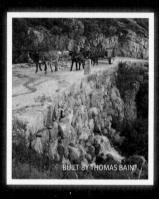

BUILT BY THOMAS BAIN

income, but the donkey cart drivers will complain that the payment for their crops is sporadic at best. However, a newly renovated guesthouse/backpackers on the left-hand side gives an indication of the benefits that tourism can bring. The village enjoys a stunning location surrounded by high mountains, and the whitewashed walls of the houses, old-world doors and scruffy smiling kids add to its charm. But it is the hospitality of the local people that really makes Heuningvlei memorable. Whether you're staying at the new guesthouse or with one of the ladies of the community who put you up in their houses, you're guaranteed a warm, genuine welcome. Many of the locals are not English speakers, but everyone waves and greets you as you step off the cart and are ushered in to your home for the night.

The accommodation is basic and you might have to share a room, but the bedding is clean and the beds are soft (sometimes a bit too soft). There's a bathroom for the shared use of the group – which never numbers more than six people. A tray with the basics for tea and coffee is always available and Mrs Ockhuis, our host, even provided towels (though these are not necessarily provided at the other guesthouses so pack your own). Although you're

you'll see a variety of reeds, colourful protea and erica, as well as rare endemic plants such as tolbos, *Leucadendron concuvum*, perdekop, *Leucospermum reflexum*, spiderbush, *Serruria leipoldtii*, and the rare Clanwilliam cedar, *Widdringtonia cedarbergensis*, that are found nowhere else in the world. Occasionally you'll catch a glimpse of some of the shy fauna of the 'Berg: agile klipspringer, grey rhebok and dassies sunning themselves on the rocks. Keep your eyes peeled when you stop to admire the view – you might spot a porcupine quill or even the footprint of the elusive Cape mountain leopard.

After a couple of hours you gain a rise and a cluster of white cottages comes into view. Heuningvlei, the end of the day's trail, is a mission village where self-sufficiency is still the norm and the local people are poor but proud. The sale of rooibos tea should in theory produce some

WHITEWASHED COTTAGES AT HEUNINGVLEI

clearly an honoured guest to be fussed over, you are very much in someone's home, and it is this proximity – the opportunity to spend time sitting around the kitchen table chatting or asking about the people in the photographs and pictures of school sports teams on the wall – that makes the stay so interesting.

Shortly after your arrival one or more of your 'chefs' will arrive to establish the time at which you'd like to dine. Dinner is usually served early in the villages and is a wholesome affair with local dishes of meatballs, roast chicken, boerewors (sausage), potatoes, vegetables and fresh salad followed by a typical home-made dessert of bread-and-butter pudding, sponge and custard or such like. If you're not careful this is a trail on which you could easily gain weight! No alcohol is available in the mission villages but you're advised in the very thorough pre-trip notes that you can bring moderate supplies of your own (the donkeys have to pull the weight up the hills, remember) in plastic bottles or wine boxes. After dinner your guide for the following day will come and discuss the programme. You have a choice of two possible walks depending on the fitness levels and/or inclination of the group (and you will have

Seventeen kilometres from Clanwilliam there is a sign on the left, indicating Leipoldt's grave. C. Louis Leipoldt (1880–1947) trained as a doctor, making his mark as a paediatrician and the first lecturer in the diseases of children at the University of Cape Town. But he preferred writing (his first piece to be published was written when he was 11). Leipoldt became a leading poet of the Second Afrikaans Language Movement, writing poetry, drama, travel books, detective stories and books on cookery. Leipoldt also wrote in English, and his book *Bushveld Doctor* reveals (given the times in which he lived) how far ahead of his time he was in much of his thinking regarding education and health care, while Leipoldt's *Food & Wine* (a trilogy of Leipoldt's *Cape Cookery*, *Culinary Treasures* and *Three Hundred Years of Cape Wine*), published in 2003, demonstrates the breadth of his interests and culinary skills.

Leipoldt was also known as a botanical explorer and several plants are named after him. From his grave, in a small shelter where traces of San rock paintings are still visible, you can see three peaks that tower over the top of the pass. These were named by the great man himself: 'Faith', 'Hope' and 'Charity'.

WEATHERED ROCKS AND HEAPS OF FUN

One of the most alluring aspects of this trail is the opportunity to visit some of the ancient rock paintings of the San people, the first inhabitants of the Cape. The Cederberg is one of the best areas for rock art in Southern Africa, with 2000 discovered sites. (The other three areas are the Drakensberg Mountains in KwaZulu-Natal, the Brandberg Mountain in Namibia and the Matopas Mountains in southern Zimbabwe.)

been asked before arriving on the trail what you think the likely choice of your group will be). The leisurely option is an easy scenic day hike of 10–12km in the hills to the east of Heuningvlei where you can enjoy some rock art sites, intriguing rock formations and wild flowers, as well as a swim in a deep pool in the Heuningvlei River. But if at all possible go for a guided hike up Krakadouw Peak. It's no mean undertaking but the views and the rock formations of the plateau are more than

WEATHERED FORMATIONS AT KRAKADOUW PEAK

ample reward. Just take it slowly and steadily.

Day 3 Krakadouw Peak
12km, 8 hours

(There is a more leisurely trail for those who do not feel up to this strenuous hike.)

This is an immensely rewarding, but strenuous, hike up one of the highest peaks in the Cederberg Mountains, led by one of the men of the village. It is important to stress that while these 'guides' know the area well they have no formal guide training and are not necessarily fluent in English so they should be regarded more as escorts. Do not expect too much from them, but if you prompt them they will open up with all sorts of interesting snippets of local knowledge.

The trail leads up from the back of the village to a rock shelter with some poorly preserved paintings. Apparently a local man lived in this shelter for 35 years while working on the road to Pakhuis Pass that you came down the previous day, and you can still see a well-preserved stone canal system which carried water to what had been his garden. Just beyond this is a stone hut at the base of Krakadouw Peak – one of the few shelters remaining in the Cederberg Wilderness Area. And it's simply a shelter with no beds

or ablutions, so when you see it you'll appreciate your Heuningvlei accommodation even more. All hikers beyond this point need to carry tents or brave the elements. From the hut the path climbs up steeply for a while but then just as you start to tire it eases off and wends its way left across a vlei with a smattering of trees before the main climb to the craggy summit. It's a stiff walk that will take 3–4 hours during which you gain some 900m, but you can take

CRACKS AND GULLIES ON KRAKADOUW

it slowly, stopping often to admire the views and the vegetation. On the way you'll see one of the Cederberg endemics, the gnarly cedar tree, as well as numerous fynbos species, so it's worth doing some pre-hike reading or carrying a (light) floral guide. There is usually water in the streams that trickle down the valleys so you can refill your water bottle and

KRAKADOUW VISTA

The Englishman's Grave is that of Lt. G. V. W. Clowes, who was killed during the Anglo-Boer War on 30 January 1901 and buried in the Pakhuis Pass, at the turn-off to Wuppertal. The Boers were pulling back over very rough mountain terrain, but as the English were outnumbered, the C.O. de List sent back for reinforcements before pursuing them. That evening, Capt. Gordon, Lt. Clowes and Pte. M. Clarke rode out to see if certain ground was passable for the horses. They pushed too far ahead and were ambushed. Gordon, who had dismounted, was hit in the foot but managed to remount and escape. Clowes was killed, while Clarke was injured and captured by the Boers. He died of his wounds and is buried in the Anglican churchyard of Clanwilliam.

Clowes's family were devastated by his death, and his mother travelled to the Cape from her home in Hertfordshire and had the present grave constructed over the simple hole where her son had been buried. For many years Mrs Clowes made an annual visit to the grave to lay a wreath on the anniversary of her son's death – a considerable act of love in the days before air travel and when the road all the way from Cape Town was untarred.

cool off at intervals. The path is well marked but rocky and uneven and at times, particularly near the top, there is some scrambling through the gullies, so care and good footing is required (the trail is not exposed). As you near the top of Krakadouw you appreciate the height you've gained. The sheer cliffs drop away dramatically below you and you look down on soaring birds. It really is an incredible place with 360-degree views over the Cederberg Mountains. The guides usually advise spending an hour on the summit so this is divided between eating lunch and exploring. You could spend days up here on the summit plateau, and it's easy to get lost, so don't wander off. The sandstone rock has been eroded into wonderful formations – you'll have fun spotting tortoises, snails,

DINE WITH THE LOCALS

camels and other animal forms and walking through deep passages where the rock walls surrounding you are several times your height. There are lots of water-filled depressions on the plateau, including a natural 'infinity pool', which has water for most of the year, right on the edge of the cliff, and there are numerous places where you can see down into deep caverns and tunnels. The hour passes too quickly, leaving so much still to explore. The descent is via the same route and takes about three hours. You'll deserve your dinner that night.

Groups

SUMMIT KRAKADOUW

STREAM CROSSING AFTER RAINS

short climbs and a long, fairly steep descent gully. The trail contours around the lower slopes of Krakadouw Peak, winding up and down through little valleys and open vleie, past some fine cedar trees and a big pool – 'our Olympic swimming pool' your guide will joke – up to the Boontjieskloof hut, another simple stone hut that was originally built to provide shelter for the forestry workers. The hut, on a big open plateau with Krakadouw as the backdrop, is magnificently sited, so it is a great place to have lunch, to swim in the nearby rock pools

who don't wish to climb Krakadouw Peak have the option of an easy day hike of 10–12km in the hills to the east of Heuningvlei. This,

to an extent, can be tailor-made to the interests of the group, taking in rock art sites, weird and wonderful rock formations and sites of particular floral interest. Your guide will point out some of the endemic species if you ask him – there are wonderfully aromatic buchu, *Agathosma distans*, for example. All routes eventually lead to one of the highlights of the day – a big, deep pool in the Heuningvlei River, where you can swim and relax in an unbelievably beautiful, tranquil setting gazing up at Krakadouw and thinking 'maybe next time!'

BOONTJIESKLOOF HUT LUNCH STOP

and appreciate the privilege of being deep in the heart of the Cederberg wilderness. After lunch the trail is flat for a while before you descend some 300m down Boontjieskloof to Grasvlei Village. This is a beautiful stretch of trail with waterfalls, steep cliffs and, as usual, some wonderfully eroded rock formations along the way. You can stop for refreshing dips in the pools of the perennial Grasvlei stream. From Grasvlei it is a short walk up the main

QUAGGAS

The quagga is a zebra subspecies that was exterminated from its habitat on the plains of the Karoo and Southern Free State in the second half of the 19th century. In October 1992 six zebras whose external appearance was similar to that of the quagga were moved to Cape Town as part of a selective breeding programme. The hope is that with successive generations the high degree of individual variation in colour and striping, characteristic of the southern plains zebra, will be reduced. Eventually individuals should emerge whose coat-pattern characters closely resemble that of the quagga.

DAY 4 Heuningvlei to Brugkraal
15km, 6–8 hours

After the steep climb of the previous day, the fourth day's hike is relatively gentle although it does involve some

valley to the little Brugkraal mission settlement, a cluster of quaint cottages with well-kept little gardens full of vegetables and flowers. The overnight accommodation is in a community guest cottage consisting of two bedrooms (one with a double bed and single bed and the other with four single beds) and a shared bathroom – basic but comfortable – and, as you experienced in Heuningvlei, the ladies of the village arrive with plates and plates of hearty fare for dinner and breakfast.

DAY 5 Brugkraal to Wuppertal
12km, 6–7 hours

The first section of the hike leads down the valley of the Grasvlei River, via Grasvlei to Agtersvlei. After retracing your footsteps back to Grasvlei (which you passed the previous afternoon) you can enjoy a swim in the big pool at the foot of the Grasvlei waterfall – though be warned that it's a scramble down a steep path and back again. Then you cross over a rustic footbridge and follow the gravel track for a short while before turning off into the indigenous vegetation between the track and the cliff above the river. There is no clear path so you wind your way through the fairly sparse vegetation,

rejoining the gravel track for a couple of kilometres to pass through Agtersvlei. Though this is one of the less interesting sections of the trail in terms of scenery and views, you regularly see donkey carts carrying wood and other provisions up and down the dirt road. There's another short cut through the bush, before the trail crosses the Tra Tra River and joins a good path through the dramatic Sassakloof gorge that leads to Wuppertal. The kloof is narrow and very beautiful – one of the highlights of the whole trail. The path goes up and down, sometimes along the river and sometimes on higher terraces, and there are several swimming pools along the way (if the river is really high after winter rain you might even have to wade at times). Eventually the path leads out of the kloof and you gain a rise to see a big settlement surrounded by trees in the valley ahead. Wuppertal Mission Village is the oldest of the settlements in the area, founded in 1830 by the Rev. Johann Gottlieb Leipoldt of the Rhenish Missionary Society and looked after by the Moravian Church since 1965. It boasts a primary school so it's full of youngsters who board during the week before returning to Heuningvlei, Brugkraal and the other outlying settlements at the weekends. Otherwise,

Sousboontjies (curry sauce beans)

Ingredients:
2 cups beans
4 cups water
pinch salt
sugar
1½ teaspoons turmeric
2 dessertspoons vinegar

Cook beans till soft
Salt to taste
Add sugar, turmeric and vinegar
Stir well and enjoy.

CEDERBERG CUISINE INTO YOUR HOME

SASSAKLOOF GORGE

BRUGKRAAL

Wuppertal is quiet and seemingly untouched by the 21st century. Once you've settled into the Kloofhuis community guesthouse it's worth taking a stroll around town before dinner. Meals

HIGHLIGHTS

The hills are alive…with the sound of music every Sunday evening in December when the local choir entertains with Christmas carols from Singkop, the hill overlooking Wuppertal.

Best view: Looking down the sheer cliffs of Krakadouw Peak from the summit plateau. Mind your step!

Best lunch spot: Boontjieskloof hut – make sure you have a dip in the deep pool just beyond the hut.

Funniest sighting: Hop onto the back of a snail.

KRAKADOUW FUN

– are well worth a visit, and there's always a tantalising smell of fresh bread from the wonderful bakery on the way into town should you be peckish. But the highlight is probably the shoe factory and shop, where the traditional *veldskoene* are made. You can watch the cobblers at work and even invest in a pair of the durable leather shoes that are made here.

DAY 6 Sevilla Rock Art Trail
4km, 2 hours

There's time for more sightseeing in Wuppertal after breakfast before you're collected around 10am and taken on a guided tour of the Sevilla Rock Art Trail on the way back to Clanwilliam. The trail, which can also be walked unguided, is one of the Cederberg's best-kept secrets, offering some of the finest examples of rock art in the area. The easy trail winds along the Brandewyn River and takes in nine sites of well-preserved rock art paintings, a legacy of the San people who inhabited the area for thousands of years. There's an excellent free pamphlet available to supplement the guides' explanations of the paintings, so once your eyes are accustomed you'll have fun picking out dancing women, elephants, quaggas (similar to zebra), eland,

KLEIN KRAKADOUW TRAIL

are a slightly more formal affair here – in the quaint Lekkerbekkie community restaurant next to the information centre. If you fancy a swim ask for directions to the Krokkedam swimming hole, about a 15-minute walk from the village along a path that starts from behind the Moravian church. The church itself, the small museum and Red Cedar Cosmetics – a small community-based project making bath and skin products using rooibos tea

BLOCKHOUSE 1901 ON THE KLEIN KRAKADOUW TRAIL

END OF DAY

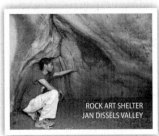

ROCK ART SHELTER
JAN DISSELS VALLEY

handprints and the striking long-legged archers with their bows and quivers of arrows. It's strange to think that big game once roamed these areas. In spring the flowers are simply magnificent in this lush area, while all year round you may catch a glimpse of dassies, baboons, bird life and occasional small game. The paintings are regularly spaced and you can return the same way if you wish so you can opt to visit as many, or as few, sites as you like. Once finished, around noon, you are transferred, with an optional quick stop at the Englishman's Grave, to your cars in Clanwilliam, ready to depart for home by 2pm. A tip though: the last five sites are less visited and therefore better preserved than the first four, so if you're pushed for time skip the early sites and concentrate on those at the far end of the valley.

Other Cederberg Heritage Route Trail Options

Both the three-night Klein Krakadouw and the four-night Groot Krakadouw trails start with a rock art trail and donkey cart ride as above. Hikers on the Klein Krakadouw Trail then have a guided hike of about 13km (taking six to eight hours) up to Krakadouw Nek and then down the Krakadouw Pass, back to a guest cottage in the Jan Dissels Valley. The scenery is very different once you are over the nek as the trail follows the valley of the perennial Dwars River stream through patches of beautiful indigenous bush and trees. En route you pass an unusual round blockhouse built in about 1901 by the British forces during the Anglo-Boer War.

Hikers on the Groot Krakadouw Trail complete the rock art trail in the Jan Dissels

Valley on their day of arrival, then on the morning of the second day take the donkey cart trip down to Heuningvlei where they have lunch, before continuing for a further 8km on a donkey cart trail via Witwater Village to Brugkraal for their second night. They then hike back up via Grasvlei and the Boontjieskloof hut to Heuningvlei (day four of the Wuppertal Trail in reverse) where they overnight, before completing the section over the Krakadouw Nek and down the Krakadouw Pass to the guesthouse in the Jan Dissels Valley for the final night, as per the final day on the Klein Krakadouw Trail.

Krakadouw

CN 86

SUMMARY

Start/finish	Clanwilliam
Group size	Minimum two, maximum six
Difficulty	Most of the hiking/walking on the Cederberg Heritage Route trails is of moderate difficulty, though the paths are often stony and uneven. Occasionally during the winter (wet) season some of the streams/rivers may be difficult to cross without removing your boots and wading. These are good trails for novice and averagely fit hikers and there are some challenging optional hikes to satisfy the macho types.
Facilities	Accommodation at the beginning and end of the trail is in comfortable guesthouses with en-suite bathrooms and all mod cons. The community guesthouses are basic (shared rooms and bathrooms and no heating in the winter for example) but clean and adequate. There are no facilities on the trail but water is available from the mountain streams.
And the kids?	Children from about 10 years old are welcome on the trails provided that they have hiking experience.
When to go	The trail can be walked year round. Spring (August to October) when the wild flowers are at their best and autumn (March to May) are ideal times. Winters are cold and sometimes wet. Summers are very hot but you can walk early to avoid the heat of the day.
Contact	CHR, Cedarberg African Travel, 027 482 2444, info@cedarberg.co.za, www.cedheroute.co.za
Other contacts	African Paddling Association (up-to-date list of rafting operators on the Doring), www.apa.org.za Amanzi Trails, 072 229 4672, info@amanzitrails.co.za Aquatrails, 073 362 6121 / 021 782 7982, info@aquatrails.co.za Beaverlac Resort, 022 931 2945 Boschkloof MTB Trails, 022 921 3533 Bundi River Adventures, 021 975 9727, info@bundi.co.za, www.bundi.co.za Bushmans Kloof, 021 685 2598, info@bushmanskloof.co.za, www.bushmanskloof.co.za CapeNature (Cederberg and Grootwinterhoek bookings), 021 659 3500, bookings@capenature.co.za, www.capenature.org.za Cederberg Escape, www.cederberg-escape.com Cederberg Oasis Hiking/MTB/4x4 trails, 027 482 2819 CITOUR Information Office (Citrusdal hiking, MTB, quad, 4x4 trails), 022 921 3210, info@citrusdal.info, www.citrusdal.info/ www.citrusdal2x4x4.co.za Citrusdal Quad Farm, 082 773 8310/022 921 3398, info@citrusdalquadfarm.co.za, www.citrusdalquadfarm.co.za Clanwilliam Tourism Info Office, 027 482 2024, cederberg@lando.co.za, www.clanwilliam.info De Pakhuys, 027 482 1879, thys@depakhuys.com, www.depakhuys.com Driehoek, 027 482 2828, www.cederberg.co.za Gravity Rafting Adventures, 021 683 3698, www.gravity.co.za

Other contacts *ctd.*	Karukareb Trails, 027 482 1675, karukareb@telkomsa.net, www.karukareb.co.za
	Kromrivier (Cederberg Tourist Park), 027 482 2807, namapip@netactive.co.za, www.cederbergtourist.co.za
	Mountain Mist MTB Trails, 027 262 5750
	Oudrif, 027 482 2397, moondance@49er.co.za, www.oudrif.co.za
	River Rafters, 021 975 9727, info@riverrafters.co.za, www.riverrafters.co.za
	Rondegat 4x4/quad bike trail, 027 482 2527 / 082 777 2757
	Sanddrif, 027 482 2825, sanddrif@cederbergwine.com, www.cederbergwine.com
	Sevilla Rock Art Trail/Traveller's Rest, 027 482 1824, travrest@clanwilliam.co.za, www.travellersrest.co.za
	Sewefontein Farm, 022 921 3301
	Trekkloof MTB, 022 921 3353 / 082 574 2773, www.gekko.co.za
	Wildthing Adventures, 021 556 1917, kat@wildthing.co.za, www.wildthing.co.za
Kit list	See general kit list, page 202
	Limit your luggage to 15kg in soft bags as space, particularly on the donkey carts, is limited.
	Specific
	🚶 Your own tipple, decanted into plastic bottles, unless boxed wine
	🚶 Slingsby's 'the map' of the Cederberg
	🚶 Wild flower book
	🚶 Guide to the rock art (guide books on the areas to be visited can be purchased in Clanwilliam)
	🚶 Magazines, biscuits or other little treats for your hosts in the communities who rarely have access to such luxuries
	🚶 Coins/phone card if you need to keep in touch with the outside world. Cellphone reception is available in and around Clanwilliam but is only occasionally available during the walks.
	🚶 First-aid kit – including personal medications, throat lozenges, lipsalve, aspirins, antiseptic cream, insect repellent. It is important to regularly check for ticks. (The community guide will have a first-aid kit during the walks but bring anything you may need during the evening/night.)
On your bike	**Around Kromrivier**
	🚶 **Tower Route, 2 hours, moderate** The route leads through fields up to the old TV relay tower on top of the peak. Return the same way or by a circular route that comes out on the Truitjieskraal Road.
	🚶 **Eco-route (MTB or 4x4), 4 hours, moderate** See the Maltese Cross from your bike or 4x4. This long, but spectacular route starts at the top of Kromrivier Pass, across Dwarsrivierberg, around Sugar Loaf and back either via Witkleigat or Gonnafontein.
	🚶 **Stadsaal Caves, 2 hours, easy/moderate** There are two alternative routes from Kromrivier – either over the Kromrivier Pass or through the fields on the Truitjieskraal Road. These can be combined to form a circular route.

On your bike
ctd.

Around Sanddrif

- Wolfberg MTB trail, 7.5km, 1–2 hours, moderate A well-marked circular trail from the car park at the base of Wolfberg Cracks takes you around the Wolfberg massif on the Jeep track, with great views of Tafelberg ahead.
- Lot's Wife MTB trail, 12.5km, 1–2 hours, moderate Another straightforward trail which heads down past the car park for the Maltese Cross and takes in some great rock formations.

Other MTB trails

- Cederberg Oasis, 40km linear and 25km circular, moderate There are two MTB route options along gravel roads from the farmhouse and a 4x4 track with extreme climbs.
- Trekkloof MTB trail, 30km, easy/moderate An undulating trail into the foothills of the Cederberg, between plantations of rooibos tea, back down into the valley to the river or Sanddrift dam.
- Beaverlac MTB trail, 10km and 14km, moderate There are two circular trails on steep, rocky farm roads from Beaverlac Resort. These can be ridden individually or combined for a longer ride.
- Sewefontein Farm, 12km (return), difficult A steep and rocky climb is rewarded by magnificent views and there are plenty of gravel roads between the farm and Clanwilliam if you want something less challenging.
- Bushmans Kloof, 18km, 1–2 hours, easy/moderate You need to be a guest to enjoy this stunning ride along the reserve's gravel roads but that is no hardship. Go in August or September to enjoy the outstanding flowers. Mountain bikes are available at the lodge.
- Algeria to Kromrivier Resort, 62km (return), moderate A good gravel road runs from the turn-off to Algeria on the N7 all the way to just short of the final tarred section before Op-die-Berg. If you're not up for the whole thing then a good ride is the section between Algeria Forest Station and Sanddrif (where you can stop for a swim or hike up to the Maltese Cross), to Stadsaal or to Kromrivier.
- Clanwilliam to Wuppertal, 40km, moderate/difficult This is a great route on a good gravel road that leads over the Pakhuis Pass, past C Louis Leipoldt's grave, the Sevilla Rock Art Trail and Bushmans Kloof Reserve, the Englishman's Grave and finally down the switchbacks to Wuppertal. Just remember that what goes down has to go back up!
- Cederberg Escape, 200km, 3 days, difficult Introduced for the first time in 2008, the Cederberg is a fully supported three-day mountain biking race consisting of three out-and-back loops from the race village at Sanddrif. Daily distances, on a mix of gravel roads, rocky Jeep tracks and singletracks, vary from 48–85km per day.

| **Short hikes** | **Overnight hiking in the Cederberg** |

The Cederberg is a wilderness area of 75,000ha with no specified, i.e. named or marked, trails but plenty of opportunity to plan multi-day hikes along the network of paths and off the beaten track. Except for basic stone huts there is no accommodation other than at Algeria and the privately owned camp sites/chalets at Driehoek, Sanddrif and Cederberg Tourist Park, so you need to be self-sufficient.

The wilderness is divided into three 24,000ha hiking blocks. Groups are limited to a minimum of three and a maximum of 12 people per day. Permits are only valid for specific blocks.

Day and overnight hikes

- Around Algeria/Driehoek (permits from Algeria or CapeNature)
- **Crystal Pools, 2 days,** return from Algeria or 8–10 hours, via Welbedacht, from Driehoek Most day hikers content themselves with the Skeurkrans route or hiking up to the waterfall above Algeria, but if you're feeling strong then the hike up to Crystal Pools via the Middelberg hut is a superb outing with a swim in a deep pool the reward for your efforts. While it's possible in a long day it's more fun to overnight at the Crystal Pool hut and return the next day.
- **Wolfberg Arch, 12km, 6–8 hours** The straightforward hike up to the arch from Driehoek takes you up the Riff (the steep section, but where there is generally water) and then onto the Wolfberg Plateau and the arch.
- **Tafelberg, 2 days** A fabulous, strenuous hike up to Spout Cave near the summit plateau of Tafelberg. Follow the path up Welbedacht Kloof from the car park at what was formerly the old forest station, or from Driehoek, then head south (i.e. turn right) along the Jeep track until you see a cairn indicating a track on the left which heads up to Tafelberg and the roomy cave.

Around Sanddrif (permits from the office)

- **Maltese Cross, 4km, 2.5–3 hours (return)** It's is a moderately strenuous climb from the car park near Sanddrif up the steep valley to the Maltese Cross, but there is water for most of the way, even in midsummer. Alternatively it's a fairly strenuous hike (which can be done in either direction) from Kromrivier, which takes you round the prominent Suikerberg (Sugarloaf Peak) and the Pup to the Maltese Cross. From the cross, head over Kokspoort and return via Disa Pool and Kromrivier Cave (20km, seven to eight hours return).
  The Maltese Cross is also accessible via the 4x4 eco-trail from Kromrivier.
- **Wolfberg Cracks and Arch** This stiff hike (Cracks – 3 hours return, Cracks and Arch – 8 hours return) is a must, but start early. The main trail goes up through the largest track and there is an alternative route for the more adventurous. The path from the top of the cracks to the arch is fairly flat and marked with cairns. Return via the same route (13km) or via the Riff (16km).

Short hikes
ctd.

Maalgat, 1km, 35 minutes This short hike is along the river from the camp site. Maalgat, or Seekoeigat (Hippo Pool), is a huge swimming hole where families can while away the day while daredevils jump in from the 10m-high surrounding cliffs.

Sneeuberg, 15km, 6–9 hours For a really good, challenging day walk follow the route up to the Maltese Cross and then continue on the trail across the broad vlei until you see a track leading up to the saddle at the base of Sneeuberg's triangular summit peak. The final stage of the ascent of the peak from the saddle is a serious scramble that should only be attempted by experienced mountaineers, but the views from the top of the saddle are impressive.

Around Kromrivier (permits from the office)

Disa Pool, 12km, 3–4 hours (return) from the car park This pretty trail up Kromrivier, past the Kromrivier Cave to the waterfall and Disa Pool at Tweede Kloof, is particularly appealing between December and February when the disas, *Disa tripetaloides*, are in flower.

Stadsaal Caves, 3 hours You can drive all the way to the caves but if you want to stretch your legs then park at the top of the Kromrivier Pass and walk down and back.

Apollo Cave/Lunar Tunnel, 12km, 7–8 hours Follow the path up the Kromrivier until you see cairns leading off to the left towards Apollo Peak.

Other short walks/ attractions

Stadsaal Caves and Bushman Paintings
Drive or cycle from Sanddrif/Cederberg Tourist Park and spend a few hours exploring the Stadsaal and Elephant caves and rock formations or make a day of it by being dropped off then walking back.

Cederberg Observatory
This is either a one-hour, 4km return hike from Sanddrif or you can park at the Observatory. The Observatory is open on Saturday evenings – weather permitting and provided that it is not a full moon – when visiting astronomers present a slide show and set up a telescope for stargazing.

Hiking in Groot Winterhoek
You can hike, and sleep out, anywhere you like in the wilderness areas – as you can in the Cederberg – but there are also marked day trails that can be combined to form a multi-day hike, overnighting at De Tronk or Perdevlei. Groot Winterhoek is greener than the Cederberg and most trails follow/cross rivers and lead through wonderful eroded sandstone rocks and outstanding flora. Be warned that all the trails lead downhill from the car park so remember you have to climb back out of the valley to get back to your car. This can be surprisingly taxing in the heat of the afternoon so leave plenty of time.

A good multi-day trail is to take the trail to De Tronk via Groot Kliphuis and Perdevlei. You can do this in one long day, or overnight at Perdevlei, then continue to De Tronk the following day before returning on the third day via the

Other short walks/ attractions *ctd.*

direct path from De Tronk to the car park. The first section, the 16km (four-hour) hike from the parking area to Groot Kliphuis, takes you through weird and wonderful rock formations, some outstanding fynbos (and disas in season) and there's a good swimming pool en route. An alternative is the easy 14km (three-hour) trail which leads from the parking area to Kliphuis, and then on to Groot Kliphuis via the Jeep track – also very scenic. From Groot Kliphuis you can continue to Perdevlei, where there is a primitive stone hut, either on a 6km footpath (one and a half hours) or via the Jeep track, which is a more demanding 7km route (two hours) but which affords magnificent views. From Perdevlei it's a 12km (two-and-a-half-hour) hike along the Klein Kliphuis River to De Tronk, with plenty of opportunities to swim en route. De Tronk has three primitive overnight huts. Leave your overnight bags at De Tronk and then follow the 5km (one-and-half-hour) trail to one of the Cederberg's most impressive sites – the vast rock pool and gorge of Die Hel. It's an easy hike to the start of the gorge but the descent into the gorge and to the pool is very steep and dangerous. No overnighting or fires are allowed at the pool or at the overhang at the start of the descent, which contains some rock art, so you need to return to De Tronk if you intend to sleep overnight.

Alternatively, if you want to do Die Hel and back to the car park in two days (or even as a long day walk) you can go straight to De Tronk on an easy 13km (three-hour) trail from the parking area following the Kliphuis River to the low-water bridge, then follow the Jeep track to De Tronk (this would be the return route if you followed the suggested longer multi-day trail). Beautiful patches of erica and numerous swimming pools are the main attractions. Alternatively, you can follow the Jeep track through outstanding fynbos all the way to De Tronk (14km, three and a half hours) and return on the trail along the Kliphuis River described above. There is no water available on the Jeep track for the first 11km after leaving (or returning to) the car park, so this is not recommended as a return route.

Other activities

Citrusdal and Clanwilliam tourism offices can supply information on the numerous hiking/MTB/4x4/rafting trails and tracks on farms around Citrusdal, Clanwilliam and the Cederberg.

4x4 and Quad Biking

The gravel roads of the Cederberg are a 4x4 enthusiast's playground, and much of the area around Wuppertal is only accessible in 4x4 vehicles. Routes include: Wuppertal 4x4 trail; Esselbank 4x4 trail; Luiperdskloof 4x4 trail; Biedouw River 4x4 trail; Kromrivier Eco-trail; Little Boy's Farm 4x4 trail; Kagga Kamma 4x4 trail; Rondegat 4X4 and quad bike trails; Citrusdal Quad Farm trails; Cederberg 4x4 offer guided excursions and basic and advanced driver training.

Rock Climbing

The Cederberg has some of South Africa's best climbing, with everything from extensive bouldering areas, bolted sport routes and long traditional routes all in spectacular settings. Top areas include Truitjieskraal (permits from Sanddrif or Kromrivier), Sanddrif Crag and Wolfberg Cracks (permits from Sanddrif) and Rocklands (permits from CapeNature) and De Pakhuys (private farm).

Rafting

The Doring River, one of the country's most exciting stretches of white water if there is enough rain during the winter months (usually July to September), is an exciting multi-day rafting adventure with Amanzi Trails, Aquatrails, Bundi River Adventures and River Rafters.

TRAIL 3

Postberg Wild Flower Trail

Postberg Wild Flower Trail

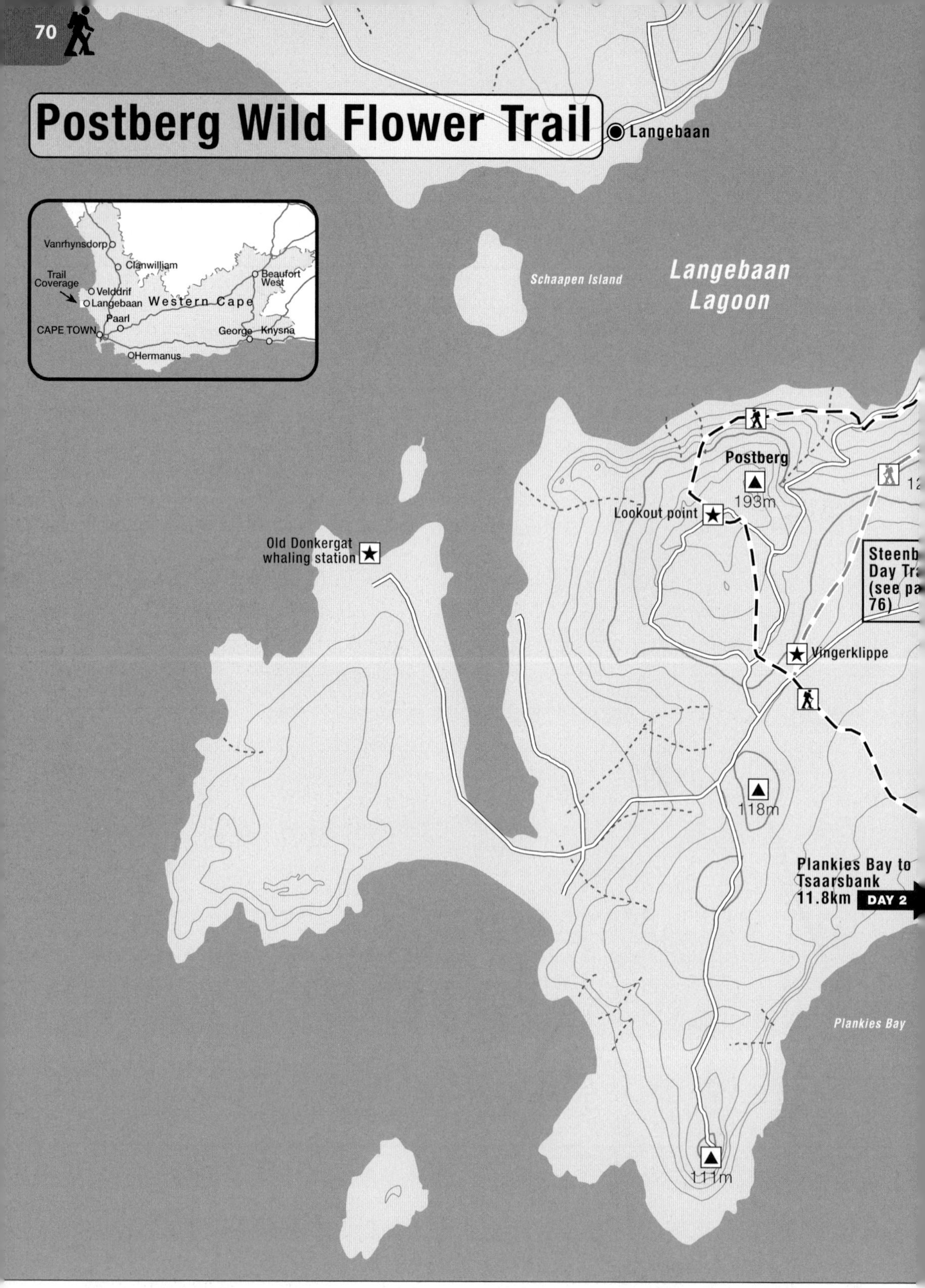

Langebaan
Vanrhynsdorp
Clanwilliam
Trail Coverage
Velddrif
Langebaan
Western Cape
Beaufort West
Paarl
CAPE TOWN
George
Knysna
Hermanus
Schaapen Island
Langebaan Lagoon
Postberg
193m
Lookout point
Old Donkergat whaling station
Steenb
Day Tr
(see pa
76)
Vingerklippe
118m
Plankies Bay to Tsaarsbank 11.8km
DAY 2
Plankies Bay
111m

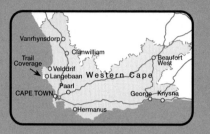

Pantelis A Lemos 1978

Kraal Bay
Houseboats

...abelkop
...38m

16 Mile Beach

...aarsbank to
...ankies Bay
...5km

START / FINISH

33°08'42 S
18°00'15 E

Braai or lunch stop

Kreefte Bay

Vondeling Island

Atlantic Ocean

Plankies Bay
Overnight Camp

4 S
2 E

Stony Head

LEGEND

Hiking	Point of Interest	Index Contour
Optional Hike	Lighthouse	Contour
Cycling	Whale Watching	Major Road
Surf Spot	Post Office	Main Road
Spot Height	Bird Watching	Other Road
Accommodation	Homestay	Hiking Trail
Boating	Fishing	Vehicle Transfer
Shipwreck	Viewpoint	R777 Route Marker
Town Spot	4x4 Track / Transport	
Waterfall	River	GPS Points

POSTBERG WILD FLOWER TRAIL

The Postberg Wild Flower Trail, in the West Coast National Park, is one of the Cape's best-kept secrets. The two-day trail is only open during the peak flower season months of August and September and, provided the weather holds, it's an absolute delight. On the first day you wander through private land past great granite outcrops and along the edge of the beautiful Langebaan Lagoon, then spend the second day on the beach before returning through the coastal fynbos to your car. The great carpets of springtime wild flowers are obviously the highlight and the extensive swathes of orange, pink and white daisies won't disappoint, but the fynbos is also superb. The reserve is well populated with animals – you'll no doubt be falling over leopard tortoises and there are ostriches aplenty, eland, gemsbok, springbok, wildebeest, bontebok (the park is outside the bontebok's normal distribution range but these were successfully introduced) and elusive bat-eared foxes, while twitchers will enjoy sightings of numerous birds of prey, oystercatchers, Egyptian geese, egrets and even flamingoes in the lagoon.

Only 12 hikers are allowed on the trail so you enjoy a real sense of wilderness only an hour from Cape Town. There is no formal portage service, and though there are loos, braais and wood at the overnight spot, you need to be totally self-sufficient in every other sense. But if you ask nicely at the entrance the park staff will (usually) schlep your tent and heavy gear to camp. Obviously it's not so easy in the morning – your pack goes on your back. But it's only a couple of kilometres back to the start of 16 Mile Beach, where you can see, and make a short detour to, your cars and dump your bags if you're really struggling, before continuing along the trail to the shipwreck. This very straightforward, well-marked hike has only one hill of any significance so it is manageable even by unfit hikers. And besides, the whole point of the trail is to go slowly and enjoy the flowers!

DISTANCE 27.3km	
DAYS 2	
DIFFICULTY EASY	

" My soul is full of longing for the secrets of the sea, and the heart of the great ocean sends a thrilling pulse through me. "
Henry Longfellow

NICE SUNDOWNER AT PLANKIES BAY

DAY 1 Tsaarsbank to Plankies Bay

15.5km, 6 hours

Park your car at Tsaarsbank and, if you don't fancy carrying your overnight bag, ask the staff at the parks board portacabin to drive it around to Plankies Bay. The information that comes with your permit advises that you should start no later than 9am as the Postberg section closes at 5pm (but in fact you have plenty of time so there's no rush). Follow the white poles and flower signboards that mark the trail across the veld towards Konstabelkop, keeping your eyes peeled for birds of prey overhead and terrestrial creatures such as dung beetles and cute little bat-eared foxes. The last time I hiked this trail I saw five foxes in as many minutes. As you head up the hill the path becomes indistinct at times but if in doubt head for the next white pole. It's not too long a climb, but from the summit – about 2km from the start and at a height of only 188m – you can see the turquoise expanse of the Langebaan Lagoon, the small quaint settlement of Oude Post and Kraal Bay with its bobbing yachts and houseboats. Jan van Riebeeck stationed a garrison at Kraal Bay in 1660 and the sea bed off Postberg is littered with shipwrecks, so cast your mind back to the 17th century when this was a thriving base. Archaeological records suggest that human occupation of the park dates back to the middle Pleistocene, while habitation by Strandlopers and Khoi people is evidenced in the middens and fish traps. On the edge of the Kraal Bay is the historical site of Oude Post 1, the remains of an old Dutch fort, while more recent discoveries include Eve's footprints, fossilized Homo sapiens footprints dating back some 117,000 years ago. Stop and explore the rock formations of the koppie, great outcrops of weathered and lichen-covered granite, then follow the path down and across the gravel road behind the houses until you get to a Jeep track which runs along the water's edge and beneath the slopes of the Postberg Mountain (193m). It's a glorious walk along the lagoon so admire the flowers and the ever-changing views. After an hour or so you reach Perlemoen Point and shortly afterwards the track starts to climb gently towards Uitkyk. On your right you'll see the old Donkergat whaling station and the military base, while behind you the view extends over the flat Schaapen Island and right across to Langebaan on the far side of the lagoon.

The trail leaves the Jeep track just before the top of the

SHEEP ISLAND

In the 1660s, the Dutch used Schaapen Island (Sheep Island) to kraal sheep traded from Khoi tribes. I find it hard to imagine now as I walk through the floral wonderland, but I read somewhere that they used these little islands to protect the sheep from being taken by lions!

PANTELIS A LEMOS WRECK 1978

KUKUMAKRANKA PLANT SPIRALLED ON GROUND

COFFEE BREAK ON ROCKS NEAR TSAARSBANK

MIND WHERE YOU TREAD

Please respect the request to stay off the sensitive dunes in the immediate areas of the ablution block and water tanks at Plankies Bay.

MARINE FAUNA

Langebaan Lagoon has over 400 species of marine fauna and is also the only known habitat for South Africa's most endangered marine mollusc, *Siphonaria compressa*.

THE KUKUMAKRANKA

An interesting West Coast plant is the kukumakranka, which has distinctive long, thin leaves that are usually spirally twisted or coiled. The attractive flowers appear in summer when the leaves have already died. In midwinter the kukumakranka produces a long club-shaped berry with a fragrant pulp in which numerous seeds are embedded. The ripe fleshy fruits were gathered to make kukumakranka brandy – one of the early Cape remedies for colic and indigestion. Traditionally, an alcoholic infusion or tincture was made from a few ripe fruits in a bottle of brandy or witblits ('white lightning'). The edible fruit was also highly valued to perfume rooms and linen.

hill, veering right through a mass of tiny, colourful yellow and orange flowers. This is a magical section so enjoy it. You'll often see buck and ostriches here – give the latter a wide berth! Eventually you arrive at the beach of Plankies Bay. Continue, with the sea to your right, over the rocky peninsula to a smaller beach at the southern end of the bay. This is your home for the night and it's exposed to the brunt of the Atlantic Coast so it can be quite a wild spot. If it's not too windy you can collect your bags from the parking area near the ablution block and pitch your tent on the beach beneath one of the granite boulders. The official camp site, however, is more sheltered: a level grassy area among the rocks near the ablution block. This is a basic site so come prepared; the only facilities are the ablution block with toilets, basins and drinking water, braai grids, wood and washing-up stands. No hot water, showers or

cooking utensils are available at Plankies Bay. If the weather is playing ball, head to the beach for sundowners and watch the sun sink into the sea before you braai your food and then let the sounds of the sea lull you to sleep.

DAY 2 Plankies Bay to Tsaarsbank
11.8km, 3.5 hours

The trail hugs the coast until you reach the small settlement of Kreefte Bay. The path leaves the Jeep track here and again takes a detour round the back of the pretty beach cottages. Opposite Kreefte Bay is Vondeling Island, literally Foundling Island, named after the young seals that once were abundant there. Now home to thousands of sea birds, the island is a rich source of guano, which was exploited during the Guano Rush of the 1940s by numerous prospectors seeking their fortunes. The dwellings are

SIGNAGE IN WEST COAST N.P.

Spare us a Thought

A TWITCHER'S PARADISE

The West Coast National Park is an extremely important conservation area for many different types of bird, including 50% of the world's population of swift terns. A total of some 255 species have been recorded in the park, including the highest population density of vulnerable Black Harrier, *Circus maurus*, in South Africa. The park surrounds the Langebaan Lagoon, which is a Ramsar Site (a site deemed to be of global significance to wetland bird species). Many of the wader species are Palaearctic migrants, so the best months to visit the lagoon are September, when the birds return weary from their transcontinental travel, and March, when large numbers of migrants are feeding heavily in preparation for the reverse journey.

If you want to observe the lagoon waders, visit the Geelbek Hide just after low tide. As the water level rises the waders are forced closer to the hide until they eventually fly off as the water recedes. You'll see all sorts of birds, including Sanderling, Little Stint, Ruff, Marsh, Terek and Curlew Sandpiper, Turnstone, Ringed and Grey Plover, Greenshank, Whimbrel, Curlew and Bar-tailed Godwit and even, in the deeper water, flamingoes and white pelicans. The isolated hide west of the Geelbek Educational Centre overlooks a saltpan and offers the chance to see Chestnut-banded Plover.

Southern Black Korhaan, Cape Spurfowl and Grey-winged Francolin, Southern Grey and Cape Penduline Tit, Ant-eating Chat, White-throated and Yellow Canary, Karoo Lark, Chestnut-vented Tit-babbler, Bokmakierie and Cape Bunting are regularly seen in the fynbos surrounding the lagoon, while the coastal islands at the mouth of the lagoon are breeding havens for Kelp and Hartlaub's Gull, Cape Gannet and African Penguin.

abandoned these days – relics of a pre-chemical era.

About an hour after leaving Plankies Bay you reach a stile over a fence, which takes you onto 16 Mile Beach where you'll see great flocks of Common Terns and Kelp Gulls and a shipwreck in the distance. There are braai places here and it's a beautiful spot to sit on the rocks and have a late breakfast or tea break. Walk along the beach for about half an hour, to the boundary fence where you'll see a flag and sign indicating the turn-off into the dunes. Turn inland here and follow the trail inland back to the road leading to Tsaarsbank and your car. Instead of turning inland at the markers, you should, however, make a short detour and carry on along the beach for 20–30 minutes to the wreck that has been in your sights for most of the day. This is the wreckage of the *Pantelis A Lemos*, an iron ore carrier that mistook South Head for North Head on her way to Saldanha in 1978.

DAY 2: GO SLOWLY AND ENJOY THE SPACE – BEACH NEAR TSAARSBANK

Start/finish	Tsaarsbank Gate, West Coast National Park
Group size	Minimum one, maximum 12
Facilities	Drinking water, toilet facilities and braais are provided at Plankies Bay, but hikers must be totally self-sufficient and bring tents, sleeping bags, stoves, cooking utensils, food, etc. There is no water on the trail other than at Tsaarsbank and Plankies Bay so carry at least two litres. There is cellphone reception most of the way.
And the kids?	There is no minimum age limit on the trail. This is a straightforward trail that youngsters will enjoy, though all hikers must be walking fit.
When to go	The trail is only open during August and September. Be warned, however, this is the Cape winter so be prepared for wet and cold weather.
Contact	West Coast National Park, 022 772 2144, patriciame@sanparks.org www.sanparks.co.za
Other contacts	Cape Sports Centre, 022 772 1114, info@capesport.co.za, www.capesport.co.za Gravity Adventures, 021 683 3698, adventure@gravity.co.za, www.gravity.co.za
Other hikes in the area	**Strandveld Educational Trail** **Day 1 • 14km, 5 hours; Day 2 • 14km, 5–6 hours** This easy, self-guided trail consists of two circular routes starting and finishing at the Geelbek Homestead, so you can hike each day with only a daypack. It's an interpretive route, largely on Jeep track, which leads through the Strandveld dunes and a section of 16 Mile Beach. If you want a leisurely stroll learning about the flora and fauna of the West Coast, this one's for you. **Day Trails** **Steenbok Day Trail, 13.9 km, 5 hours** The Steenbok Day Trail follows the route of the Postberg Wild Flower Trail up to Konstabelkop. At this point, follow the Steenbok signboards left towards the granite spires of Vingerklippe (finger rocks), then down to Plankies Bay where you join the route of the Postberg Trail before veering off left back to Tsaarsbank. Again, this trail is only open during the spring flower season and can accommodate 20 people.
On your bike	Bikes are not allowed in the Postberg section but mountain bikers can ride on the tar and gravel roads and tracks in the rest of the national park There is no charge for riding these trails, other than normal park entrance fees.
MTB trails	**Seeberg** There are two options on this route that starts at the Langebaan gate and are marked by green and red signs respectively. **The Green Trail, 13km, 1 hour** This easy circular trail starts at the Langebaan gate and turns right off the tar down on the old Bottelary dirt road (lift your bike over the chain) and joins up with the original old 'white road' where you will turn right. Turning left here is not permitted as there is a bush reclamation project underway. This brings you back out at the Seeberg Bird Hide and it's an easy ride back to the gate.

MTB trails *ctd.*	**The Red Trail, 17km, 1.5 hours** This includes some sandy and bushy terrain so is more challenging for fit riders. The trail basically follows the same route as the Green Trail, but has two deviations. The first is a short out-and-back route off to the right up the steep Seeberg lookout road to the top, after which you rejoin the tar road and continue towards Geelbek. The second deviation requires you to turn left at Mooimaak. Follow the Red Trail signs around Mooimaak and down along a circular route back to the tar road where you continue as on the Green Trail. **There are also two cycling routes on the tar:** Langebaan gate to Geelbek, 30km, 2–3 hours (return) Langebaan gate to Kraal Bay, 70km, 4–5 hours (return)
Paddling	Guided paddling trips and kayak hire are available on the lagoon through Gravity Adventures.
Kiteboarding	Langebaan Lagoon is a popular place to learn kiteboarding and the reliable winds attract kiteboarders from all over the world, so on most days the sky above the azure lagoon is full of colourful kites. There are several schools in Langebaan, including Cape Sports Centre, where you can attain the basic internationally recognised IKO kiteboarding certification.
Game-viewing/ birding	During the wild flower season (August and September) visitors can explore the spectacular Postberg section of the reserve in their own vehicles, viewing game or admiring the flowers at their leisure. The bird hides near the Geelbek Homestead are accessible year round.

CAMPING AT PLANKIES BAY

Rocky shores

TRAIL 4

Hoerikwaggo
Tented Classic

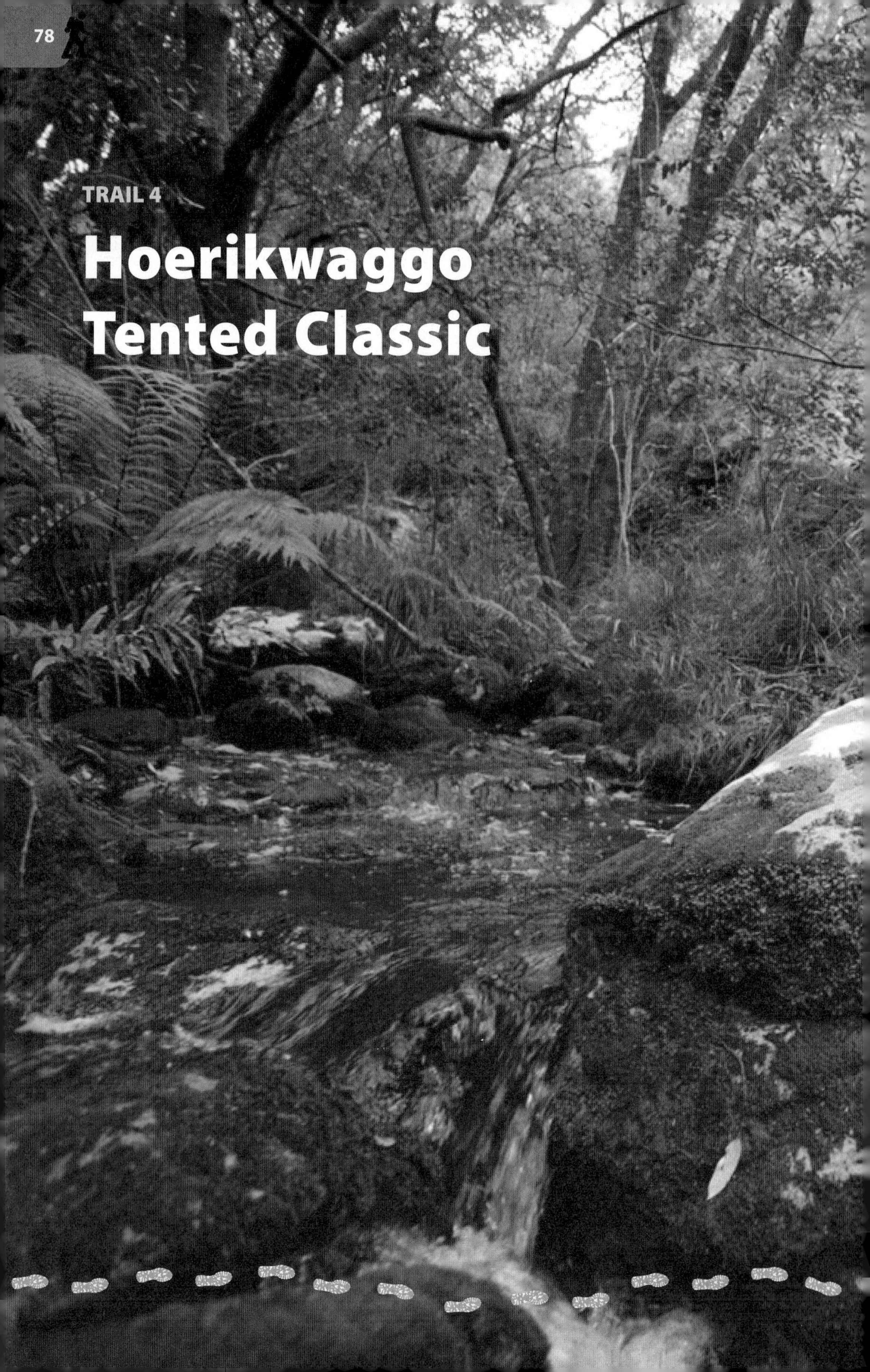

Hoerikwaggo Tented Classic

Western Cape

Clanwilliam
Beaufort West
CAPE TOWN
Paarl
Strand
George
Knysna
Mossel Bay

Trail Coverage

To Paarl

N2

Table Bay

Cape Town

V & A Waterfront

Three Anchor Bay

Kirstenbosch Botanical Gardens

TABLE MOUNTAIN

Deer Park
Platteklip Gorge

Nursery Ravine

Hely-Hutchinson Reservoir

844

Lower Cablecar Station
33°57'23 S
18°24'13 E
989m
Vic Rese
Cableway

TWELVE APOS

Lions Head

Camps Bay

FINISH

Camps Bay

Lui Bay

M6

Atlantic Ocean

LEGEND

🚶	Hiking	★	Point of Interest		Index Contour
	Optional Hike		Lighthouse		Contour
🚴	Cycling		Whale Watching		Major Road
	Surf Spot	✉	Post Office		Main Road
▲	Spot Height		Bird Watching		Other Road
🏠	Accommodation		Homestay		Hiking Trail
	Boating	🎣	Fishing		Vehicle Transfer
	Shipwreck	📷	Viewpoint	**R777**	Route Marker
●	Town Spot		4x4 Track / Transport	⊕	GPS Points
	Waterfall		River		

N

TRAIL 4

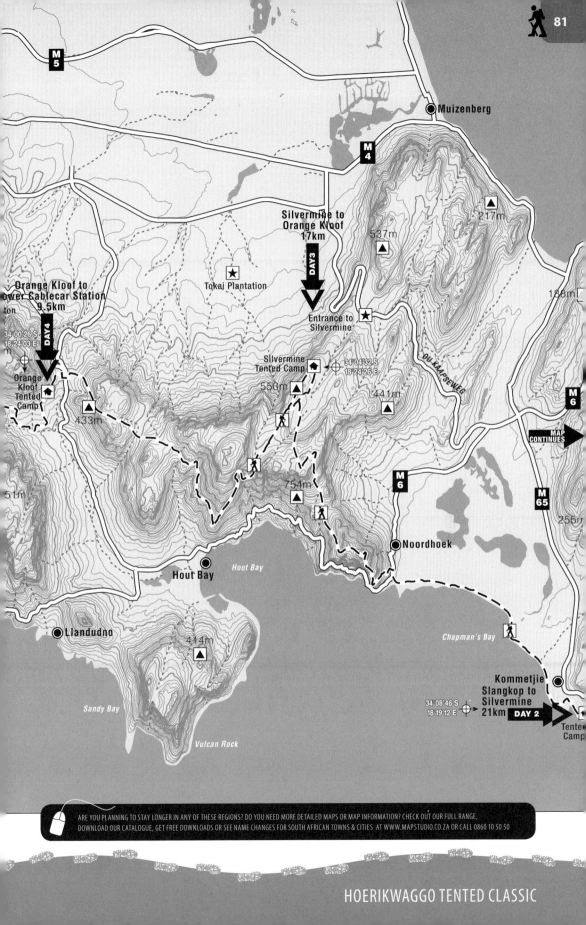

M5

Muizenberg

M4

217m

Silvermine to
Orange Kloof
17km

537m

188m

DAY3

★ Tokai Plantation

Orange Kloof to
lower Cablecar Station
9.5km

ton

Entrance to
Silvermine
★

34 00'26 S
18 24'03 E
m

DAY4

OU KAAPSEWEG

Orange
Kloof
Tented
Camp

Silvermine
Tented Camp

34 04'32 S
18 24'26 E

550m

441m

433m

M6

51m

MAP
CONTINUES

754m

M6

M65

255m

Noordhoek

Hout Bay

Hout Bay

Llandudno

414m

Chapman's Bay

Sandy Bay

Kommetjie
Slangkop to
Silvermine
21km

34 08'46 S
18 19'12 E

DAY 2

Tented
Camp

Vulcan Rock

ARE YOU PLANNING TO STAY LONGER IN ANY OF THESE REGIONS? DO YOU NEED MORE DETAILED MAPS OR MAP INFORMATION? CHECK OUT OUR FULL RANGE,
DOWNLOAD OUR CATALOGUE, GET FREE DOWNLOADS OR SEE NAME CHANGES FOR SOUTH AFRICAN TOWNS & CITIES AT WWW.MAPSTUDIO.CO.ZA OR CALL 0860 10 50 50

Hoerikwaggo Tented Classic

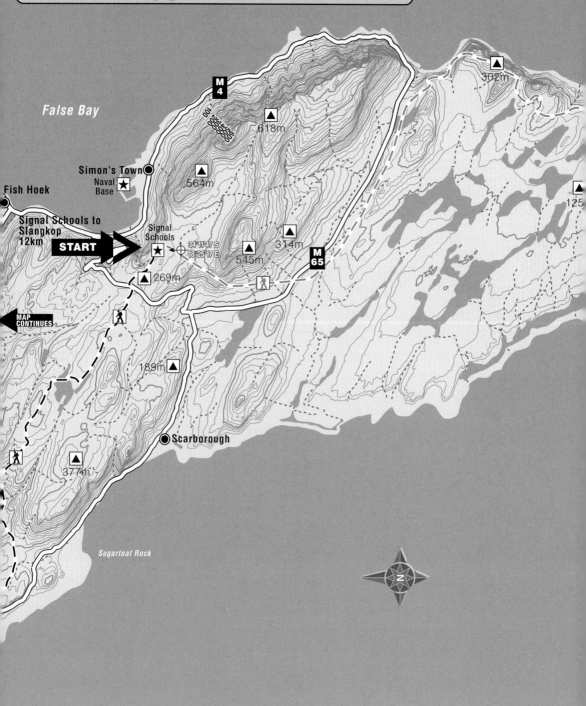

False Bay

M4

618m

Simon's Town

Naval Base

564m

Fish Hoek

Signal Schools to Slangkop 12km

START

Signal Schools

34°11'47 S
18°25'17 E

545m

314m

M65

302m

125

269m

MAP CONTINUES

189m

Scarborough

377m

Sugarloaf Rock

N

Cape Point

▲ 266m

Cape of Good Hope

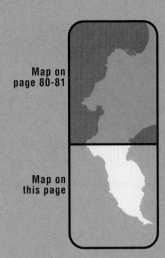

Map on
page 80-81

Map on
this page

Atlantic Ocean

LEGEND

🚶 Hiking	★ Point of Interest	—— Index Contour
🚶 Optional Hike	Lighthouse	—— Contour
🚴 Cycling	Whale Watching	—— Major Road
🏄 Surf Spot	✉ Post Office	—— Main Road
▲ Spot Height	Bird Watching	—— Other Road
🏠 Accommodation	Homestay	– – Hiking Trail
Boating	🎣 Fishing	– – Vehicle Transfer
Shipwreck	📷 Viewpoint	R777 Route Marker
● Town Spot	4x4 Track / Transport	⊕ GPS Points
Waterfall	– – – – River	

HIGHLIGHTS

Few trails anywhere in the world compare with this superb guided, portaged and self-catered hike on Cape Town's iconic Table Mountain. Although moderately strenuous, the Hoerikwaggo Tented Classic is a luxury, or slackpacking, trail where you are guided and your bags are driven around from camp to camp, leaving you free to explore the mountain, the beaches and the fynbos with only a light daypack. What makes this trail really special is not only the high-quality guiding and the beautiful eco-friendly and uniquely designed overnight camps, but also the price – it is unbelievably good value. When it's completed, the full five-night, six-day Hoerikwaggo Tented Classic will allow hikers to follow the 100km mountain chain of the peninsula all the way from Cape Town to Cape Point through the Table Mountain National Park (TMNP). At the moment it is still work in progress; three of the five overnight camps are open – at Kommetjie, Silvermine and Orange Kloof – so hikers can spend one, two or three nights on the trail, while the fourth overnight camp, at the old forestry station above Smitswinkel Bay (near the entrance to the Park's Cape Point section), should have been completed by August 2009. Whether you sign up for a two-, three- or four-day trail you can't fail to be impressed by the outstanding scenery, and as you walk you'll learn about Hoerikwaggo, the 'Mountain in the Sea', its flora, fauna and the previously disadvantaged local people who built this trail. Don't go expecting a walk in the park – the distances are taxing and there are big hills to climb. But when you arrive in camp at night you'll do so with a sense of satisfaction and with a new appreciation for the magnificent Table Mountain National Park.

> DISTANCE 58.5km
> DAYS 4
> DIFFICULTY MODERATE
> MTB THREE ROUTES (SEE PAGE 95)

Table Mountain National Park
Kleinplaas Dam

66 *The mountains are calling and I must go.* 99
John Muir

STRETCH BETWEEN THE SIGNAL SCHOOL AND SLANGKOP

DAY 1   Signal Schools to Slangkop

12km, 5–6 hours

This is the easiest day of the trail. From the Signal Schools, high in the mountains above Glencairn, the trail initially follows the Kleinplaas Dam Trail, a fairly flat, undemanding route through the fynbos on the top of Red Hill. The vegetation is sparse and the views are extensive so it's worth stopping often to look at these unfamiliar vistas down to Cape Point and north to Chapman's Peak, to the big

WHALE BONES AT SLANGKOP CAMP

NEAR KOMMETJIE

peak of Karbonkelberg above Hout Bay, and even as far as the main table. This area burnt in 2008, so the bulbous plants – particularly the orchids – are prolific and extremely beautiful. You skirt the rugged Grootkop, or if you want a little diversion you can ask to climb this 390m peak. The trail veers right around the dam, with the boggier sections protected by

a boardwalk, then continues to a second dam where you can have a swim.

Look at the fynbos as you continue on the good, undulating path towards Slangkop – particularly the wonderful ericas and lilies. The settlement of Ocean View comes into sight on your right and beyond it you can see the great white expanse of Noordhoek Beach, which you'll be walking tomorrow. It's a stunning view – usually the water is a brilliant blue and you might see the odd surfer in the waves.

If it's a good day (it can get very windy in these parts) then the old observatory station on Slangkop is a good place for lunch. The buildings are derelict but afford great views over Kommetjie and along the coast. You'll see the distinctive white Slangkop lighthouse, the second tallest lighthouse in the country, down below, and if you look carefully you'll also spot the

ORANGE KLOOF TENT

tented camp that is your home for the night.

It's a steep downhill from the viewpoint, after which you cross over the road and follow the boardwalk through magnificent lichen-covered milkwoods to the back of the camp. The entrance is from the beach so you cross the dunes on a boardwalk leading to the coastal track, before

WATER ON TAP

On the top of the mountain the guides will point out a water tank. This is a baboon watering station placed there to encourage the primates to stay high in the hills during the dry summer months rather than come down to the residential areas where they are considered a pest.

SLANGKOP LIGHTHOUSE

THE CRAWL UP CHAPMAN'S PEAK

veering off along a path made of big round boulders to the camp gate. As you approach through the indigenous garden you pass a huge whale bone. The camp is close to an old whaling station and the coastal theme is very evident in the style of construction and décor.

Slangkop is a windy spot and though the camp is quite well protected by the vegetation several design elements have been incorporated so as to minimise the exposure to the elements. The braai area is enclosed while the tents are domed (in contrast to the A-framed structures at the other two camps, Orange Kloof and Silvermine) to reflect the movement of waves and wind as well as to encourage the prolific coastal vegetation to creep over and act as camouflage. As with all the highly imaginative and beautifully constructed Hoerikwaggo camps there are lots of inspired touches, including overhead lighting concealed in whale vertebrae and great views from the decks of the tents and the main area.

DAY 2 Slangkop to Silvermine
21km, 8–10.5 hours

From the Slangkop camp you head back to the coastal path. If you didn't check out the lighthouse the previous night then it's worth a photo stop. Operational since 1919, the lighthouse is the tallest cast-iron tower on the South African coast, with a massive 30m from base to balcony and a light that is visible for 30km out to sea. The path leads past great fields of kelp, then onto Kommetjie beach. Very up-market houses line the shore and pretty little boats bob in the sheltered bay – the shallow basin, according to the guides, was a natural fish trap for Strandlopers. Once past Sunset Beach you scramble over the rocks to the long, deserted stretch of Noordhoek Beach, where you can kick off your shoes and walk barefoot. The rusty wreck of the *Kakapo* makes a good spot for a break while the guides fill you in on her sad demise. The *Kakapo* was bound for Sydney when she ran aground one misty night in 1900. Soon after leaving Cape Town, the skipper mistook Chapman's Peak for Cape Point and headed east – right up onto the beach. It must have been an embarrassing, and of course costly, mistake! Keep your eyes peeled as you hike. A multitude of sea birds, including African Black Oystercatchers, as well as some rare mammals such as Cape clawless otters, subsist off this coast, while whales

BONES OF THE *KAKAPO* WRECK – 1900, NOORDHOEK BEACH

All Hoerikwaggo camps are designed to 'touch the earth lightly'. Developments are designed to have the least possible impact on the natural and cultural landscape, and to reflect both internally and externally the sense of place evoked by the intrinsic qualities of the landscape. Emphasis is placed on new and innovative ideas and approaches to energy-efficient design and on encouraging responsible custodianship of the resources by hikers.

As part of this goal, the tented camps have been built almost entirely of alien vegetation chopped down from within the TMNP. The advantages of this approach are many: not only does it create work for disadvantaged communities and aid fynbos restoration, but it saves around 30% of the timber costs commercial wood retailers would charge. The tents are built on wooden decks with connecting boardwalks so the scarring of earth is minimised by the approach of 'poles in holes'. No concrete is used – only light dagha mixes are used where absolutely necessary, otherwise it's a combination of crushed and compacted stone.

and dolphins are often seen just out to sea. Noordhoek Beach is popular with horse riders, dog walkers and surfers and occasionally you'll even see camels on its extensive white sands. It's quite a wild stretch of coast but if it's a calm day you might want to have a swim at the far end before heading up a steep little path through the coastal forest to Chapman's Peak Drive. A sturdy wooden ladder aids the climb up the first steep section, then you contour and climb gradually on a gentle track heading north towards Hout Bay. This is a new path, exclusively used for the trail and specially constructed by a largely female workforce funded by the Department of Environmental Affairs and Tourism's (DEAT) Social Responsibility Projects.

A lookout over Hout Bay and the Sentinel makes a good spot for a tea break before the final steep push to the summit of Chapman's Peak. The view from the top is truly awesome – you look back all the way across Noordhoek Beach to the lighthouse where you started this morning and across the busy harbour of Hout Bay to the sheer cliffs of the Sentinel, a popular base-jumping spot. Rest and refresh yourself before following the well-trodden path down to the saddle between Chapman's and Noordhoek peaks. The next stage, the sustained, steep climb up Noordhoek Peak, catches many hikers out, so take it easy and stop often to admire the views and the flowers. You're in the heart of the Cape Floral Region World Heritage Site, so enjoy these

NOORDHOEK BEACH

HOERIKWAGGO TENTED CLASSIC

Table Mountain is a 'park for all, forever' (as the marketing slogan for TMNP goes), but it's still a big mountain where the weather can change quickly. Obviously the guides are qualified in mountain leadership and will get you down safely if conditions get tough, but you must go prepared. Wear sturdy footwear (with a good grip) and carry a fleece and rainproof jacket in your daypack, as well as plenty of water as, particularly in summer, there is little to be had on the mountain.

According to local legend, Jan van Hunks, an 18th-century pirate, gave up life at sea to live on the slopes of Devil's Peak. As he was sitting on the mountain smoking his pipe one day, a stranger approached and asked for some tobacco. A smoking contest ensued and Van Hunks finally defeated the stranger, who turned out to be the devil. The cloud of tobacco smoke that they created covered the whole mountain like a tablecloth – as the famous white cloud still does when the southeaster is blowing.

WATSONIA SMILES ABOVE ORANGE KLOOF

ABOVE HOUT BAY

unique floral specimens while you can. Despite the vast number of flower species on the mountain, the guides are fairly knowledgeable and they carry flower books, which they can consult when in doubt. What you'll see will obviously depend on the time of year that you're hiking but there are usually erica and protea in flower, while at times pelargoniums and watsonia cover the slopes with bright purples and pinks, and if you're lucky you might also see delicate blue disas on the path. The last time I hiked this trail I was extremely fortunate to be in the company of a flower fundi who pointed out some unusual green, fly-pollinated *Leucadendron ferraria* and the *Gladoli carnusa* with its white flower and red stripes which apparently guide insects into the pollen. Even if you're a regular hiker on Table Mountain, as I am, you'll probably see plants that you've never seen before and it really makes you appreciate the narrow habitats of many of the endemics – and the reason why the Cape Floral Region is worthy of World Heritage status and has to be protected.

Once you gain the ridge, stop to savour the view back to Kommetjie and the Atlantic coastline for the last time. You're now heading over the watershed so you will be looking over the Silvermine valley towards False Bay for the rest of the day. After a brief spell on a Jeep track the path leads through the fynbos again heading towards the Silvermine Dam. The red-tasselled ericas are

SILVERMINE

magnificent and the scent of buchu fills the air. You can see the tented camp in the distance, and after a steep downhill the path leads past the dam and down a boardwalk by the stream until you cut up and over the road to the Silvermine camp. (If you are doing the two-day Slangkop Trail you leave the path at the Silvermine Dam car park.)

The theme behind Silvermine is mountain fynbos because, you guessed it, the camp looks out over fynbos-covered slopes. In deference to one of the main attractions of the reserve, the superb rock climbing on the east-facing sheer sandstone cliffs, the walls of the communal lounge/kitchen building are covered with artificial climbing holds – so that enthusiasts can hone their skills on this funky bouldering wall. (If you're fit and think you'll have the time and energy to enjoy the crags, you could also pack your sports-climbing gear in your overnight bags as the lower Silvermine crags are only a 15-minute walk from the camp.)

The camp buildings are constructed from alien vegetation, cut and sawn on site, and gabion-type wire mesh cages filled with broken stones. Again, there are great little touches that reflect the care that went into the design of the camp, such as lights made from burnt protea stands, wonderful showers, big wooden beds and a deep fireplace in the shade of a yellowwood tree.

DAY 3 Silvermine to Orange Kloof
17km, 6–8.5 hours

From the Silvermine camp you head north to the nek between Noordhoek Peak and Constantiaberg. It's a very pleasant start to the day as the gradient is not too strenuous and once again you are surrounded by magnificent fynbos and towering peaks. The trail skirts around Constantiaberg – easily identifiable from the radio mast on its top – to a lookout above Blackburn Ravine where the views are simply incredible. You then contour around again until you reach a waterfall, where you'll stop for lunch, before the path climbs briefly again and then descends the slopes of Vlakkenberg Mountain, through an area of cleared alien vegetation, towards Constantia Nek. This is a rather unsightly stretch, but what follows more than compensates. Once over the main road (where you would leave the trail if hiking the two-day Silvermine section) you enter the restricted area of Orange Kloof – a magnificent wilderness area that contains some of the last

Commonly known as the 'pride of Table Mountain', the red disa is the emblem both of the Mountain Club and of Western Province sports teams. Once common, the population of this colourful orchid has been decimated by collectors and is now endangered and protected. However, the bright red flowers can occasionally be seen in the lesser-known ravines and on waterfall cliffs between January and early March.

RED DISAS

BELOW WOODHEAD DAM WALL

BETWEEN CHAPMAN'S PEAK AND SILVERMINE

The Table Mountain Aerial Cableway was inaugurated by the then Mayor of Cape Town on 4 October 1929 and has been upgraded three times, most recently in October 1997. To date, some 18 million passengers have ridden it up to the top of Table Mountain.

SECTION FROM ORANGE KLOOF TO WOODHEAD DAM

According to TMNP, prehistoric people first left evidence of their habitation in what is now Table Mountain National Park more than 600,000 years ago. Tools of these Early Stone Age hunter-gatherers were found in a depression near the Cape of Good Hope. The Middle Stone Age inhabitants (dating from 200,000 to 40,000 years ago) also left evidence of their life on the peninsula. Fossils from around 8000BC indicate that by that period the inhabitants of the region had developed bows and arrows, which they used to hunt. San (or Bushmen) hunter-gatherers relied on the seashore for most of their food. This resulted in the Dutch naming them Strandlopers (beachcombers).

Antonio de Saldanha was the first European to land in Table Bay. He climbed the mighty mountain in 1503 via the natural break of Platteklip Gorge and named it 'Table Mountain'.

indigenous forest found on the main table. The Orange Kloof camp, in the shadow of the towering Eagle's Nest and Constantia Ridge, is only a short walk away. Again, you have to hand it to the camp designers – despite being less than half an hour from Cape Town city centre you feel deep in the cradle of the mountains in this wonderfully secluded setting. There's no traffic and no cellphone reception, only the tinkling of the stream and twittering of the birds. The

theme here is very much of the forest and the tents are linked by boardwalks and arranged around a central open space. One of the highlights is the raised lookout deck. It's a perfect sundowner spot so make sure you put those beers in the fridge as soon as you arrive.

DAY 4 Orange Kloof to lower cable car station

9.5km (or if the emergency route down Kasteelspoort is used, 11.1km), 4–5 hours

The final day takes hikers from the camp through the indigenous forest and up Disa Gorge onto the mountain along paths that you cannot access unless you have a special permit or are on the Hoerikwaggo Trail. Initially you wander beneath the canopy of yellowwoods, milkwoods, red alder and Cape beech, then head up a beautiful kloof

FERNS IN DISA GORGE

ABOVE ORANGE KLOOF

adorned with ferns. Disa Gorge is named after the Cape's most famous flower, the striking red *Disa uniforma*, and if you're on the trail in late January/February you might see this beautiful orchid on the steep, shaded banks. But at any time of year this is a delightful hike as the sides of the gorges are covered with rich green mosses, ferns and little flowers.

The guides will tell you that Cape clawless otter still live in the Disa River. You'll be lucky to see one,

ENTRANCE TO THE WOODHEAD TUNNEL 1891

not least because they are nocturnal animals, but you do occasionally see their droppings – with tell-tale fragments of crab shell – as you climb.

As you reach the top of the gorge the path narrows and can become quite treacherous, so watch your step – it's quite a drop so you don't want to slip. Shortly you arrive at the bottom of the Woodhead Reservoir dam wall, built in 1897 to supply water to the burgeoning city of Cape Town. This makes a good place for a short break before you climb up the steps to join the main path where, for the first time on the trail, you'll probably meet other hikers. From the reservoir the path leads across the back table, through the delightful Valley of the Red Gods and up to the upper cable car station. The views along the way are mind-blowing – at times you can see both the Atlantic and False Bay coasts and all the way down to Cape Point. The guides stop frequently to point out flowers, butterflies and colourful endemic sunbirds and sugarbirds and to remind you of the richness and incredible diversity of this floral kingdom, so it's as much an interpretive journey as a hike. Once you've admired the views of the city, Lion's Head, the Twelve Apostles and Devil's Peak from the lookout points at the upper

cable car station, you descend the mountain via the 'Rotair' revolving cable car – an adventure in itself. As the car turns you see the steep face of the mountain's upper buttress, across to the Waterfront and Robben Island and down into the city bowl. Your bags will be ready for collection at the lower cable car station.

THE TWELVE APOSTLES

It is not clear when the buttresses along the western side of the mountain acquired the name the Twelve Apostles. Their original Dutch name was 'De Gevelbergen' (Gable Mountains). A quick squiz at a map reveals that there are actually 14 buttresses and that none bear any biblical names, though the peak at the end of the Twelve Apostles path is called Judas Peak. Starting from the main table end the buttresses are: Porcupine, Jubilee, Barrier, Valken, Kasteel, Postern, Wood, Spring, Slangolie, Corridor, Grootkop, Separation, Grove and Llandudno Corner.

HOERIKWAGGO GUIDE

SUMMARY

Start/finish	Big Tree car park, Signal Schools, Red Hill/lower cable car station, Tafelberg Road
Group size	Minimum six, maximum 12
Difficulty	This is a moderately strenuous trail, with some steep climbs and uneven terrain.
Facilities	Accommodation is in extremely comfortable tented camps with shared bathrooms. A full range of pots, pans, crockery and cutlery is provided and a fire on which you can braai is lit by the camp staff in the evening. There are no facilities on the trail and water is not available other than from the mountain streams.
And the kids?	Children 12 years old and upwards are welcome on the trails.
When to go	The trail can be walked year round. Spring (August to October), when whales are often spotted off the coast and when wild flowers are at their best, and autumn (March to May) are ideal times. Winters are cool and sometimes wet.
Contact	Hoerikwaggo Tented Classic, 021 465 8515, hoerikwaggobookings@sanparks.org, www.hoerikwaggotrails.co.za
Other contacts	Abseil Africa, 021 424 4760, info@abseilafrica.co.za, www.abseilafrica.co.za Cape of Good Hope Hiking Trail, 021 780 9204, jacquelines@sanparks.org, www.sanparks.org/parks/table_mountain/tourism/overnight_hikes.php Cape Town Tandem Paragliding, 076 892 2283, www.paraglide.co.za Downhill Adventures (guided mountain biking trails), 021 422 0388, www.downhilladventures.com Hoerikwaggo Table Mountain Trail, 021 465 8515, hoerikwaggobookings@sanparks.org, www.sanparks.org/parks/table_mountain/ht/tm/default.php Mountain Club of South Africa, 021 465 3412, mcsacapetown@iafrica.com, www.mcsa.org.za South African Hang-gliding Paragliding Association (for up-to-date information on paragliding clubs): www.sahpa.co.za TMNP mountain guides, 021 465 8515/9
Kit list	See general kit list, page 202
Overnight hikes in Table Mountain National Park	**The Hoerikwaggo Table Mountain Trail** *Day 1: Wash Houses to Overseers Cottage (including a cable car ride if the weather permits), 9.5km, 5 hours* *Day 2: Overseers Cottage to Kirstenbosch, 9km, 4.5 hours* The two-day Hoerikwaggo Table Mountain Trail is a guided, portaged and self-catered luxury trail which showcases the most spectacular section of Table Mountain. Although hikers must be able to negotiate uneven terrain and a steep descent, the pace is slow so the trail is suitable for those who are not hard-core hikers. The standard of guiding is excellent so this is very much an interpretive trail, with the guides pointing out and identifying the magnificent fynbos species, the birds and the fauna that you see along the way and outlining the history and myths associated with the iconic peak.

Overnight hikes in Table Mountain National Park *ctd.*

The first night is spent at the Wash Houses – more of a boutique guesthouse than a hiker's hut. Then in the morning it's a short walk up to the lower cable car station where (weather permitting) hikers are whisked to the top of the mountain by means of the cable car. After you've enjoyed the amazing views from the revolving car and from the viewpoints at the top, the guides lead the way to the Maclear's Beacon (the highest point at 1086m), then over to the luxurious Overseers Cottage for the night. There's time for a short hike on the top of the mountain on the second morning before you descend Nursery Ravine to the Kirstenbosch National Botanical Garden, where the trail ends.

A minimum of two and a maximum of 16 people can be accommodated on the trail.

www.sanparks.org/parks/table_mountain/ht/tm/default.php

Cape of Good Hope Hiking Trail

Day 1: Entrance gate to overnight huts on Vasco da Gama Peak, 23.3km (with a shorter 19km option), 7–10 hours
Day 2: Vasco da Gama huts to entrance gate, 10.5 km, 4 hours

This two-day self-guided trail through the Cape of Good Hope section of the Table Mountain National Park (TMNP) is an absolute gem. Day one leads from the entrance gate to the Atlantic Coast, through swathes of colourful flowers and past herds of Cape mountain zebra, bontebok, eland and other plains game, and along a coastal path that is not open to day hikers. The scenery is glorious; the path leads past empty golden beaches, from which you'll often see whales and dolphins, then along the spectacular cliff path between the reserve's premier attractions – the Cape of Good Hope and Cape Point. After overnighting at the wonderful huts on the flank of Vasco da Gama Peak, the route on day two completes the circle, along the dramatic cliffs and wild beaches of the False Bay coast and back to the gate. Although it's not particularly steep at any stage, don't underestimate this trail – 33.8km is a long way in two days if you're carrying a pack so my advice would be to pay the extra bucks to have your bag (and your cooler bag of beer and meat) delivered to the hut. A minimum of one and a maximum of 18 people can be accommodated on the trail. The three huts, which each sleep six, are equipped with showers, flush toilets, mattresses, cutlery, crockery, pots and pans, braais and grids, which you can purchase at the gate and have delivered (along with your bags, if you have any sense!).

Day hikes

Plattklip Gorge, 2.5km, 1.5 hours (one way) The deep nick in the flat top of Table Mountain, known as Plattklip Gorge, is visible from a considerable distance and this was the first route by which Table Mountain was climbed. The first known ascent was by Admiral Antonio de Saldanha, commander of the Portuguese fleet that sailed into Table Bay in 1503.

The path, which starts about a kilometre and a half beyond the lower cable car station on Tafelberg Road, is so popular that it's nicknamed Adderley Street (after the main street in the city) by the locals. That said, it's incredibly steep and direct and there is no shade except in the narrow section at the top, so don't

Day hikes *ctd.* underestimate it, but the route is easy to follow and therefore provides a good, safe ascent or descent route, particularly in bad weather. Take water and be prepared for some knee jarring on the way down.

Skeleton Gorge, 4km, 2 hours (one way) This shaded trail, which starts at the Kirstenbosch National Botanical Garden, is steep but well marked and fairly straightforward. There are, however, a couple of ladders over the very steep sections, which can become slippery when wet. This was the favourite ascent of Field Marshal Smuts, a keen mountain walker, so the route is also known as the Smuts Track.

Nursery Ravine, 4km, 2 hours (one way)   This is a pleasant, if at times unrelentingly steep, uphill route which starts from the contour path just to the left of Skeleton Gorge. As with Skeleton Gorge, the first section through the wooded gorge is wonderfully tranquil. The route follows the stream, passing pockets of indigenous forest in which birds can be heard singing. About halfway up the path leaves the shade of the ravine and takes you up the right-hand slope in a series of zigzags. The views down the ravine are magnificent and there are well-maintained wooden steps aiding your way. A final steep wooden staircase brings you out under the steep cliffs of the dramatic Castle Rocks. Turn left here and follow the easy path over the stream. Magnificent stands of protea and fynbos flank the trail, which brings you to a four-way junction. A right turn will take you around Cleft Peak to Breakfast Rock and the Smuts Track, where you can descend by Skeleton Gorge.

Kasteelspoort, 3km, 1.5 hours (one way) There's no shade on this popular trail so as a result it affords incredible views. I thoroughly recommend this as a late afternoon hike when the sun sinks into the Atlantic and Lion's Head and the Twelve Apostles glow burnt orange in the evening light. Park at the top of Theresa Avenue on the Rontree Estate, then follow the concrete Jeep track up until it divides. Stay on the main track, which goes right, and continue up for about 100m until you can see a green signpost on the contour path above you. Leave the Jeep track and take the narrow path directly up the mountain to the signpost – you will see the cairn marking the way just after a big rock on the left. The signpost directs you over the contour path and on up.

Lion's Head, 2km, 1 hour (one way) There is no easy way to the top of Lion's Head, since the top section involves some scrambling, but the prominent triangular peak separated from the main table is without a doubt the most popular climb on Table Mountain. Tradition dictates that this be done as a full-moon walk, but it has become so popular that you can expect long queues at the chains and on the upper section if you opt to follow the crowd. Although the route is well marked and obvious, don't be fooled into thinking this is just a hike. There is a steep rock face to be negotiated, either by a scramble up through the rock bands or with the help of chains – which are definitely not for the vertiginous. Nevertheless, you will be astounded to see dogs, hikers with kids on their backs and people of all shapes and sizes enjoying the challenge. There is no shade on the route so go early or late, particularly in the heat of summer.

Guided hikes	Trained Table Mountain National Park guides may be hired to guide these trails.
MTB trails	**Silvermine, 7.5km, 1.5 hours, moderate** The Silvermine Mountain Bike Trail up Noordhoek Peak is only 7.5km but the first half contains a steep, serious climb that should not be underestimated (fortunately the steepest part is aided by a short cement strip but it's still a tough ride). The trail starts at the trail marker by the parking area next to the Hoerikwaggo Trail Silvermine camp. Once you reach the viewpoint over Hout Bay the climb is almost over, then it's downhill all the way back to the dam wall and down the tar road to your car.\n\n**Tokai Plantation, various options (easy to extreme)** The Tokai Forest is probably Cape Town's most popular mountain biking venue, with a network of gravel roads and some challenging singletrack.\n\nRoute maps are available at the entrance to the picnic site just down the road where you pay your entrance fee. From the gate, follow the main gravel road up to the Vlakkenberg Nek (5.6km). From here, if you have the lungs and legs, you can continue on a steep tar road for 4.9km to 'The Mast' on the top of Constantiaberg (927.8m). For the singletrack, turn right on Vlakkenberg (instead of continuing up to the mast) and try your luck on the switchbacks down. If that's too technical there's another section of singletrack starting on Level 5. From Level 5 you can also ride through to Silvermine on a fairly straightforward Jeep track.\n\n**Deer Park, various options (easy to difficult)** Most of the gravel roads below Tafelberg Road are open to cyclists, so you can choose your entry/exit point and length of ride. Now that Tafelberg Road is blocked off to vehicles from just beyond the path up Devil's Peak, the disintegrating tar road, which becomes a gravel track leading towards the King's Blockhouse, is a fairly easy option. Access points to Deer Park from the top of Derry and Pepper roads in Devil's Peak Estate, Deer Park East Drive in Vredehoek, Molteno Road in Oranjezicht and Glencoe in Higgovale are more challenging as they head pretty much straight uphill from the start.
Abseiling	The jumping-off point for Abseil Africa's 112m abseil adventure, one of the highest commercial abseils in the world, is just in front of the restaurant on the top of Table Mountain, close to the upper cable car station. The views are awesome and though it feels terrifying to be first walking down the rock and then dangling in space, the operators have you on a safety rope so you can relax and enjoy the amazing views. Allow at least 40 minutes to walk up to the top again from the bottom of the abseil on Fountain Ledge.
Rock climbing	Table Mountain offers a vast number of traditional and sports-climbing routes on excellent rock. For guides and information contact the Mountain Club of South Africa.
Paragliding	There are few things to beat soaring around Lion's Head in a paraglider, descending to over Camps Bay or Clifton Beach to land at La Med for sundowners. Tandem paragliding flights are available off Lion's Head with Cape Town Tandem Paragliding, while experienced pilots should contact SAHPA for details of local clubs and flying conditions.

TRAIL 5

Boland Hiking Trail

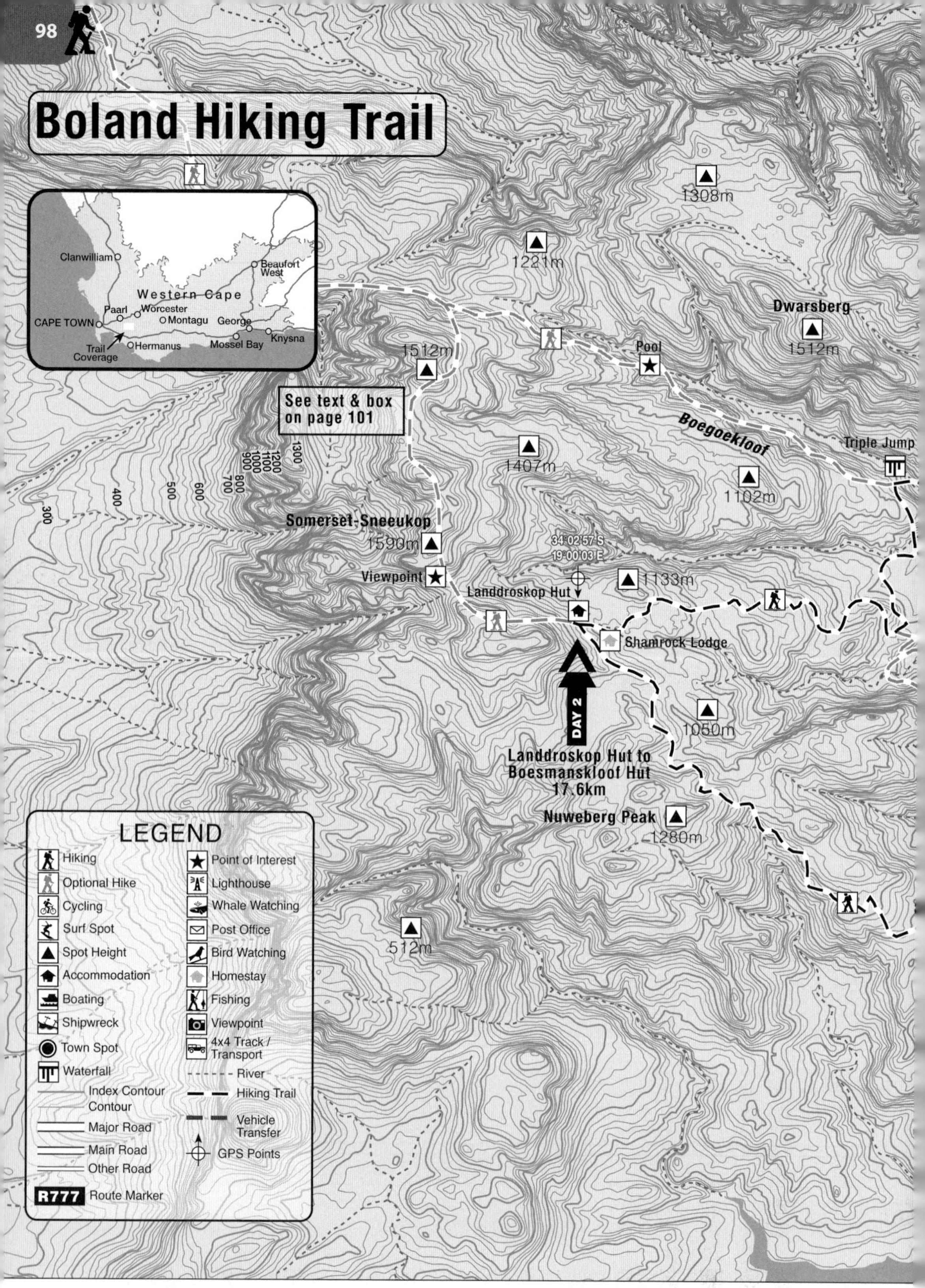

Boland Hiking Trail

See text & box on page 101

1308m

1221m

Dwarsberg

1512m

1512m

Pool

Boegoekloof

Triple Jump

1407m

1102m

Somerset-Sneeukop
1590m

34°02'57 S
19°00'03 E

Viewpoint

Landdroskop Hut

1133m

Shamrock Lodge

DAY 2

Landdroskop Hut to Boesmanskloof Hut 17.6km

1050m

Nuweberg Peak
1280m

512m

Western Cape

Clanwilliam

Beaufort West

CAPE TOWN

Paarl
Worcester
Montagu
George
Knysna

Hermanus
Mossel Bay

Trail Coverage

300 400 500 600 700 800 900 1000 1100 1200 1300

LEGEND

Hiking		Point of Interest	
Optional Hike		Lighthouse	
Cycling		Whale Watching	
Surf Spot		Post Office	
Spot Height		Bird Watching	
Accommodation		Homestay	
Boating		Fishing	
Shipwreck		Viewpoint	
Town Spot		4x4 Track / Transport	
Waterfall		River	
Index Contour Contour		Hiking Trail	
Major Road		Vehicle Transfer	
Main Road		GPS Points	
Other Road			
R777 Route Marker			

TRAIL 5

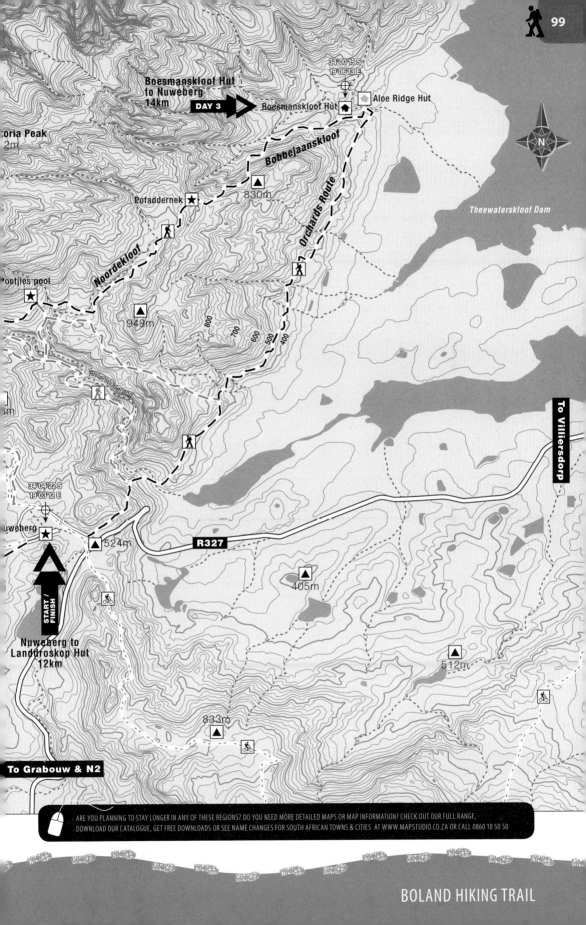

Boesmanskloof Hut
to Nuweberg
14km **DAY 3**

34·00·15 S
19·06·13 E

Boesmanskloof Hut

Aloe Ridge Hut

oria Peak
2m

Bobbejaanskloof

830m

Pofaddernek

Orchards Route

Theewaterskloof Dam

Noordekloof

ootjies pool

949m

800

700

600

500

400

Riviersonderend

34·04·22 S
19·03·12 E

uweberg

524m

R327

405m

START / FINISH

Nuweberg to
Landdroskop Hut
12km

To Villiersdorp

512m

833m

To Grabouw & N2

ARE YOU PLANNING TO STAY LONGER IN ANY OF THESE REGIONS? DO YOU NEED MORE DETAILED MAPS OR MAP INFORMATION? CHECK OUT OUR FULL RANGE,
DOWNLOAD OUR CATALOGUE, GET FREE DOWNLOADS OR SEE NAME CHANGES FOR SOUTH AFRICAN TOWNS & CITIES AT WWW.MAPSTUDIO.CO.ZA OR CALL 0860 10 50 50

BOLAND HIKING TRAIL

The popular Boland Hiking Trail is an easily accessible, yet magnificent, outing into the Cape fold mountains. Though only an hour out of Cape Town, the Boland Trail takes you into wild country as it weaves its way between the towering peaks of the Hottentots-Holland and Franschhoek mountains, over tumbling streams and through patches of forest. There are various routes of one to three days through rugged mountain wilderness and beautiful fynbos, covering distances of between 5km and 50km. One attraction of the trail is its suitability for big groups, as each of the two overnight sites has two large huts with bedrooms, bunk beds and mattresses, which can be booked separately. The fairly strenuous three-day circular trail is described below.

DISTANCE 43.6km	
DAYS 3	
DIFFICULTY STRENUOUS	
MTB TWO ROUTES (SEE PAGE 106)	

> ‘Go to the mountains and get their good tidings.’
>
> John Muir

SCENERY NEAR BOESMANSKLOOF HUT

LANDDROSKOP, SHAMROCK

DAY 1 Nuweberg to Landdroskop hut via the Sphinx Route
12km, 3–4 hours

From the car park the trail follows the gravel road until just past the reserve office, then cuts right into the forest climbing slowly until the edge of the plantation. The Jeep track swings right then heads uphill, about 4km from the start (when you can see the firebreak in front of you), and contours briefly to the left before the climb begins

in earnest. The path, which is clearly marked with footprints, heads steeply up towards a rock outcrop known as the Sphinx. I guess the person who named it thought it looked like the famous Egyptian Sphinx but I don't really see the resemblance. This is a good place for a tea break; you've knocked off nearly half of the day's distance so you can relax and enjoy the views. The trail then continues along Palmietpad, which contours under Nuweberg and Landdroskop

peaks around the headwaters of the Palmiet River to the huts. There is normally water in the tributary streams so you can cool off along the way, and the views and stands of protea and erica are impressive. Don't get too excited when you spot the overnight huts on the spur off to your right; they're visible for quite a long way off but the distance is deceptive. The trail continues some way up the valley then doubles back, so it's further than it looks, although mostly downhill.

LANDDROSKOP HUT

The two large mountain huts, Landdroskop and Shamrock, are geared very much for hiking groups and have a big central room with four bedrooms radiating off it, an inside central fireplace surrounded by benches, and tables, benches, braais and washing troughs outside.

TYPICAL BEDROOM

DAY 2 Landdroskop to Boesmanskloof
17.6km, 7 hours

There are a number of options from Landdroskop. If you only want one night out on the trail you can take the quick descent route back to Nuweberg on the Jeep track (8km, two hours). The most popular option, however, is the three-day trail, which follows the Jeep track (often marked as the Sneeukop Road) for just over 3km, then at an obvious signposted trail junction heads left (north) down towards the Riviersonderend River. Pass the sign off to Riviersonderend (a popular kloofing trip, see page 105) on your right and continue on the track, which contours around a spur before climbing and traversing around another junction. The Boegoekloof Trail comes in from the left at this point, but you descend to cross the river via the suspension bridge at Red Hat Crossing. Stop and swim in the pools here, or at least have lunch on one of the rocks in the river and take in the view. The trail then heads steeply uphill and soon you're high enough to spot the Jeep track coming down from your previous abode, the Landdroskop hut, and to look down into the rugged gorge below. This is a fabulous stretch of trail, but at the time

(a popular kloofing trip, see page 105)

THE MACHO OPTION

If you really want a tough day or two you can head west from Landdroskop hut (on the trail that leads over to Jonkershoek), past the impressive peaks of Landdroskop and Somerset-Sneeukop, then turn right to join the Boegoekloof Trail at the junction below Guardian Peak (a left turn here would take you to Jonkershoek). Continue down the kloof, crossing it several times and swimming at the pool at the base of the waterfall. There's a bit of a climb out at the end as the path leaves the river then descends again to the junction above Triple Jump Falls where you can either return to Nuweberg (thus completing a good two-day, one-night circular route) or join the Boesmanskloof trail as above. This extra loop adds another 10km or so to the hike so should only be undertaken by the fit (and foolish?), but it really is a spectacular section of trail which I would thoroughly recommend to those undaunted by a 30km day.

RESTIOS ABOVE LANDDROSKOP

BOLAND HIKING TRAIL

The Boland Mountain Complex, part of the Cape Floral Region Protected Area World Heritage Site, spans an area of over 110,000ha and comprises five contiguous nature reserves: Hottentots-Holland, Kogelberg, Jonkershoek, Assegaaibosch and Limietberg.

When the 18th-century Dutch settlers realised that there were Khoisan living in those mountains, they named them the Hottentots-Holland, as in the Holland of the Hottentots. Evidence of Late Stone Age occupation found in the Hottentots-Holland Mountains suggests that man has inhabited this area for some 250,000 years. Europeans settled in the Boland Mountain Complex less than three decades after colonising the Cape, and in 1692 Simon van der Stel granted a number of freeholds in the Jonkershoek Valley.

of writing it was ravaged by fires, so it looks like a lunar landscape. The gradient eases off for a while, then you descend to another river with a sign indicating the start of Suicide Gorge. The gorge is narrow and drops steeply here so you soon understand why following the river downstream on the Suicide Gorge kloofing trip is quite an undertaking. Before crossing the river hike upstream for five minutes and you'll come to a beautiful pool, Pootjiespool, which you simply have to swim in. If you're feeling brave you can scramble up to the top of the waterfall for an exciting bum-slide down the steep, grassy waterfall.

The fynbos in the next section of the trail escaped the burn so it is a pleasant interlude after traipsing through the blackened earth. And, since there is no sign of habitation in the valley, you really feel deep in the mountains here so take it slowly and admire the flowers.

There's another opportunity to swim and cool off at the next river crossing, but even if you choose not to stop for long, at least fill your water bottles – you have a long hike up Noordekloof and over Pofaddernek and there's no guaranteed water until the overnight huts.

The trail climbs steeply (again) out of the river valley, then at the junction heads left up towards the nek, basically staying parallel to the river. The route going off to your right is an emergency escape route which cuts back to join the Orchard Route quite near the end of the trail (that you will do on day two). But your way is up. It looks a long way but the leucadendrons are splendid and the gradient is kind, so within an hour or so you're at the saddle – not so bad after all.

If the views back down Noordekloof and over to the peaks of Nuweberg, Landdroskop and Somerset-Sneeukop are impressive,

THE MACHO OPTION – BETWEEN LANDDROSKOP AND JONKERSHOEK

LANDDROSKO
KURKTREKKE
SWARTBOSKL

POOL ON BOEGOEKLOOF SECTION

BOEGOEKLOOF SECTION

what lies before you is breathtaking. The great buttresses (with wonderful names like Baboon's Castle) and gullies of Noordekloof Peak flank the left-hand side of the valley, which drops away (worryingly) steeply, while the Theewaterskloof Dam shimmers in the late afternoon light. Fortunately the path down Bobbejaanskloof to the Boesmanskloof hut is not as knee jarring as you expect when you try to pick out the route, but it is long and relentless, so steel yourself. The views, however, make it all worthwhile, particularly if you're fortunate enough to be hiking late in the day when the mountains often take on a blue hue. The protea too are magnificent during the descent – great head-height stands flanking the path. Stop and look back – bet you're glad you don't have to start the day by trekking *up* this pass (known as Tandseer or Toothache) first thing in the morning, which of course

you'd have to do if you did the circle in reverse. Finally you reach the bottom of the kloof and climb slightly to the right before contouring round to the junction marking the route back to Nuweberg. From here it's a short downhill to the suspension bridge that leads to the rather tired-looking Boesmanskloof hut. Take care, and go one at a time when crossing the bridge. The swing can be disconcerting but it's also easy to cut your hands on the metal side rails.

DAY 3 Boesmanskloof to Nuweberg
14km, 2–3 hours

This easy route back to Nuweberg is also known as the Orchard Route, as for the most part it contours around the hillside overlooking farms, with, you guessed it, apple orchards! Be warned, however, that there is a sting in the tail in the form of a steep climb out from the weir about

Some 150 bird species, including Cape Sugarbird, Orange-breasted Sunbird and Victorin's Warbler, have been recorded in the reserve. Mammals include grysbok, grey rhebok, duiker and klipspringer, as well as highly elusive leopard, caracal, black-backed jackal and Cape clawless otter. The southern rock agama is commonly encountered in rocky habitats and you may also be fortunate enough to spot the rare strawberry frog. The Hottentots-Holland Mountains are also home to the only known population of the endemic dwarf crag lizard.

Apparently larger game species such as bontebok, red hartebeest and the rare Cape mountain zebra have been reintroduced into the Hottentots-Holland and, if all goes to plan, visitors will soon be able to see Cape buffalo. Quite a scary thought!

4km from the end, so save your energy, you're going to need it! From the overnight huts at Boesmanskloof you re-cross the suspension bridge, then climb a short way up the hill to the sign indicating the way back to Nuweberg. Soon you leave the big mountains behind and follow a path that contours above the farms, orchards and dams of the flat plains below. It's an uneventful, if pleasant, undulating trail (with swimming holes around the 3.8km and 7.5km marks) which finally comes out above the Riviersonderend River. Here the trail snakes down, cutting far left, then back right to the new bridge over the river. Stop and cool off here. It may only seem a short way (4km) to go on the map but trust me, you have a long haul ahead. In fact, if you've had your eyes open during the descent you might have been thinking 'where on earth does that trail on the other side of the river go? Glad I'm not going that way'. But

you are, though a little voice in your head is screaming 'surely you can contour round?' From the river the trail heads into the trees for the last of the shade, then keeps climbing until you eventually cross into another valley and head down towards the Nuweberg gates. It's pretty much downhill all the way until you hit the gravel road that leads back to your car – a rather anticlimactic end to an otherwise scenic trail. The good news is that there are hot showers in the car park, so pack a towel and change of clothes.

LUNAR LANDSCAPE AFTER FIRE – NUWEBERG TO BOESMANSKLOOF BEFORE SUICIDE GORGE

Start/finish	Nuweberg
Group size	Mimimum two, maximum 60
Facilities	There are two huts, each sleeping 30 people, at each of the overnight sites, equipped with bunks, mattresses, braai area, firewood and water. Each hut has four rooms, which can be booked separately. There is usually water in the streams that cross the trail and fairly regular cellphone reception.
And the kids?	Children over 10 years old are allowed on the trail.
When to go	The trail can be walked year round but hikers should go prepared for extreme weather, particularly during the winter months of July and August.
Contact	CapeNature Reservations, 021 659 3500, bookings@capenature.co.za, www.capenature.co.za

Other contacts	Dirtopia Trails, Thandi Dirtopia Trails, Lourensford Classic, 021 884 4752, theteam@dirtopia.co.za, www.dirtopia.co.za Frixion Adventures, 021 447 4985, brett@frixion.co.za, www.frixion.co.za Gravity Adventures, 021 683 3698, adventure@gravity.co.za, www.gravity.co.za Lebanon MTB Trail, 021 844 0248, info@oaklane.co.za, www.oaklane.co.za Oak Valley MTB Route, 021 859 2510, mail@oak-valley.co.za, www.oakvalley.co.za Oudebosch Office, 028 271 5138 Tri Active Events Management, 021 844 0975, info@triactive.co.za, www.triactive.co.za
Kit list	See general kit list, page 202
Day hikes	**Boegoekloof, 24km, 8 hours** The CapeNature pamphlet describes the out-and-back route up this vegetated kloof as 'fairly easy'. I beg to differ. I'd grade it as moderate, or even moderately strenuous, as the terrain is uneven, the path is often quite overgrown at the top of the kloof, and you've got quite a climb out from the river back to the Jeep track at the end of the day. But regardless, it's certainly a scenic day out in the mountains with plenty of water en route. **Groenland Mountain, 22km, 7 hours** This scenic and moderately strenuous out-and-back route starts across the road from the main reserve gate and winds up the flanks of the Groenland Mountain, offering superb views over the Hottentots-Holland Mountains, as well as spectacular fynbos and birding opportunities. From the top you can see for miles over the towns of Grabouw and Villiersdorp, the Theewaterskloof and Eikenhof dams and, on a good day, all the way to the sea. **Palmiet Blind Trail, 6km, 2 hours** This easy route along the river has Braille plates, so it is designed for blind and disabled persons. It's unsuitable for wheelchairs and is closed during the winter due to the risk of flooding.
Kloofing (November to April only)	**Riviersonderend, 15km, 6 hours • Suicide Gorge, 17km, 5 hours** Kloofing, or canyoning as it is sometimes called, is an extreme sport, which means you must be well prepared, fit and, of course, brave. Think hiking through the mountains, scrambling down waterfalls and launching yourself from rock crevices into icy waters metres below while repressing the urge to scream. The Hottentots-Holland Reserve is the mecca of kloofing in South Africa. There are just so many kloofs to explore in the Western Cape, but Riviersonderend and Suicide Gorge are perhaps the best known and most accessible. You can get a permit to explore on your own but unless you are experienced and know the kloof, go with a guiding company such as Frixion Adventures. Beginners could start with the beautiful Riviersonderend Gorge, a 24km (roughly seven-hour) route that starts just off the main Boland Hiking Trail. This is very much a mountain-river experience; there are no abseils and the highest compulsory jump is a mere 7m (although that's pretty high when you haven't done it before!).

Kloofing *ctd.*

The neighbouring Suicide Gorge is for the more experienced and courageous. It starts with a two-hour hike high into the mountains and an optional waterfall slide. Then it's a steep downhill all the way for 17km, with plenty of jumps (the highest is 14m) and swims – allow about nine hours. And if you really want a challenge you can go down Suicide and back up Riviersonderend Gorge.

If you are planning a kloofing adventure, note that it is inherently dangerous. Minimise the risk by observing the following safety tips.

The weather can turn quickly in the mountains so go prepared. Wear a wetsuit and carry food, emergency gear and warm clothing in a waterproof pack.

Once you're in the gorge the only way out is to continue down the river, so go prepared for a long, strenuous day. You won't get cellphone reception in the kloof so you're on your own.

Never jump without testing the water. Cape mountain water is very dark due to the natural tannins in the water, and the rocks underneath can be invisible, especially in shadows.

Land feet first, legs together, with your arms at your sides. **Never, ever dive.**

MTB trails

Groenland Mountain, 22km, 2–3 hours

There's an easy trail around the reserve offices through the plantation, but much more interesting is the trail that goes up to Groenland Mountain. Soak in the views – on a clear day you can see all the way to Hermanus and Kleinmond – then return the way you came, or exit at Lebanon or Twaalfontein Farm.

Jonkershoek Nature Reserve, 15 or 30km, 1 hour or c3 hours

The Jonkershoek Mountains make for scenic riding. The easy, circular 15km route starts at the reserve entrance and follows the undulating gravel road along the valley floor.

The 30km moderately strenuous ride climbs through the plantation to a scenic lookout point. Then it's pretty much downhill all the way on some challenging single- and Jeep track to the Eerste River, which you follow past the Fire Lookout and Kleinplaas Dam to the gate.

Wiesenhof, 7km, 2 hours

This circular trail, largely on good singletrack and rated as easy to intermediate, starts at the Wiesenhof Wildpark and takes you up into a game reserve, where you can enjoy the wildlife and the magnificent scenery as you ride.

Dirtopia Trail Centre Porcupine Trail, 15km, 1.5–2 hours (with another 3km Black Route singletrack option)

This technical trail at the Delvera agri-tourism complex near Stellenbosch was built by the same crew that is responsible for the Tokai, Jonkershoek, Lebanon and Thandi MTB trails. One of the Cape's premier singletrack destinations, it has over 5km of technical constructed singletrack and an additional 3km Black Route for advanced riders.

MTB trails *ctd.*

Dirtopia Trail Centre Farm Trail, 7.25km, 45 minutes to 1 hour
This short non-technical route on farm roads between the vineyards offers a great view from the top and is suitable for the whole family. Bikes can be hired at the trail centre that also boasts a fun Terrain Park and Pumptrack.

Palmiet, 26km, 5–6 hours
This easy to moderate trail starts at the Oudebosch office of the Kogelberg Nature Reserve. After the initial short section of singletrack, the trail is largely along Jeep track up to Stokoe Bridge where you can swim and chill before returning the same way.

Oak Valley, 21km, 2–3 hours
This tricky route starts at the farm gate and leads through vineyards, orchards and oak forests. Almost half the trail is on singletrack and there are a couple of serious hills to challenge fit and experienced riders.

Thandi Dirtopia De Rust Trail, 24km, 1.5–2.5 hours
This scenic loop through orchards, vineyards and fynbos near Grabouw showcases the spectacular scenery, floral spendour and biodiversity of the Groenlandberg Conservancy.

Thandi Dirtopia Thandi Trail, 8.5km, 30–45 minutes.
This short but challenging trail includes over 4km of singletrack and can be combined with the De Rust Trail.

Lebanon MTB trails
There's something for all on these scenic trails that start and finish at Oak Lane Cottages. Popular options include the easy Yellow Trail (7.3km, one hour), the easy to moderate Green Route (10.1km, one hour) and the moderately difficult Blue (17.1km, two to three hours) and Red trails (23.6km, three to four hours).

Lourensford Classic
The annual event held on the Lourensford Estate above Somerset West and organised by the Dirtopia team includes a Family Fun Ride (15km), intermediate event (34km) and an advanced course (62km).

Hottentots-Holland 4x4 trail
The trail, which starts at either Sir Lowry's Pass or at the Nuweberg gate, leads through beautiful mountain scenery. If you start at Sir Lowry's Pass then factor in some extra time to explore the famous Gantouw Pass where there's a national monument with old cannon and ox wagon track embedded into the rock.

Green Mountain Eco Route MTB, quad bike and 4x4 trails
Tri-Active Events Management offers guided trails of various lengths in the Elgin Valley and around the Groenland Mountain.

River rafting

Gravity Adventures offer one- and two-day rafting trips down the lower section of the Palmiet River in the Kogelberg Nature Reserve. In the summer this is a fun, easy adventure, while winter rain brings an exciting whitewater challenge.

TRAIL 6

Whale Trail (De Hoop)

Whale Trail (De Hoop)

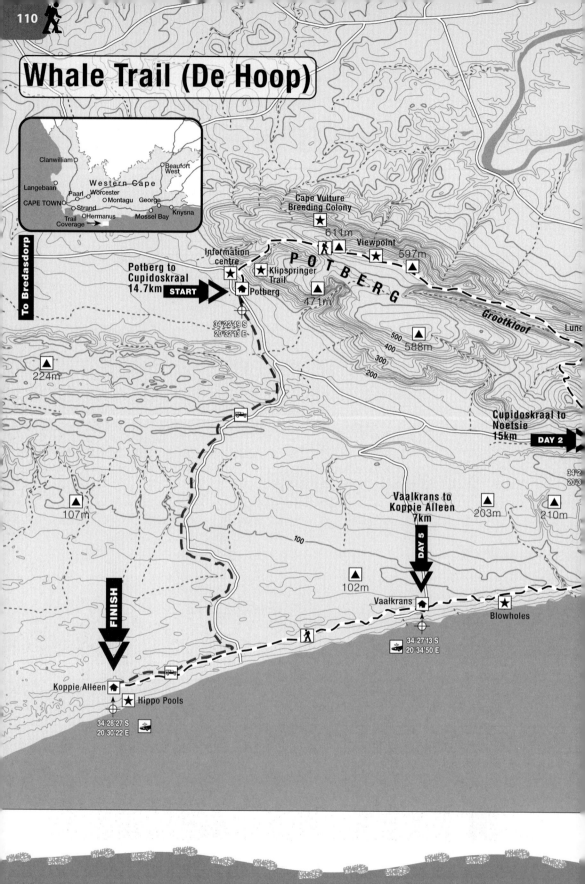

Western Cape

Clanwilliam
Beaufort West
Langebaan
Paarl · Worcester · George
CAPE TOWN · Montagu · Knysna
Strand · Mossel Bay
Trail Coverage · Hermanus

To Bredasdorp

Cape Vulture Breeding Colony

611m

Viewpoint

597m

Information centre

POTBERG

Klipspringer Trail

START
Potberg to Cupidoskraal 14.7km

Potberg

471m

Grootkloof

Lunc

34°22'49 S
20°32'18 E

500
400
300
200

588m

224m

Cupidoskraal to Noetsie 15km
DAY 2

34°2
20°3

107m

203m

210m

Vaalkrans to Koppie Alleen 7km
DAY 5

100

102m

FINISH

Vaalkrans

Blowholes

34°27'13 S
20°34'50 E

Koppie Alleen

Hippo Pools

34°28'27 S
20°30'22 E

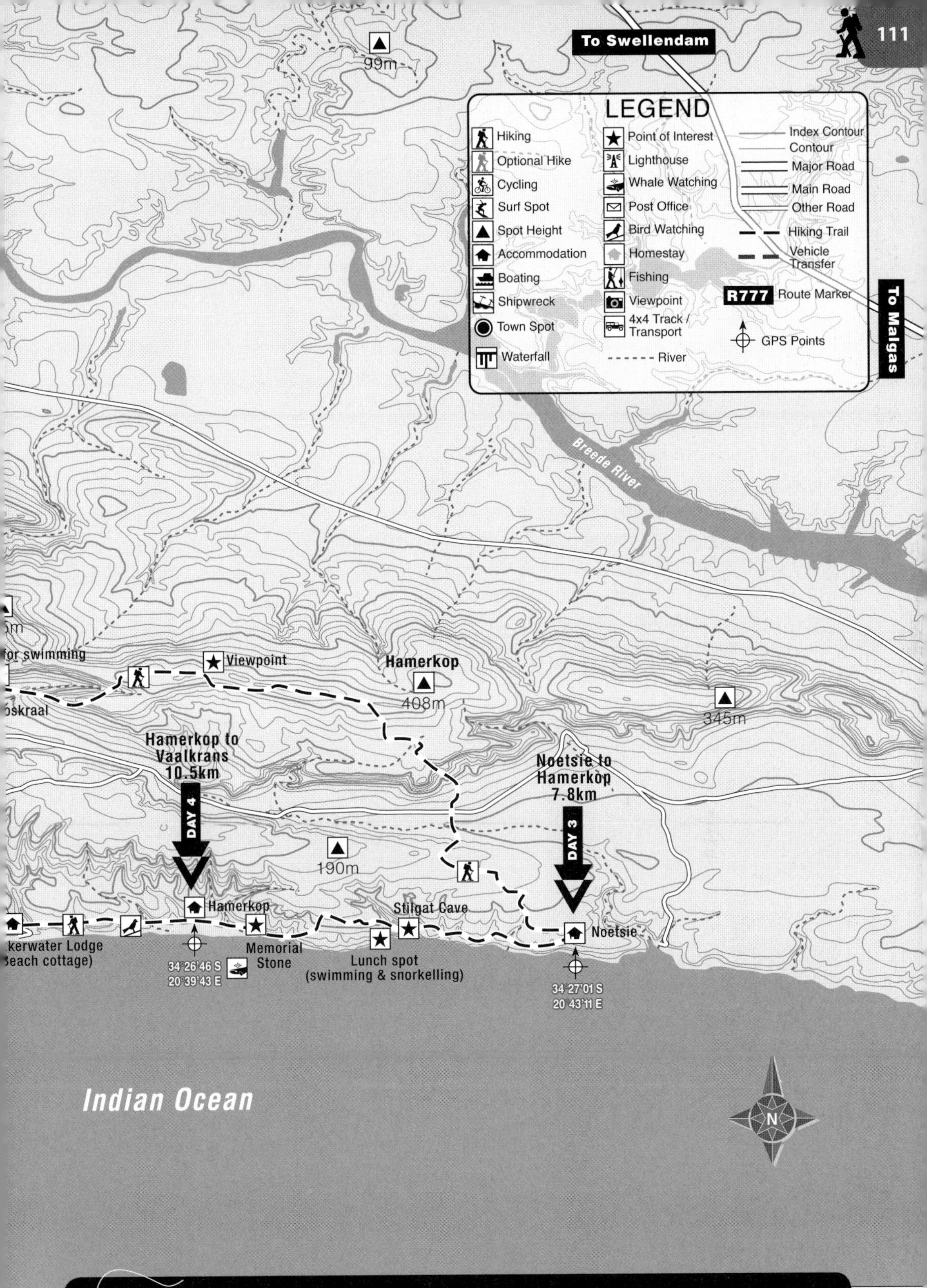

To Malgas

99m

LEGEND

🚶 Hiking	★ Point of Interest		Index Contour
🚶 Optional Hike	🗼 Lighthouse		Contour
🚴 Cycling	🐋 Whale Watching		Major Road
🏄 Surf Spot	✉ Post Office		Main Road
▲ Spot Height	🏠 Bird Watching		Other Road
🏠 Accommodation	🏠 Homestay		Hiking Trail
🚣 Boating	🎣 Fishing		Vehicle Transfer
Shipwreck	📷 Viewpoint	R777 Route Marker
● Town Spot	🚙 4x4 Track / Transport	⊕ GPS Points
🎋 Waterfall	- - - River	

Breede River

for swimming

★ Viewpoint

Hamerkop
▲ 408m

▲ 345m

oskraal

Hamerkop to Vaalkrans 10.5km

Noetsie to Hamerkop 7.8km

DAY 4

DAY 3

▲ 190m

🚶

🏠 Hamerkop

Stilgat Cave

🏠 Noetsie

kerwater Lodge
(Beach cottage)

⊕ 34°26'46 S
20°39'43 E

Memorial Stone

★ Lunch spot
(swimming & snorkelling)

⊕ 34°27'01 S
20°43'11 E

Indian Ocean

N

WHALE TRAIL (DE HOOP)

The Whale Trail, through De Hoop Nature Reserve, is an absolute gem – a five-day, self-catered, self-guided trail that suits virtually any type of hiker. And since only hikers have access to this part of the reserve (and they're limited to 12 per day), you really enjoy a wilderness experience. The overnight huts are comfortable, well-equipped cottages with flush loos, hot showers, solar lighting and spacious kitchen and living areas, and there's the (sensible) option of having your bags (and cooler boxes) portaged between the huts. De Hoop is CapeNature's flagship reserve, the heart of the Cape Floral Region Protected Area World Heritage Site, and the flora is incredible. It's also a haven for twitchers and the best CapeNature reserve for game-viewing. If you hike between May and December there's an excellent chance of spotting whales, but there's plenty to impress year round. The trail leads through varied and magnificent scenery as it meanders from the sandstone hills of Potberg Mountain over an outcrop of craggy limestone hills and then through patches of thicket, stunning fynbos and wild flowers to the rugged coastline. Daily distances are not too taxing so you have plenty of time to chill out, swim from the sandy beaches, explore the rock pools, picnic in the sweet-smelling fynbos or simply sit at a vantage point staring out to sea. What a treat.

DISTANCE 55km
DAYS 5
DIFFICULTY MODERATELY STRENUOUS
MTB TWO ROUTES (SEE PAGE 118)

66 Don't grow up too quickly, lest you forget how much you love the beach. 99

Michelle Held

SCULPTURED CLIFFS BETWEEN HAMERKOP AND VAALKRANS

KLIPSPRINGER POTBERG TRAIL

DAY 1 Potberg to Cupidoskraal
14.7km, 7–8 hours

Most hikers arrive the night before they start walking and stay in the Potberg hut, a lovely old farmhouse in the eastern section of the reserve. If you've paid for portage, black boxes are provided to pack your belongings into; these are then transported to the next hut. (If you've underestimated the number you'll need you can pay the officer on duty for additional boxes.) The first section, to the 611m summit of Potberg Mountain, is one of the most taxing parts of the whole trail, so don't be perturbed if you're sweating by the time you reach the top. The fynbos is magnificent here so you can take plenty of

LEAVING POTBERG

HAMERKOP HUT

breaks. It really is worth taking a flower book or going with someone who knows their fynbos – many of the species here, including the ground protea, are endemic, i.e. found nowhere else in the world. The Potberg cliffs are also a refuge for the last breeding colony of Cape Vultures in the Western Cape, so you may be fortunate to spot these big birds soaring above you.

From the top – a good tea spot – you can see right across the reserve to the sea. To the west lie vast dune fields and Cape Agulhas, the southernmost tip of Africa. The Breede River winds its way through the wheat fields in the north, and beyond that tower the jagged peaks and ridges of the Langeberg Mountains. From the summit it's largely downhill to the second hut. The trail leads through more glorious, dense

fynbos along the watershed above Grootkloof to the Melkhout River – a good lunch spot where you can swim and recuperate before the final short climb to the Cupidoskraal hut. There's also a dam just beyond the hut, so you have the option of a dip once you've dumped your bags. Cupidoskraal, on the edge of a grove of trees, is spacious and offers great views as well as some luxuries such as outdoor showers.

DAY 2 Cupidoskraal to Noetsie
15km, 7–8 hours

You might fancy a refreshing dip in the dam before heading off up through the fynbos-covered mountains again. The views are just awesome as the trail follows the crest of the range through

De Hoop Marine Reserve, the largest Marine Protected Area in Africa, extends 5km out to sea from the eastern border of the De Hoop Nature Reserve to well beyond the western border (incorporating the area adjacent to the Overberg Test Range). The Southern African continental shelf is at its broadest here on the Agulhas Bank, and varying sea temperatures, high wave energy and the meeting of the cold Benguela and warm Agulhas currents contribute to a variety of habitats with a huge diversity of marine organisms. At least 250 species of fish occur in the Marine Protected Area, dolphins and seals can be seen in the waters off the coast year round and southern right whales calve and mate in the sheltered bays of De Hoop each year between May and December.

DE HOOP MARINE RESERVE

If you don't like the waves, chill out in the stunning Stilgat pools. Otherwise there are plenty of inviting spots along the beach.

DAM ABOVE CUPIDOSKRAAL HUT

The caves that you pass soon after leaving Noetsie are the best for picnics. Sure, it's a bit early to stop, but these bizarre rock formations just beg to be explored – and it's a short day so you're in no rush.

The landscape and flora of De Hoop are extraordinarily diverse thanks to the mountain-to-coast connection and the fact that seven major habitat types exist in the reserve. De Hoop Nature Reserve is unique among the protected areas of the Cape Floral Region World Heritage Site in conserving Cape Floral Region lowlands and is one of only two nature reserves where this limestone fynbos is conserved.

citrus-smelling buchu and colourful heath. You're now on limestone hills – hard dunes that support only thin, poor soils – and you'll notice the change. Protea dominate here: great swathes of cone bushes, orange pincushions and rarities like the Bredasdorp protea, a striking red sugarbush that has a very localised, restricted distribution. De Hoop harbours 70 endemic limestone fynbos species, so spend a bit of time here admiring these rarely seen plants. Look under the bushy cover at the smaller flowers and grasses – there is just so much to see if you really look.

If you're fortunate enough to be hiking in springtime you'll find this next section a mass of colourful wild flowers. Throughout spring and summer you'll see butterflies, sunbirds and sugarbirds flitting from plant to plant, lizards sunning themselves on the rocks and tortoises

crossing the path. If you're really fortunate you might see endangered Cape mountain zebra in the rocky areas on the descent to the coastal plain.

Once you reach the plain you'll again notice a change in the predominant vegetation. The fynbos of this section burnt in 2006 and the relatively young plants make good grazing, so you'll probably see buck, perhaps even De Hoop's famous white-faced bontebok, as you hike towards the Noetsie hut.

PATH DOWN TO CUPIDOSKRAAL HUT

CUPIDOS KRAAL HUT

Fynbos is a fire-dependent ecosystem, so controlled burns like these every 12–15 years are vital to its regeneration.

Noetsie consists of two attractive A-framed, thatched huts or *kapstylhuisies* – in the style used by local farmers for their holiday homes – that sit on the edge of the bay. Unfortunately there are a few design faults that are really a nuisance, like having to go outside to the back of the kitchen hut to go to the loo and there being no indoor braai area (both inconvenient, especially when it's raining). Still, the outside *lapa* (fireplace) is great when the weather's good.

DAY 3 Noetsie to Hamerkop
7.8km, 3 hours

The path now follows the coastline, a glorious walk through coastal fynbos and along the beach. You pass various interesting wind- and wave-sculpted overhangs and caves in the cliffs, and since it's only a short hike to the next hut you'll have plenty of time to explore these and the colourful tidal pools. At low tide you can see big circular depressions carved out of the grey, wave-cut platform – reminiscent of Chinese paddy fields. A good diversion is to scramble down the chain ladders to explore the pools near Stilgat cave.

STILGAT CAVE

The Cape mountain zebra is one of the rarest mammals in the world. It's easily distinguished from Burchell's zebra, the most common zebra in Africa, by its smaller size, lack of shadow stripes, reddish-brown nose, prominent dewlap, white stomach and gridiron pattern on the rump. The Cape mountain zebra was on the brink of extinction at the turn of the century but the numbers multiplied rapidly since the 1980s. The first descendants of the present population of De Hoop, which now numbers about 50 animals, were introduced to the reserve in 1963.

This is a good place to snorkel and laze around and you can scramble back along the coast to the cave (much easier than scrambling down the cliff near the cave itself). From here it's a bit of an up-and-down slog to Hamerkop, but when you see the white sandy beach you're as good as home. This is a really beautiful hut, just back from the beach, with a terrace from which you can scan the sea for whales. De Hoop is world-renowned as one of the world's most important nursery areas for southern right whales and during the season they can be seen breaching very close to the shore here.

DAY 4 Hamerkop to Vaalkrans
10.5km, 5–6 hours

The trail to Vaalkrans starts off with a long section along the beach where you'll hike past shell middens and spot

oystercatchers, cormorants and numerous gulls. At about the halfway mark you'll see Lekkerwater Lodge on the cliffs – a gorgeous beach cottage that is available for hire. This is the only time you might see other people in

STRETCH OF BEACH BETWEEN HAMERKOP AND VAALKRANS

this part of the reserve but your trail brochure, and signs on the beach, request that you stay clear and respect the privacy of the guests. The trail then leaves the beach onto the craggy coastal

The Cape Griffon Vulture is endemic to Southern Africa, with colonies occurring in the Drakensberg, Eastern Cape, Limpopo and in the Magaliesberg. The Potberg colony, which currently numbers around 75 birds (out of an estimated 12,000 birds in the whole of Southern Africa), declined to around 45 birds in the 1980s, but thanks to cooperation of local farmers it is now on the increase again.

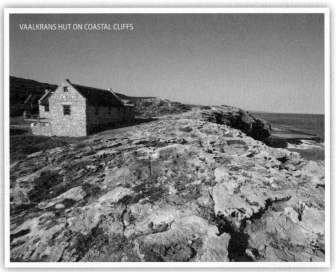

VAALKRANS HUT ON COASTAL CLIFFS

fringe, through a wonderful stretch of dune vegetation interspersed with exposed sandy dunes where myriad tracks in the sand indicate the presence of the little antelope, mice, reptiles and birds that inhabit the clumps of succulents and evergreen shrubs. The overnight cottage at Vaalkrans is also superb – it is right on top of spectacular limestone cliffs so it offers a fantastic view out over the coast. You can't swim safely at the hut so if you fancy a final dip, head back to the beach once you've settled in.

DAY 5 Vaalkrans to Koppie Alleen
7km, 3 hours

The trail takes you along the beach or on the coastal cliff for most of the way and is an easy, short finale. You pass ancient middens; layers of bones and shells deposited by the Strandlopers who once roamed these shores. The rock pools – deep, enclosed turquoise gullies fringed by seaweed that looks like ferns – are incredible, and there are pretty beaches and great swimming spots such as at Hippo Pools. As you near Koppie Alleen you'll find other people on the beaches and coastal footpaths – quite a shock after four days of having the reserve to yourselves. The final section is along a boardwalk to the ablution block and then it's a short walk to the car park from where a shuttle bus will transfer you back to your cars at Potberg. But it's worth continuing on a little to the magnificent dunes of Long Beach. The high dunes here are an excellent viewpoint for one last look back along the trail and over the extensive dune field west of De Hoop. The marketing slogan says it all: the Whale Trail 'is not just a retreat, it's a total surrender'.

BEST FOR BEASTIES

De Hoop boasts 86 mammal species and is by far the most interesting of the Western Cape national parks/reserves if you're into spotting beasties. Big herds of bontebok – those gorgeous antelope with the white stripes down their faces – and Cape mountain zebra are often seen on the plains. (Watch out for them from the road as you're shuttled back to your car.) You also often see eland, grey rhebok, klipspringer and baboon. Yellow mongoose, caracal, leopard and Cape clawless otter inhabit the reserve but are rarely seen. You are, however, sure to see tortoises, including the Cape Floral Region endemic, the parrot-beaked tortoise.

TREAD LIGHTLY

Be careful when walking on the rock platforms at low tide as they're incredibly fragile and you can see plenty of evidence of damage by hikers. Tread lightly in this delicate marine landscape so that others too can enjoy its unique beauty.

RUGGED COASTLINE – VAALKRANS TO KOPPIE ALLEEN

SUMMARY

Start/finish	Potberg/Koppie Alleen
Group size	Bookings are only taken for two groups of six or one group of 12 hikers.
Facilities	Accommodation on the trail is excellent – it should be a blueprint for other new trail facilities. Braai grills, wood, candles, a kettle, cutlery and crockery are provided for use at the hut and, refreshingly, each has recycling bins. There's no water between the huts (except on day one). There is a shuttle bus transfer at noon from Koppie Alleen, where the trail ends, back to the car park near the Potberg hut where you left your car.
And the kids?	Children over eight years old are allowed on the trail so it's great for family groups.
When to go	The trail can be walked year round but the whales are usually only seen from May/June to December. The flowers are also at their best from July to September. During the summer months you're likely to experience mosquitoes, horseflies and other insects.
Contact	Cape Nature Reservations, 021 659 3500, bookings@capenature.co.za or visit www.capenature.co.za.
Other contacts	Potberg Challenge, Mariaan Dunn, 028 424 2840, ouplaas@whalemail.co.za, or Niel Neethling, 082 896 3545, potteberg@whalemail.co.za, www.potberg.blogspot.com, www.pedalpower.org.za (on-line entries)
Kit list	What you take will largely depend on whether you opt for the portaged option or not. But if you opt for portage it's worth keeping your belongings to one 68l box (or cooler box). It costs R300 to be transported. See general kit list, page 202

Specific
- Two water bottles – there's no water between the huts except on day one
- Binoculars
- Bird book
- Flower book
- Marine identification guide
- Swimming costume and kikoi
- Mask and snorkel
- Insect repellent
- Strap for your box (if taking the portaged option)

On your bike	Mountain bikers can explore on any of the management roads in the western sector of the reserve.

Popular routes include:
The scenic circular drive from the reserve office (11km, one hour, easy).
The dirt track from the office to Koppie Alleen and back (30km return, two to three hours, easy to moderate).

Potberg Challenge
The Potberg Challenge is an annual MTB and running event held in August, which starts at the Potberg entrance to De Hoop and offers four challenging and fun MTB routes in the reserve and surrounding farms: the 75km Whale Route,

BREATHTAKING VIEW FROM THE BIG HILL ON DAY 1

On your bike the 55km Eland Route, the 32km Bontebok Route and the 10km Vulture Route,
ctd. as well as a duathlon (a half marathon and the 32km Bontebok MTB Route), a
half-marathon and a fun run – a wonderful day out for the whole family.

Short hikes in De Hoop

If you can't spare the time or can't get a booking on the Whale Trail you can at
least enjoy the scenery at the start and end of the trail on one of these short
trails.

Beach/coastal walk (open-ended linear trail)

Day hikers can walk on the beach, back along the Whale Trail from Koppie Alleen
or on the dunes to the west. Use the boardwalk to get to the water's edge and
walk to your left if you want to explore rock pools, limestone cliffs and rocky
outcrops.

De Hoop Vlei Trail, 15km, 3 hours

The Vlei Trail starts at the reserve office in the western sector of the reserve and
offers three alternative routes – the Grebe Trail (15km, three to four hours), the
Heron Trail (8km, two to three hours) and the Coot Trail (5km, one to two hours).
All offer outstanding scenery and fynbos and the full trail gives hikers great views
of the vlei, so it is perfect for birders.

De Hoop Klipspringer Trail, 6km, 2 hours

This short hike in the foothills of the Potberg Mountain starts at the car park at
the Potberg Environmental Centre. The trail meanders through the fynbos, past
the pools in the Potberg River and Black Eagle Cave, and there's a chance of
spotting Cape Vultures overhead.

Potberg Trail, 10km, 4 hours

This moderately strenuous hike climbs up through the fynbos to the top of the
Potberg Mountain. From the summit, at 611m, there are awesome views over
the Breede River to Witsand in the south and all the way to Swellendam in the
north.

TRAIL 7

Swellendam Hiking Trail

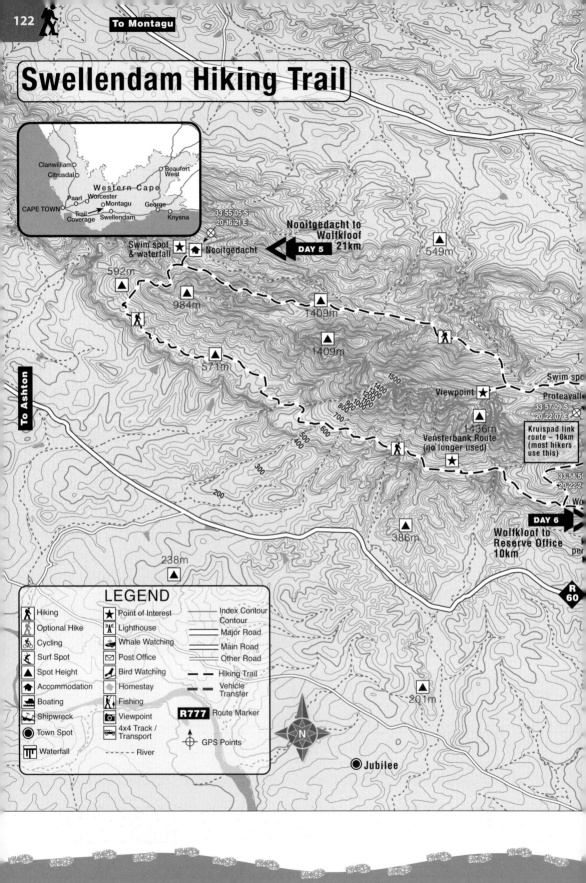

Swellendam Hiking Trail

To Montagu

To Ashton

Western Cape

Clanwilliam
Citrusdal
Beaufort West
Paarl
Worcester
Montagu
George
CAPE TOWN
Trail Coverage
Swellendam
Knysna

33 55'05 S
20 16'21 E

Nooitgedacht to Wolfkloof 21km

DAY 5

Swim spot & waterfall

Nooitgedacht

549m

592m

984m

1409m

1409m

571m

1500
1400
1300
1200
1100
1000
900
800
700
600
500
400
300
200

Swim spot

Viewpoint

Proteavalle

33 57'09 S
20 22'07 E

1436m

Vensterbank Route (no longer used)

Kruispad link route – 10km (most hikers use this)

33 58'50
20 22'2

Wo

DAY 6

Wolfkloof to Reserve Office 10km

386m

238m

201m

R 60

Jubilee

LEGEND

Hiking		Point of Interest	Index Contour
Optional Hike		Lighthouse	Contour
Cycling		Whale Watching	Major Road
Surf Spot		Post Office	Main Road
Spot Height		Bird Watching	Other Road
Accommodation		Homestay	Hiking Trail
Boating		Fishing	Vehicle Transfer
Shipwreck		Viewpoint	
Town Spot		4x4 Track / Transport	R777 Route Marker
Waterfall		River	GPS Points

N

TRAIL 7

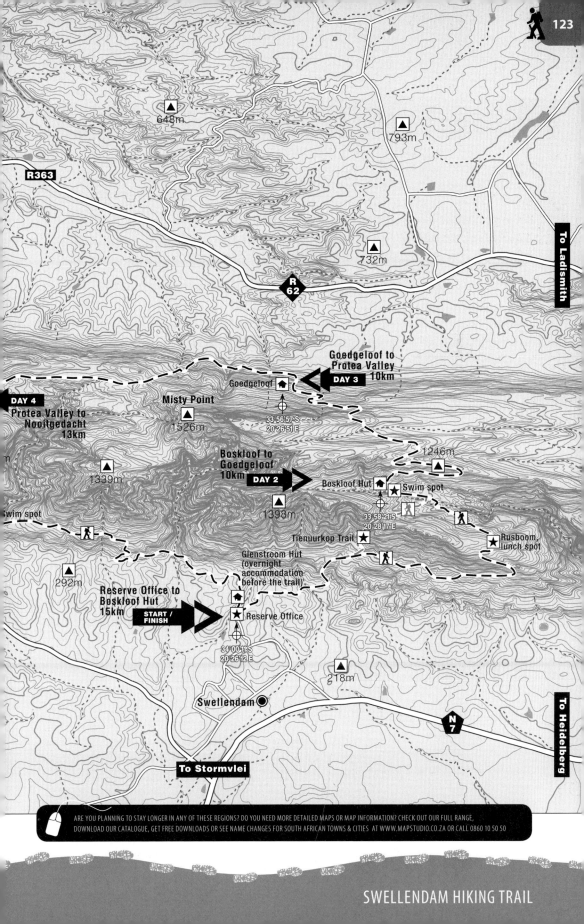

To Ladismith

R363

R 62

648m

793m

732m

Goedgeloof to Protea Valley 10km   **DAY 3** ◀

Goedgeloof

33 56 57 S
20 26 51 E

DAY 4 ◀
Protea Valley to Nooitgedacht 13km

Misty Point
1526m

1246m

Boskloof to Goedgeloof 10km   **DAY 2** ▶

1339m

1398m

Boskloof Hut   ★ Swim spot

33 58 21 S
20 28 17 E

Swim spot

Tienuurkop Trail ★

Rusboom, lunch spot ★

292m

Glenstroom Hut (overnight accommodation before the trail)

Reserve Office to Boskloof Hut 15km

START / FINISH ▶

★ Reserve Office

34 00 11 S
20 26 12 E

218m

Swellendam ●

To Heidelberg

N 7

To Stormvlei

SWELLENDAM HIKING TRAIL

HIGHLIGHTS

This spectacular trail through the Langeberg Mountains gives you a real sense of being in mountain wilderness. The well-maintained trail, which broadly circumnavigates the Marloth Nature Reserve, leads though magnificent mountain fynbos, over tumbling mountain streams and past sculpted rock formations. It's a strenuous undertaking with some steep climbs and descents but the rewards for the self-sufficient hiker are enormous. This is a trail for those who enjoy getting away from it all, and even though 22 hikers are allowed on the trail at any time you rarely see another soul other than on the day-hike sections. The fynbos is particularly fine, especially in October/November when Protea Valley really lives up to its name and many of the erica species are in bloom. The reserve is rich in bird life and you'll occasionally spot graceful rhebok on the lower slopes or klipspringer along the way. The rustic hikers' huts, simply equipped with bunks, mattresses and long-drop loos, are beautifully located and well maintained, and the views along the way will lift your soul. Shorter trail options from overnight to five-day routes are possible but the full six-day trail must rate as one of the finest and easiest opportunities to really immerse yourself in the wilderness on offer in the Western Cape.

> **DISTANCE** 79km
>
> **DAYS** 6 DAYS. SHORTER ROUTES (2- TO 5-DAY HIKES) ARE ALSO POSSIBLE
>
> **DIFFICULTY** STRENUOUS
>
> **MTB** A NETWORK OF TRAILS RANGING FROM 5 TO 15KM
>
> **BEST SWIMMING SPOT** POOL AT BOSKLOOF HUT
>
> **BEST LUNCH SPOT** LOOKING DOWN AT THE VENTERSBANK

MOUNTAIN STREAM NEAR BOSKLOOF HUT

❝ My grandmother started walking five miles a day when she was sixty. She's ninety-three today and we don't know where the hell she is.❞
Ellen DeGeneres

DAY 1 Reserve office to Boskloof hut
15km, 4–5 hours

Sign in at the reserve office then park your car under the trees. Note that there's a cold shower at the parking area – a welcome opportunity to clean up a bit when you come off the trail. A photocopied map is available from the extremely enthusiastic, knowledgeable staff at the office. One of the things I like about this trail is that every half kilometre is marked on the path, so you know exactly how far you've gone and what pace you're going at. The trail heads down to the Glenstroom hut some 500m away. The two wooden huts, where you can overnight before starting the trail, have single beds and bunks, an inside toilet and shower and a small kitchen and braai area. Follow the trail from the huts down a gentle path to a braai area in the trees then up some steps to the edge of the plantation. The mountain biking sign at the base of the steps might make you chuckle – the mountain bikers around here are clearly quite hardcore! The path then heads up the mountain via a firebreak before contouring a little then descending a steep slope via a series of zigzags to the river at Koloniesbos, the original site of the first huts and now another picnic area.

Once you've crossed the river the trail starts in earnest and you get a taste of what's to come: a steep uphill which can be very wet after heavy rain. More contouring brings you to a waterfall – take care as you cross the stream. The Tienuurkop Trail – which you'd return on if you were doing the overnight hike to and from Boskloof – comes in on the left, then some respite from the heat is offered by Wamakersbos, a pretty section of indigenous forest largely consisting of rooiels, Cape beech (boekenhout), yellowwood, stinkwood and ironwood. Originally forests covered a much larger area but fires and the felling of trees for timber means that there are now only isolated patches in the damper kloofs. After a long descent to the point where the Appelsbos circular trail branches off back to the office the sustained uphill really begins. From the 7.5km marker the well-maintained path climbs gradually for a couple of kilometres through wonderful swathes of erica,

leucadendrons and watsonia. A scenic viewpoint with a tree and rock outcrop is a good stop for a tea or lunch break, then you reach the watershed after about 10km. The scenery changes at this point and you see dramatic cliffs and fold mountains off to your right. There's a little waterfall near the top of the hill, then you start heading left. You can see right up the valley towards the Boskloof hut, but the path contours at a fairly high level, dropping down a couple of times before contouring round until the turnoff to Tienuurkop, where it drops down to a swing bridge over the river where you can cool off in the pool. From here it's a spectacular hike up the valley to the hut. Boskloof hut is a beautifully located wooden structure fronted by a surprisingly well-tended 'lawn'. It consists of two rooms of bunk beds sleeping 20 and a verandah on which you can sit and survey the big peaks of Tienuurkop and Elfuurkop. There are tables and benches where you can cook and eat, but you must carry your

> ## DON'T QUARREL
>
> The old maps of the Swellendam Hiking Trail (sadly no longer available) refer to Twistnietvallei – meaning 'do not quarrel'. No one seems to be quite sure why but it's possibly because it drops down into one of the most isolated areas of the reserve and people will need to rely on each other till they get to Nooitgedacht hut at the end of the day.

INDIGENOUS FORESTS DAY 1

BOSKLOOF HUT

GLENSTROOM HUT – OVERNIGHT ACCOMMODATION BEFORE THE START OF THE TRAIL

BOSKLOOF HUT
← PLAAT-EAST
TIENUURKOP

WAMAKERSBOS →

APPELSBOS CIRCLE
← ROUTE

The rare ghost frog was discovered in the area only recently. If you're very lucky you might hear its call – a clear, high-pitched 'tink' every second. The name 'ghost frog' might come from the fact that Rose's ghost frog occurs in Skeleton Gorge in Table Mountain, which was once a location where local people brought the bodies of their dead.

rubbish to the next hut, where you can leave it in the rubbish bins. Though the facilities on the trail are rustic, the huts have been well thought out. When you utilise one of the two long-drop loos you'll understand what I mean –

these really are loos (labelled as gents and ladies no less) with views. You can collect water from a stream running past the hut but if you want to bathe head slightly up the main river to an awesome pool – a five-minute walk but well worth the effort.

DAY 2 Boskloof to Goedgeloof
10km, 4 hours

Day two starts with a long uphill (as does virtually every day on this trail, you'll soon discover) up Drosterpas. Stop often and look back. The views of the hut, the ridge on the other side of the valley and east to the magnificent folded cliffs of Meulkloof are terrific. Tree ferns along the sides of the path provide an interesting break from the lush protea – it's clearly quite damp in this valley. The path then levels out and contours back along the northern side of Boskloof for a couple of kilometres before you get a

series of steeper zigzags by which you gain the nek. This is marked by the big, dramatic and photogenic Vulture Rocks – a good tea spot. You can see the path that you followed the previous day and the steep Tienuurkop Trail (the popular return route on the overnight trail) and the very different landscape on the other side of the watershed – more of a gentle plateau than on the Boskloof side of the ridge. The views of the distant mountains are spectacular, each with their gently inclined northern slope and dramatic southern scarp.

The trail heads up again following the ridge and crosses the Zuurplaats stream before climbing steeply again past Knuckle Rock out of this second valley. The next valley is a wetland; again you head west, dropping down to cross the stream and then climbing steeply on the far side to Het Goedgeloof Nek where you're met by views of fields, dams and rolling hills with deep

TYPICAL FYNBOS LANDSCAPE

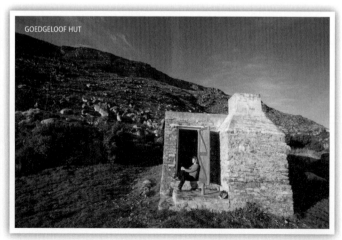

GOEDGELOOF HUT

LOO WITH A VIEW – GOEDGELOOF HUT

valleys cut into their flanks.

You can see from the map where you're heading for the night, but the trail to Goedgeloof is longer than you think, with many ups and downs, and it seems like an eternity before you see the hut. The scenery on this northern side of the range is very different to that of the Swellendam side – much more like that of the Cederberg, with big burnt orange, wind-sculpted sandstone boulders and cliffs. There are some great spots to stop for tea and to admire the view – one of the best being a grassy overhang at about the 8km mark where you can shelter out of the wind and see a remarkable variety of erica species. Keep your eyes peeled for rhebok and birds of prey – you'll often spot Black (Verreaux's) Eagles and Jackal Buzzards overhead.

Finally you descend steeply to Goedgeloof, which is in the foothills of the range and close to a big dam. There are two stone buildings, a big wooden dining area with taps, and showers, which makes this a comfortable, spacious overnight spot – and again you'll find both ladies' and gents' loos. If you're up to the scramble, the big rock above the loos makes a great sundowner spot.

It's certainly not wilderness here; actually it's a bit of a shock to come so close to farms and inhabited areas, but at night there is remarkably little light pollution so you can gaze at the stars.

TYPICAL FYNBOS LANDSCAPE

DAY 3 Goedgeloof to Protea Valley
10km, 4 hours

The trail descends further from the hut and you can't help regretting the loss of height – on this trail it really is a case of what goes down has to go up again. Sure enough, after about 3km you're faced with a steep, sustained climb back to Warmwaternek. The trail then dips just over the ridge following it up the magnificent valley that now unfolds in front of you. The daunting peak of Misty Point, the highest peak in the reserve, dominates the view behind you, while ahead yet more inviting peaks form the skyline. You can see the Protea Valley hut snuggled against the southern flanks of the

In 1795 Swellendam was, for approximately three months, one of the capitals of the world. The inhabitants of Swellendam were at that time angered by the high taxes and the maladministration of the Cape Dutch East India Company and without much ado they declared themselves an independent republic. Shortly afterwards, however, the British occupied the Cape and the new republic, consisting of a mere 20 houses along the river valley, disbanded again.

SWIMMING HOLE AT NOOITGEDACHT

range, in a very inviting spot. The trail now contours around, keeping roughly the same altitude before doubling back down to the hut itself along a track that is almost a corridor of *Protea aurea*, *nerifolia* and *eximia*. This is another great wooden mountain hut, right next to a river, so you can wander upstream a bit to find a suitable bathing pool. The protea are generally at their best in winter and early spring, particularly the *Protea aurea* which flowers in June/July.

DAY 4 Protea Valley to Nooitgedacht
13km, 4–5 hours

The majority of hikers cut back from the hut on the Kruispad route, or if they're strong, over the spectacular, but infrequently trodden, Ventersbank route, spending their fourth and last night at the Wolfkloof hut. But this is to miss one of the most spectacular sections of the trail, so try to give yourself an extra day to do the full whack. If you've chosen this route head west in the morning up the steep climb from the hut to Dwariganek where the path divides. Even if you feel a trifle weary, leave your pack at the junction and hike for another kilometre and a half up the Ventersbank route to the great chasm that provides a window through the mountains back towards Swellendam. It's an incredible feature – a great rupture in the rock where the green slope just seems to tumble away in front of you. When you can see the trail winding around the western side of this great gash and have taken the obligatory photos of the geological phenomenon, turn around and return to your bags. I guarantee that if the visibility is good you'll concede that it was well worth the effort. From the nek the trail drops sharply. On your right incredible folded mountains flank Twistnietvallei and you can make out where the trail rises again in the distance. But for now it's knee-jarring stuff – down, down, down. Watch your step; the path is uneven and steep but the fynbos and the views of the great range of peaks to your left – Leeurivierberg, Middelrivierberg and Klipspringerkop – are just mesmerising. Again you climb to

VIEW FROM THE NEK TOWARDS THE NOOITGEDACHT HUT

Luiperdnek, then descend – another climb, another steep descent. But there's plenty of water on the trail so take it slowly and stop often to enjoy the views, the flowers and the flitting sunbirds and sugarbirds. Look back at the descent from the nek. Bet you're glad you're doing this trail in reverse! Finally after a few more ups and downs the main valley appears to curve around to the left and the path flattens out. The Nooitgedacht hut is hidden from view in a side valley just off to the right. If there's been a bit of rain the river here may be in flood so be prepared to take off your shoes and wade before the short climb back up to the hut.

NOOITGEDACHT HUT

The compact hut, a stone structure of two rooms and a covered dining/kitchen area, is in a gorgeous spot overlooking an overgrown river valley (access is too difficult to collect water here so rather go back down the path a short way to the pool in front of the waterfall). Out the back is a roughly mown lawn with a few stands of arum lilies. You feel like you're miles from anywhere in this hidden place and it would be fantastic to spend more time here to explore this secondary valley. In October the *Protea repens* is at its most

STUNNING FYNBOS BETWEEN PROTEA VALLEY AND NOOITGEDACHT

WINDOW THROUGH THE VENTERSBANK CHASM

MIST IN THE VALLEY BELOW NOOITGEDACHT HUT

BETWEEN NOOITGEDACHT AND WOLFKLOOF

FOREST SCENERY DAY 5

of the range and look out over cultivated fields and dams. At about 6.5km the path leaves the Jeep track, heading uphill before contouring round the slopes of Klipspringerkop. You're now looking at the other aspect of the big peaks whose slopes you traversed yesterday – Klipspringerkop, Middelrivierberg and the great 1623m-high bulk of Leeurivierberg. Patches of purple and pink erica colour to the mountain flanks. Although the map indicates that today's route is fairly flat, it lies. The trail is quite undulating as it descends

WOLFKLOOF HUT

to cross the river valleys before climbing again the other sides, and even though your pack will be lighter than when you started out you still feel the weariness in your legs by the end. You cross the river that has cut the steep valley from the nek between Middelrivierberg and Leeurivierberg, and notice from the map that there were plans to build another hut here, Middelrivier. It's an obvious site, but the plans never came to fruition. The Ventersbank route comes in from the left, in an area that was burnt in 2008, and

majestic here, but the fynbos is beautiful at any time of year. For Ben Swanepoel, manager of the Marloth Reserve, this is a special place: 'I almost always find leopard spoor around this hut, and on many nights here, they have stolen their way into my mind and invaded my dreams. I once found fresh scat just outside the hut complete with ear tags and hooves of a calf from the farm below!'

DAY 5 Nooitgedacht to Wolfkloof
21km, 8–9 hours

This is a long day so get going early. Once you've regained the main trail you contour round on a narrow track until you reach a Jeep track, which you follow for roughly 3.8km. Although not as pleasant as walking on the mountain paths, it's a fairly attractive section of the trail. The scenery changes again as you return to the southern slopes

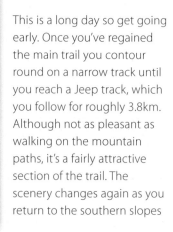

then comes a rather tricky adventurous descent into Leeukloof. Heed the warning signs; although there is some protection on the rocky slope take care particularly if it's wet – the rocks can be incredibly slippery, and since you have to cross the river just above a waterfall it's not somewhere you want to slip. If it's hot, rest a while, cooling off in the stream in the shade of Klein Houtbos, another patch of indigenous forest, before climbing out of the kloof. A couple of kilometres later, just after the Kruispad route junction, you start the steep zigzagging descent to the Wolfkloof hut. The hut, a big wooden structure not unlike the Protea Valley hut, has two rooms with 22 beds and a big *lapa* area with a braai. If you want to braai, cross the river to the end of the Jeep track on the other side where you can collect firewood. The river is not particularly deep but there are pools in which to cool off and enjoy the mountain wilderness. Occasionally, during heavy rains, the river can become impassable, in which case hikers are advised to wait until the water level drops, or to phone the

office. The reserve staff will then accompany stranded hikers out via a different route through farmlands on the western side of the river.

DAY 6   Wolfkloof to office
10km, 4 hours

From the stream the trail climbs steeply out of the valley and contours around the flanks of Eenuurkop before dropping through an

INDIGENOUS FOREST ON DAY 6

area of plantation – a rather unsightly, despoiled area after the pristine wilderness that you've enjoyed for the last five days. You follow a Jeep track down, first through the trees, then through a cleared area before the path heads into the trees again. Finally you cut right along a pleasant 4x4 track skirting the municipal dams, which eventually brings you back to the reserve offices and houses.

VIEW FROM WOLFKLOOF HUT

Start/finish	Marloth Nature Reserve, just outside Swellendam, about two and a half hours east of Cape Town
Group size	Minimum two, maximum 22
Difficulty	This is a strenuous trail, which should only be attempted by fit and experienced hikers equipped with good-quality wet/cold weather gear. Although the trail is well marked, the lack of access through adjacent private property and the risk of getting lost means that hikers must not leave the trail at any stage.
Facilities	Drinking water, bunks, mattresses and primitive toilet facilities are provided at the huts, but hikers must bring all their own bedding, cooking utensils, food, etc. Perennial water points are marked on the trail map and there is cellphone reception at many of the high points on the trail. Take precautions against ticks.
And the kids?	Children over 13 years old may hike the trail but anyone attempting this trail must be fit and able to carry a relatively heavy pack.
When to go	The trail can be walked year round. Spring and autumn are the wettest periods but are probably the most pleasant for hiking, particularly since many of the fynbos species flower in spring and early summer (September to November). Winters are cold but surprisingly drier than the autumn and spring months, though snow is a distinct possibility.
Contact	For reservations phone CapeNature, 021 659 3500, bookings@capenature.co.za, www.capenature.co.za For more detailed information on the trail, day hikes and MTB trails, ring the Marloth Reserve, 028 514 1410.
Other contacts	Arangieskop Hiking Trail, 023 615 8037, mbarnes@breeland.gov.za Bontebok National Park, 028 514 2735, reservations@sanparks.org, www.sanparks.org Marloth MTB routes, 028 514 1410
Other trail	**Arangieskop Trail, Robertson** *Distance/days on trail: 21km, 2 days • Difficulty: strenuous* The circular Arangieskop trail is not for sissies; it involves steep climbs on both days and can get quite treacherous in bad weather. But if you're after a weekend trail that offers stunning mountain views, a physical challenge and a luxurious overnight hut then look no further. In fact, it's so special that I have my reservations about publicising it! That said, the fact that it's such a strenuous trail should keep the numbers down. Get fit for this and pack light, or you'll suffer. Apart from the overnight hut – one of the finest I have ever stayed in – the highlights include the spectacular scenery, the swimming holes, wonderful rock formations, magnificent fynbos and a true sense of wilderness. *'Despite being born as recently as March 1992, this is the mother and father of all trails. It is destined to become to the Western Cape what the Otter Trail is to South Africa – the pride of all trails.'* Mike Lundy, Weekend Trails in the Western Cape

Other trail *ctd.*

Day 1 • 9.5km, 6–7 hours

The trail starts in the Dassieshoek Nature Reserve just outside Robertson where, should you wish, you can overnight at the Dassieshoek hut. Drive through the gates past the picnic site and park at the trailhead just beyond the stream. The trail starts to climb almost immediately – gradually but consistently. After 20 minutes or so you'll come to a rock, which indicates the 8km mark. Don't get excited. That means 1.5km down, 8km to go! Nonetheless, it's always encouraging to have markers to monitor your progress.

The scenery is already spectacular and if you're struggling, take heart, it gets even better. All around is beautiful fynbos so you can make plenty of excuses to stop and smell the flowers. Soon after the 6km (to go) mark the path levels out then drops down to a beautiful stream with great pools surrounded by tree ferns and indigenous trees. Chuck off all your clothes and skinny dip – you deserve it. Then enjoy a tea or lunch break in the shade and fill your water bottles before heading on up. The bad news is that you've lost a lot of height and the next stage is tough. First you follow the stream before heading steeply up the side of the ravine on a series of steep zigzags. Again the trail flattens out for a short while, becoming steeper again before you reach the plateau. If you tire, admire the rugged scenery and the wonderful eroded cliffs and rock formations – reward for your efforts indeed. Once on the grassy top the views are breathtaking and best of all, the overnight hut is right there, built into the rock. Punch in the code and let yourself into your home for the night. The hut, which sleeps 23 in a number of rooms (as opposed to dorms, and some even have double beds if you please), is luxurious, with a fireplace, flushing loos and hot showers (thanks to a donkey boiler). If this option appeals, stoke up the fire as soon as you arrive otherwise you'll have to settle for the Spartan approach! The kitchen has everything you could possibly need – even dishwashing liquid is supplied. Firewood is stored under the balcony so if it's a nice evening you can braai and eat outside while enjoying the lovely views over the Koo Valley. But before you do so (if it's not too windy) leave the hut and follow the route of the second day up to a big table-like rock – the perfect spot to enjoy sundowner drinks and snacks.

Day 2 • 11.7km, 6 hours

The start of the trail is a bit daunting but aim for the aerials – they look high but it's not such a bad walk if you pace yourself carefully. The mountain scenery will take your breath away, but also look out for some weird rock formations along the path – perfectly square bubble holes about the size of your fingernail. Checking them out makes a good excuse for a breather. Then finally scramble up the rugged rocks on a zigzagging path until you top out on the summit of Arangieskop. The view from the beacon, at 1850m, is spectacular, and you can see clearly the route you came up the day before. Don't forget to sign the visitors' book and record your achievement for posterity. From the top the path drops down steeply then swings left into a valley flanked by rooiels where there's a swimming hole, which is the ideal place to cool off and have a tea break. The

SUMMARY

Other trail *ctd.*	path crosses the river a couple of times but then comes a rude shock. Instead of continuing down the river the path cuts left and up a steep gully – not what you're expecting at all! Once out of this valley the path contours around the hill and into the next valley at the end of which you cross a stream before climbing once again. This is the last hill; from the top the path zigzags down but be warned it's further than it looks so fill up at the stream as from there it's still about an hour and a half to the end. (One of my friends was quite incredulous at reading this. She thought the final section was 'interminable', as not only do the yellow footprint markers suddenly disappear, causing insecurity, but the trail seems to be heading off in completely the wrong direction from the car, which it does – even more insecurity. So perhaps I should say *at least* one and a half hours to the end!) As you approach Dassieshoek you cross a number of Jeep tracks, but just ignore them and carry on down to the trailhead with a proud spring in your step. Just before you reach the end there's a causeway over a stream that's deep enough to wash off all the dust and sweat – what a bonus as you can now hop in your car all clean and shiny.
Day hikes in Marloth Nature Reserve	**Tienuurkop, 11.5km, 6.5 hours** This strenuous route takes hikers from the reserve office through fynbos and patches of indigenous forest to the summit of Tienuurkop at 1195m. The views from the top make the effort worthwhile.
	Twaalfuurkop, 8.5km, 4 hours This demanding trail takes you to the peak of Twaalfuurkop (1428m) and back. It's a steep climb so take it easy and enjoy the fynbos, the bird life in the patches of indigenous forest and the far-reaching views over the town of Swellendam and the Overberg.
	Marloth Flower Route, 5.5km, 2.5 hours This easy hike begins and ends at the reserve office and takes hikers through magnificent stands of protea and erica, as well as patches of afromontane forest.
	Koloniesbos, 6km, 2.5 hours This fairly easy circular hike begins and ends at the reserve office and leads through the fynbos into the beautiful indigenous forest of Koloniesbos where you will see yellowwood, stinkwood and ironwood trees.
	Duiwelsbos, 5km, 2 hours This fairly easy hike through the fynbos and Duiwelsbos forest to a small waterfall begins and ends at the reserve office.
	Die Plaat, 8.5km, 4 hours This easy route climbs to a contour, which you follow through patches of indigenous forest and fynbos, above Duiwelsbos and Koloniesbos. Keep your eyes open for various small animals and birds.
	Day Hikes in Vrolijkheid Nature Reserve There are two trails in this pretty reserve in the Elandsberg Mountains some 15km outside Roberston, both of which offer good birding and occasional sightings of buck. Permits are self-issued at the reserve gate.

Rooikat Trail, 19km, 7–8 hours

This circular trail follows an undulating course through the reserve, taking hikers to the summit of Witkrantz, the highest peak, and over smaller peaks such as Kranskop and Klein Spitzkop. The views are outstanding and it's a moderately challenging trail that will appeal to hikers unable to face the challenge of Arangieskop.

Heron Trail, 3km, 1 hour (return)

This easy trail is ideal for bird lovers as it basically gives access to the hides on the two dams. Even if you're not a birder, the trail is still worth doing, particularly in the spring when the fynbos is magnificent.

MTB trails

Marloth MTB trails, 1–15km, 30 minutes to 2 hours

The network of trails in the reserve consists largely of forestry roads with some sections of singletrack and can be extended to include a loop through the town of Swellendam and surrounding areas (largely on dirt roads). Be careful if it's wet; much of the surface is hard packed clay that can get dangerously slippery.

Suurbraak MTB trail, Barrydale, 5–30km, 30 minutes to 2 hours

This is great cruising country with a selection of easy to intermediate trails of 5km to 30km, largely along gravel roads through farmland and pine plantations.

Bontebok National Park, 5–40km, 30 minutes to 3 hours

It's a case of making your own route along the gravel roads of this scenic little reserve just outside Swellendam, home to the attractive bontebok.

TRAIL 8

Oystercatcher Trail

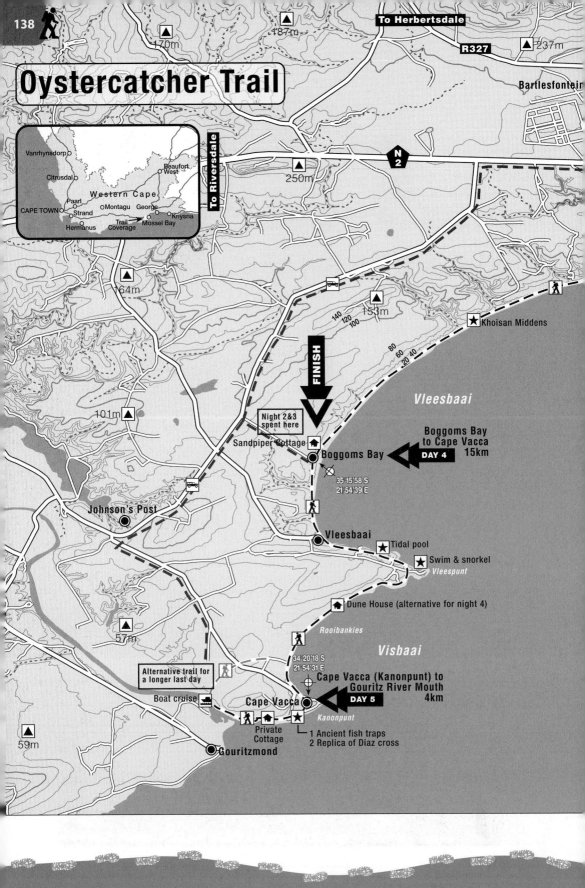

Oystercatcher Trail

To Herbertsdale

R327

237m

Bartlesfontein

170m

187m

To Riversdale

N2

250m

Western Cape

Vanrhynsdorp

Citrusdal

Beaufort West

Paarl

CAPE TOWN

Strand

Montagu

George

Knysna

Hermanus

Trail Coverage

Mossel Bay

164m

153m

140 120 100

★ Khoisan Middens

80 60 20 40

101m

FINISH

Vleesbaai

Night 2&3 spent here

Sandpiper Cottage

Boggoms Bay to Cape Vacca 15km **DAY 4**

Boggoms Bay

35 15'58 S 21 54'39 E

Johnson's Post

Vleesbaai

★ Tidal pool

★ Swim & snorkel *Vleespunt*

🏠 Dune House (alternative for night 4)

57m

Rooibankies

Visbaai

34 20'18 S 21 54'31 E

Alternative trail for a longer last day

Boat cruise

Cape Vacca (Kanonpunt) to Gouritz River Mouth 4km

Cape Vacca

DAY 5

Kanonpunt

Private Cottage

★ └ 1 Ancient fish traps 2 Replica of Diaz cross

59m

Gouritzmond

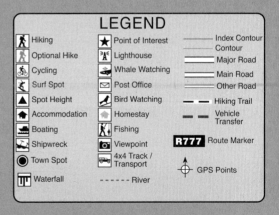

243m

Settling in
START

Point Village to Dana Bay
15km
DAY 2

34 10'54 S
22 08'50 E

Mosselbaai

KwaNonqaba

Point Village
St Blaize Cave
Cape St Blaize

Mossel Bay

197m

34 10'46 S
22 02'22 E

Dana Bay

178m

Onkruidrots

DAY 3

Dana Bay to Boggoms Bay
12km

Oyster Bay

Caves

Golf Course
Pinnacle Point

Indian Ocean

N

LEGEND

Hiking	Point of Interest	Index Contour	
Optional Hike	Lighthouse	Contour	
Cycling	Whale Watching	Major Road	
Surf Spot	Post Office	Main Road	
Spot Height	Bird Watching	Other Road	
Accommodation	Homestay	Hiking Trail	
Boating	Fishing	Vehicle Transfer	
Shipwreck	Viewpoint	**R777** Route Marker	
Town Spot	4x4 Track / Transport	GPS Points	
Waterfall	River		

OYSTERCATCHER TRAIL

The Oystercatcher Trail, which is centred round the pretty village of Boggoms Bay, just west of Mossel Bay, is another glorious coastal hike. The fully catered and portaged trail has received numerous accolades, including being listed as one of *Getaway Magazine*'s 'Top 5 hiking trails in South Africa' (2004), one of the BBC's '30 walks to do before you die' and *National Geographic Traveller*'s 'Top 50 tours of a lifetime' for 2007 and 2008. It's one of the most luxurious of the new genre of slackpacking trails so expect to be thoroughly spoilt. From the Point in Mossel Bay the trail heads west from the Cape St Blaize Cave, initially along dramatic orange cliffs and through coastal fynbos, before descending to the coast. Here you feel like a modern-day Strandloper, hiking the sandy beaches, gathering white mussels, checking out the marine life of the tidal pools and learning about the endangered African Black Oystercatcher and a diverse array of other birds and coastal organisms. The trail is varied, the distances quite manageable for even relatively unfit hikers and the scenery along this unspoilt, wild piece of coast is quite stunning, but it's the quality of the guiding and the little spoils along the way that make it so special. At the end of days one and two you can avail yourself of sauna and spa facilities or even arrange a massage, while on the final day you're treated to a champagne and oysters farewell. When you arrive in your overnight Sandpiper Cottage you'll find wine and beer in the fridge and the fire and candles lit. Nothing is overlooked. If you thought hiking trails were all about roughing it then this one's a surprise.

Although the full trail is 47km, a number of flexible trail packages are offered. You can hike for anything between two and five days, moving to new accommodation at the end of the trail each day, or you can stay in the same place and be ferried to the trailhead each morning. Whichever option you choose you'll come away enlightened and refreshed, and, since part of the trail fee is ploughed back into conservation, you also have the feel-good factor of having made a valuable contribution to the sustainability of this beautiful stretch of coast.

> **DISTANCE** 47km
>
> **DAYS** 5
>
> **DIFFICULTY** EASY TO MODERATE

66 *Today oysters are considered an aphrodisiac but it's rumoured that the extinction of the old Strandlopers was probably due to them becoming sterile due to the high iodine content of molluscs. So take care!* 99
Fred Orban, trail developer

CLIFF PATH A FEW KILOMETRES BEYOND CAPE ST BLAIZE CAVE

DAY 1 Settling in

Hikers overnight in the bright, roomy self-catering flats at Point Village, a magnificent spot with great views over the ocean. At 6pm there's a Meet and Greet and a discussion of the programme for the next few days, after which a special Oystercatcher Trail dinner (from a menu which amazingly includes vegetarian, halaal, wheat-free, prawn and seafood dishes) is served in the Kingfisher Restaurant – a popular whale-watching spot. If you arrive earlier in the day, there are plenty of glorious beaches to explore, as well as the sights of Mossel Bay itself. The Cape St Blaize lighthouse, which has been operational since 1864, is one of only two manned lighthouses on the South African coast, while the Dias Museum Complex, with its superb shell museum and aquarium, maritime museum and the famous Post Office Tree, is definitely worth a visit.

DAY 2 Point Village to Dana Bay
15km, 4–5 hours

Day one initially follows the route of the Cape St Blaize hiking trail – a well-marked path from the famous Cape St Blaize Cave near the Point in Mossel Bay. Hikers are met in the morning by one of the most interesting guides that I met while researching this book – the charismatic Willie Komani. Willie, who's been the chief guide on the trail since its inception, is a fount of knowledge and his passion for the coast is infectious.

Before you start the hike you visit the cave, a large overhang that was once a

CAPE ST BLAIZE CAVE

Strandloper dwelling. Here, by way of introduction, Willie outlines the history of the area, the archaeological significance of the many similar caves in the rocky coastline and the Strandloper traditions. Then you climb up to the clifftop path, stopping to catch your breath at the top and to admire the view. The waves crash onto the jumbled boulders below – the lichen-covered rocks glowing an incredible orange. This is an unstable area of high

> **SOME LIKE IT HOT**
>
> Mossel Bay is very proud of its reputation of having one of the mildest all-year climates in the world – apparently second only to Hawaii!

In 1500 Pedro de Ataide, returning from the East, left a letter in a shoe or iron pot under a large tree, warning of troubles he had encountered near Calcutta. In 1501 João da Nova, commander of the Third East India Fleet en route to India, found the letter and the tree became South Africa's first post office. The large milkwood tree is now a Provincial Heritage Site. Mail posted in the shoe under the tree gets the special post office tree frank.

precipitous cliffs undercut by the power of the waves. Willie points out the beautiful fynbos species and curses the existence of the aliens, explains the uses of the wild herbs and generally entertains as you walk. After about 6km the trail traverses a new golf course development, Pinnacle Point, through which hikers have right of way. It's a bit incongruous to be stomping through such a manicured area but it's quite hilarious to stop and watch some of the golfing antics. This is a tricky course, particularly in

PINNACLE POINT CAVES

the wind, and a good few tee shots end up on the beach.

Keep your eyes peeled for golf balls as you head down on the trail back to the coast. After a couple of kilometres you pass more vast caves that are clearly being excavated. Then, if the weather's fine, have a welcome swim on the deserted beach of Oyster Bay. The day ends with a short stroll through coastal thicket to Dana Bay from where a local taxi ferries you to your home for the next two nights, the quaint Sandpiper Cottages of Boggoms Bay, a little down the coast.

You now begin to appreciate the care and effort that has gone into making this trail a memorable experience. The renovated fishermen's cottages are warm and welcoming with tastefully decorated en-suite rooms, kitchen and lounge areas and gardens. If you arrive late you'll find a fire blazing in your cottage, the candles glowing,

FOSSILISED ELEPHANT BONES ON A MIDDEN

SANDPIPER COTTAGE

cold beer in the fridge and red wine and sherry on the table – you could not be more comfortable if you were at home. And if you feel like a bit of pampering you can take advantage of the spa or massage facilities at the leisure centre before more welcome drinks and a comprehensive slide show and informative talk about the trail's namesake, the vulnerable African Black Oystercatcher, which will pull at your heartstrings. In keeping with the 'local is lekker' ('local is best') approach that is central to the trail, dinner is likely to be a traditional meal of bobotie, fried fish or a braai, served up by Lena, one of the local ladies, and accompanied by fine wine.

DAY 3 Dana Bay to Boggoms Bay
12km, 4 hours

You're dropped back on the trail at Dana Bay, the point you finished yesterday, then head out along the beach back to Boggoms Bay. The empty coastline is flanked by dune fields with rocky promontories sticking out at intervals into the sea. Despite their endangered status there are oystercatchers in abundance on the rocks and the beach and Willie will point out their characteristic red beaks and legs, the locations of the nest and explain more about the

Oystercatchers, *Haematopus sp.*, inhabit most continental sea coasts. There are 13 species of oystercatcher worldwide, nine of which occur in the southern hemisphere. The northern hemisphere species have been recorded flying great distances between breeding and non-breeding areas, whereas the African Black Oystercatcher, the largest of all the species and the only oystercatcher that breeds in Africa, is a largely resident shore bird. Adults have jet-black plumage, pinkish legs, a long dagger-like orange-red bill, red eye and red eye ring. Females are larger and heavier with longer bills and each female can lay up to three sets of eggs per season – if the first eggs hatch then they lay no more, but if the first or second nest is destroyed for any reason then all is not lost. Although you'll see a refreshing number of birds as you hike along this coastline, there are no more than 5000 birds in the world – making the African Black Oystercatcher rarer than the southern right whale. The birds are threatened by unwitting beach users who by their presence during the bird's feeding time at low tide can result in the chicks starving to death. A pair of oystercatchers mates for life, and if one of the pair dies the other remains solo, or may be seen on the beach with another pair.

A common misconception is that the birds eat oysters. In fact they don't – rather they eat limpets and mussels that they take off the rocks at low tide.

BOGGOMS BAY

EDEN
REHABILITATION AREA
PLEASE KEEP OFF
SENSITIVE VEGETATION

FRANSMANSHOEK
**Bewarea / Conservancy
Lid / Member**
U BETREE HIERDIE GEBIED
OP EIE RISIKO.
YOU ARE ENTERING THIS
PROPERTY AT OWN RISK

OYSTERCATCHER TRAIL

THE CAPE OF COWS

Cape Vacca (the Cape of Cows) was where, from the 15th century, the old Portuguese seafarers traded cattle with the Khoisan. The cape was sighted in 1488 by Bartolomeu Diaz, who, after landing in Walvis Bay, was driven far beyond the Cape of Good Hope by a violent storm. When calm weather returned he sailed once more in an easterly direction and, when no land appeared, turned northward. In so doing he became the first navigator from the northern hemisphere to sight the east coast of Southern Africa, finally landing at Mossel Bay. A replica of the vessel used by Diaz in his 1488 voyage was built in Portugal and sailed to Mossel Bay in 1988 to commemorate the 500th anniversary of Diaz's trip. It is now housed in the museum.

DAY 3 KANON DUINE – NAMED AFTER THE *LA FORTUNE* THAT SANK IN 1763

OLD FISHERMAN'S SHACK FRANSMANSHOEK

birds' behaviour and chances of survival as more and more people use the coastal areas. Dolphins too are regularly sighted and occasionally you'll see the blow of whales. You stop for a break and a swim at Blind River, a closed river valley roughly 3km from Dana Bay, then continue for another 3km or so until you stop for lunch near a large mound. Shell middens are a typical feature of this coastline, the legacy of the Khoi and San people who had once roamed this coast. Some are huge and formed from a variety of different shells. You can stop to swim or explore the rocks and dunes anywhere the fancy takes you along the final stretch of beach before hiking up through dunes to the beautiful white cottages of Boggoms Bay back to the Sandpiper Cottages. Springer Bay and Kleinbos, eco-estates adjacent to Boggoms Bay, are great examples of eco-sensitive housing

developments. The fishermen-style cottages are widely spaced, solar powered, similar in size and design and, very importantly, have no external light so there's a quaint, traditional feel about the place – like being in Paternoster or somewhere on the West Coast – and in the evening the absence of light pollution means you can see the moon reflected on the ocean, and the star-filled sky.

DAY 4 Boggoms Bay to Cape Vacca
15km, 4–5 hours

It's back to the beach again on day four and if you've taken the advice in the pre-trail information you'll have brought along a mussel permit so that you can eat oysters off the rocks and exploit the rich seam of white mussels close to Boggoms Bay. Once you've learnt the drill of feeling for the mussels with your feet you can spend

DAY 4 LUNCH STOP – RED ROCKS OF FRANSMANSHOEK

hours shuffling around in the water for the molluscs. The oystercatcher too hunts the sand mussel by touch, digging its dagger-like beak into the sand. You'll also find brown mussels clinging to the rocky outcrops, so if you're there at low tide you can gather some for the evening braai. Then it's on again along the beach, until, about 4km into the hike, you head up onto a coastal path that leads through coastal scrub along the rocky shore past more ancient Strandloper middens and rocky pools. Every time you stop to cool off in the sea or to peer into the tidal pools, Willie will collect some interesting species of plant or marine life to show to you, all the while explaining the characteristics of the plant, shell, mollusc, starfish or urchin. Many of the wild herbs you pass have traditional and medicinal uses: the aromatic buchus which were used for medicinal purposes, the poisonous milk of the asbos vygie – one of five poisons used by the Bushmen – and the Christmas berry bush which is used to treat wounds. The trail then regains the coastal path and approximately 8km from Boggoms Bay you arrive at a small stone fisherman's shack on a promontory where a surprise lunch of pasta, salad and koeksisters is spread out. This old building houses a small information centre with samples of the local fauna, flora and marine life displayed, as well as accounts of the French man-o-war *La Fortune*, which sank nearby at Fonteinjies, near Fransmanshoek, in 1763. Cannon from this wreck have since been salvaged and can be seen at the coastal resort of, you guessed it, Kanon. Southern right, humpback and beaked whales are regular visitors to the bay from September until December, so keep your eyes peeled on the sea if you're hiking at this time of year.

The day ends with another pretty section of beach flanked by high dunes. A small section of these massive dunes has been approved by the authorities as a 4x4 track so you might see vehicles churning up the sandy slopes. If you have the energy it's worth climbing to the top of one of the dunes to enjoy

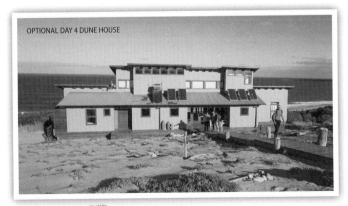

OPTIONAL DAY 4 DUNE HOUSE

STYLE NEAR GOURITZ RIVER MOUTH

OYSTERCATCHER TRAIL

OYSTERCATCHERS

will also include any mussels that you managed to collect. Then you can sit out listening to the sound of the waves, taking in the salty air and admiring the star-filled skies before turning in.

DAY 5 Cape Vacca to Gouritz River Mouth
4km, 1.5 hours

It's hard to leave this spectacular place but the last day on the trail, which again stays on the coastal path above the beach, has some interesting diversions. There is replica of a Diaz cross at Cape Vacca and at low tide the old fish traps are visible, prompting Willie to explain their construction and the traditional methods of fishing practised by previous wanderers of the coast. The wild flowers are particularly striking along this section, with brightly coloured aloes and pretty

vygies providing wonderful photo opportunities. The path follows the river inland at the Gouritz River estuary to where a boat awaits. Then it's a short cruise up-river checking out the birds before disembarking for a champagne and oysters brunch back at the Sandpiper Leisure Centre – the perfect end to the ultimate in luxury trails.

An alternative for hikers wanting a longer walk on the last day is to follow the above trail to the river mouth. Then, after a swim, continue up-river for a short distance and follow a footpath which loops back over the hill and meanders through a private nature reserve with the most magnificent indigenous coastal thicket, a great variety of bird species and even a few small buck and zebra, before being transported back to the Sandpiper Leisure Centre for the champagne and oysters farewell.

a bird's-eye view along the coast. Once you've run down the dune and cooled off with a swim it's only a short walk to the overnight spot, the magnificent Cape-style beach cottage at Kanonpunt, also known as Cape Vacca. This is my favourite spot on the trail, a private cottage right out on the promontory with awesome views of the rocks and the crashing ocean. Dinner is another superb meal of salad, fresh bread and a fish braai, served up by Pieter and his wife Katrina, which

RELICS EN ROUTE

FAREWELL MEAL AT THE SANDPIPER LEISURE CENTRE – OYSTERS

Start/finish	Point Village Accommodation, Mossel Bay/Sandpiper Cottages, Boggoms Bay
Duration	Five days, with two- to four-day options
Group size	Minimum six, maximum 12
Difficulty	This is a straightforward, flexible trail that is ideal for novice hikers and family groups. The emphasis is on getting out and enjoying nature rather than on racing to the finish.
Facilities	The trail is guided and portaged, with accommodation in luxury guest cottages and one private beach house. The food is excellent and wine, beer and (in Boggoms Bay) spirits too, can be purchased. Hikers have access to the spa and sport facilities at the leisure centre in Boggoms Bay and massages are available on request as an optional extra.
And the kids?	Children aged eight years and upwards are welcome.
When to go	The trail can be walked year round except during the December school holidays. Spring (August to October), when whales are often spotted off the coast and the wild flowers are at their best, and autumn (March to May) are ideal times.
Top tip	Buy a permit for collecting molluscs before you head out on the trail. Doing the white mussel shuffle is really fun.
Contact	Sandpiper Safaris, 044 699 1204, stay@sandpipersafaris.co.za, www.oystercatchertrail.co.za
Other contacts	Bonniedale Farm, 044 695 3175 Dennehof, 023 541 1227, www.dennehof.co.za Eden Adventures, 044 877 0179, www.edenadventures.co.za Face Adrenalin, 042 281 1458, www.faceadrenalin.com Garden Route Trail, 082 213 5931, www.gardenroutetrail.co.za Hunter Gatherer Trail, 044 699 1204, stay@sandpipersafaris.co.za, www.oystercatchertrail.co.za Outeniqua Nature Reserve, 044 870 8323, www.capenature.co.za Wildthing Adventures, 021 556 1917, www.wildthing.co.za
Kit list	See general kit list, page 202
On your bike	There are no specific mountain biking trails in the vicinity, but if you bring your own bike you can explore the farm roads and tracks to the coastal lookouts. A popular outing is along the seasonal wetland nearby which has the most amazing and varied species of water birds.
Other multi-day trails	**Hunter Gatherer Trail, Mossel Bay, Western Cape, 45km hiking, 10km kayaking, 5 days** The five-day Hunter Gatherer Trail follows a similar route to the Oystercatcher Trail along the Southern Cape Garden Route coast. The trail is geared for families and active sorts on a more modest budget who want to get a feel for the lives of the beachcombers who once roamed the coast and the challenges facing the coastline today. The trail starts at Vlees Bay and ends at the Gouritz River, with hikers spending the first two nights in a tented camp at Vlees Bay and nights three and four at Pondokkie at Boggoms Bay, where there's a dorm sleeping

Other multi-day trails ctd.

four, a double room and a tent. To a large extent each group decides the daily distances they hike/paddle from the base camp, so they can push the mileage to 60km walking and 25km on the kayaks if they want.

On day one arriving hikers are given maps and aerial photos with key points of interest – the location of middens, oystercatcher nests, etc. – and there's an introduction to the area which includes its ecology and history and a discussion of the lives, and legacy, of the Khoisan people who once subsisted off this coast. On the second day the trail takes hikers past Fransmanshoek, where, if the tide is low, there is great snorkelling, and to Fonteintjies to view the dune middens and fish traps. On the third day a guide takes hikers to the beach and dunes in the direction of Dana Bay, while day four consists of a kayaking trip on the Gouritz River for a day of bird-watching and fishing. Daily walking distances are between 12km and 20km depending on the fitness/interests of the group. Hikers must provide their own sleeping bags and cook for themselves, but have the option of self-catering or buying daily food and braai packs. Bring a permit if you want to fish or collect white mussels or mussels and oysters off the rocks.

Garden Route Trail, Western Cape, 63km, 5 days

The five-day Garden Route Trail takes hikers along the beaches, nature reserves and back routes of the Garden Route from Wilderness National Park to Brenton on Sea just outside Knysna. The first night of this superb guided, portaged and catered hike is spent at the Ebb and Flow Rest Camp in Wilderness National Park, then hikers walk along the beach to Sedgefield, past the fossilised dunes and wonderful rock pools of Gerike's Point, to Myoli near Sedgefield. The trail then heads inland with nights three and four being spent in the rondavels overlooking the Goukamma River. Trail developer/guide Mark Dixon is a passionate and knowledgeable twitcher/nature lover, a superb cook and an absolute fundi on the coast, who'll show you the secrets that lie off the popular tourist route. The trail, which includes a day of canoeing on the Goukamma River, can be catered to different interests and fitness levels and shorter hikes are available.

Day hikes in the area

Mossel Bay
Cape St Blaize, 15km, 4–5 hours

This linear day trail (also the first day of hiking on the Oystercatcher Trail) starts at Bats Cave in Mossel Bay and ends at Dana Bay. It's of only moderate difficulty and the rugged coastal scenery, rock formations and caves are spectacular. A map and brochure are available from the Mossel Bay Publicity Association but no permit is required.

Wilderness National Park
Pied Kingfisher Trail, 10km, 3–4 hours

This circular trail follows the edge of the Serpentine flood plain, then takes hikers along the boardwalk on the edge of the Wilderness Lagoon to the Touw River Mouth. After a glorious section along the beach to Wilderness Village it finishes back at the Ebb and Flow Rest Camp.

Day hikes in the area *ctd.*

Half-collared Kingfisher Trail, 3.8km, 1–2 hours

This short walk through the forest along the side of the Touw River offers hikers the opportunity to see many of the forest birds and yellowwood trees for which the area is famous.

Giant Kingfisher Trail, 7km, 3–4 hours

The highlights of this easy to moderate trail are the pools and pretty waterfall at the end where you can swim and picnic.

Brown-hooded Kingfisher Trail, 5km, 2–3 hours

A popular bird-watching trail, the Brown-hooded Kingfisher Trail takes hikers through the forest to a magnificent pool in the Klein Keurbooms River.

Cape Dune Molerat Trail, 6km, 2–3 hours

This short circular trail in the area between Rondevlei and Swartvlei is a great trail for twitchers but it also offers great views and beautiful fynbos.

Outeniqua Nature Reserve

Cradock Pass Trail, 12.4km, 5–6 hours

This strenuous historic trail follows the tracks scoured into the rocks by the ox-wagon wheels of the settlers crossing the Cradock Pass across the Outeniqua Mountains. Highlights include the spectacular mountain scenery, outstanding views back to the coast and magnificent fynbos and Karoo veld.

The trail ends on the north side of the Montagu Pass, so either arrange transport back from here or make a circular hike of it by hiking down the Montagu Pass back to the start – an additional 10.9km (three hours).

George Peak, 17.2km, 7 hours

The trail up George Peak is steep and very strenuous but don't let that put you off. The pristine mountain fynbos and the views from the summit over the Outeniqua Mountains, back over George to the sea, across to the Montagu Pass and all the way to the Swartberg Mountains are quite mind-blowing. The weather can change rapidly in the high mountains so pack warm and waterproof clothing, as well as plenty of water (once you cross the river near the start water is only available just below the final climb to the saddle between George and Cradock peaks). The trail can be combined with a climb of Cradock Peak.

Cradock Peak, 19km, 8 hours; 21.1km (9 hours) if combined with the George Peak

This very strenuous trail, a must for fit peak baggers and those who love far-reaching views, follows the same trail as that up George Peak until you reach the saddle. From here head left and up the ridge that leads to the radio mast on the summit of Cradock Peak. The final section involves a short rock scramble so be particularly careful on this and the steep slippery sections in bad weather.

Pass-to-pass day walk, 4.7km, 3 hours

The linear Pass-to-pass walk links the Montagu and Outeniqua passes and passes through magnificent fynbos. If the weather is fine the views from the high mountains are spectacular so take the 2.6km detour to the summit of Losberg. As with the previous trails hikers should go prepared for inclement weather and carry plenty of water. Organise transport to get back to the start.

MTB trails	**Montagu Pass, 30km, 6 hours (return), moderate**

This straightforward but scenic route from George to Herold on the northern side of the Outenique Mountains takes you on the gravel road over the historic Montagu Pass – one of the oldest and most famous passes in South Africa, built in 1847.

The Ostrich Tour, ±280km, 5 days, moderate

The Montagu Pass is also the first stage of Mountain Biking Africa's five-day, four-night Ostrich Tour from George to Knysna. The initial climb takes you over the spectacular Outeniqua Mountains and into the Klein Karoo. On day two you cycle through the Kamanassie Mountain Reserve to Black Eagle Falls, then continue through Uniondale onto the old wagon trail over the Potjiesberg Mountain to the top of the famous Prince Alfred's Pass before finally finishing in Knysna.

Three Passes Tour, 57.5km, full day, moderate

Dennehof offer a ride down the Montagu Pass as part of their guided Three Passes Tour. First they drop you off at Meiringspoort where you cycle 17km downhill through the poort, then on to Montagu Pass for an easy 6km uphill and 14km downhill, then you finish off with the Swartberg Pass – only 1.5km uphill followed by a swooping 19km down. The tour includes bikes, safety gear, water bottles and backup.

Outeniqua Nature Reserve

There are no marked trails but you can cycle along the scenic dirt roads of the reserve.

Bonnievale, 35km and 120km

Bonnievale offers a choice of two difficult/extreme routes both starting at Bonniedale Farm. The 35km trail takes you along farm roads and the 120km trail is circular with steep slopes, brutish climbs and some extreme downhill challenges along a combination of Jeep track and purpose-made singletrack trails.

Canoe trails	**Wilderness National Park**

All these self-guided trails start at Eden Adventures where you can hire single, double and triple canoes equipped with paddles, buoyancy aids, waterproof containers and a map.

Touw River waterfall, 5km canoeing, 4km walking, 3 hours

Paddle up the Touw River through the indigenous forest, which is rich in bird life. After about 40 minutes of easy paddling you will reach a point where it becomes too shallow and too narrow to continue. Leave the canoe on the right-hand side of the river and follow the path up onto the bank. There you will come across a stunning new 2km-long boardwalk that will take you straight to the waterfall. Relax, swim, picnic and return via the same way.

Canoe trails *ctd.*	**Island Lake via Serpentine, 12km, 4–5 hours** To reach Island Lake it takes a couple of hours of paddling through reed beds on the meandering Serpentine River, a tributary of the Touw River. At one stage – just after a bridge – the reeds become very overgrown but if you push on through for about 20m the river opens up again and the going gets easier. Island Lake has a picnic site so once you're refreshed return the same way. **River Mouth, 4km, 1.5 hours** The paddle to the beach and back gives you a different perspective on the town of Wilderness and a chance to picnic on the beach or play in the waves.
Abseiling	There's a short 25m abseil at Ebb and Flow Rest Camp available for groups, and an adventurous 45m drop next to a roaring waterfall in Kaaimans River where you land in a boat at the bottom of the falls.
Kloofing	Eden Alley, on the upper Kaaimans River, is a stunning full-day kloofing trip that includes being lowered down waterfalls on a rope. The gorge is at times only 1m wide yet over 80m deep. The half-day Cappuccino Canyon on the lower Kaaimans is great for beginners and experienced kloofers alike. It's a wider gorge with more jumping opportunities, all of which are optional.
Bungee/ bridge swing	If you fancy a quick adrenalin fix head to the Gouritz Bridge where Face Adrenalin give you a taste of freefall on their bungee jump. If you prefer to stay upright then try Wildthing's bridge swing, a stomach-churning 50m drop where you reach speeds up to 120km/h.

DAY 3 BETWEEN DANA AND BOGGOMS BAY

TRAIL 9

Swartberg Hiking Trail

To Prince Albert

Swartberg Hiking Trail

Recommended Routes (Our author route shown on map)
De Hoek → Gouekrans → Bothashoek → Ou Tol → Bothashoek → De Hoek
OR
3 day option: De Hoek → Gouekrans → Bothashoek → De Hoek
2 day option: Ou Tol → Bothashoek → Ou Tol

909m

1532m

1734m

22 07 35 S
33 20 11 E

1497m

1567m

Daantjie Se Gat

Bothashoek

Bothasho
Goue
13

33 20 49 S
22 02 38 E

Ou Tol

Oliewenberg

1815m

1700
1600
1500

1750m

Albertberg

1672m

1400
1300
1200

Ou Tol to Bothashoek (via Jeep Track) 13.8km **DAY 3**

Bothashoek to Ou Tol 12.8km **DAY 2**

R328

1100

Swartberg Pass

1000

900

1006m

809m

810m

N

LEGEND

🥾 Hiking	★ Point of Interest		Index Contour
Optional Hike	Lighthouse		Contour
🚲 Cycling	Whale Watching		Major Road
Surf Spot	✉ Post Office		Main Road
▲ Spot Height	Bird Watching		Other Road
🏠 Accommodation	Homestay	– – –	Hiking Trail
Boating	Fishing	– – –	Vehicle Transfer
Shipwreck	Viewpoint	**R777**	Route Marker
● Town Spot	4x4 Track / Transport		
Waterfall	– – – River	⊕	GPS Points

Vanrhynsdorp
Citrusdal
Western Cape
Beaufort West
Paarl
CAPE TOWN
Strand
Oudtshoorn
George
Mossel Bay
Knysna
Trail Coverage

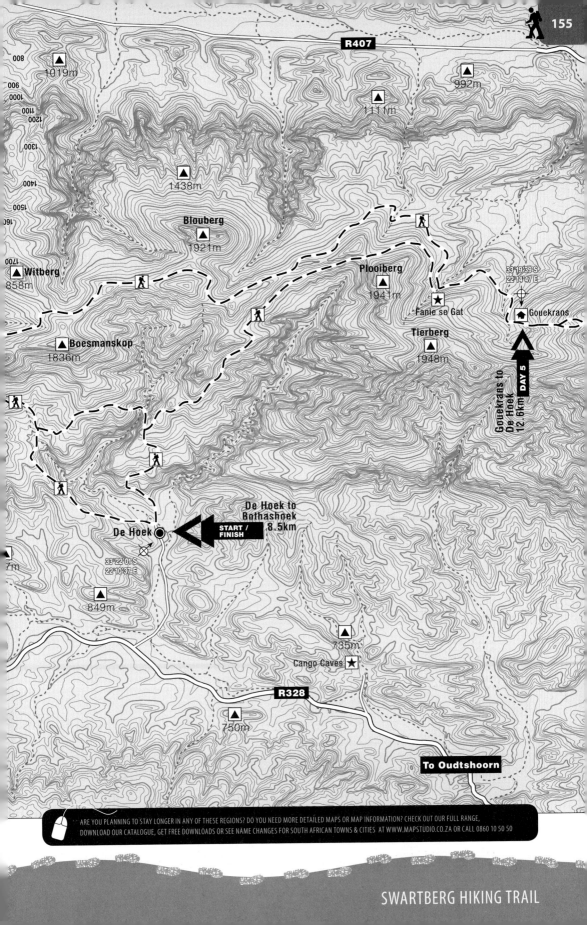

R407

▲ 1019m
800
900
1000
1100
1200
1300
1400
1500
1600
1700

▲ 992m

▲ 1111m

▲ 1438m

Blouberg
▲
1921m

Plooiberg
▲
1941m

33°19'39 S
22 14'47 E

▲ **Witberg**
858m

Fanie se Gat ★

⌂ **Gouekrans**

▲ **Boesmanskop**
1836m

Tierberg
▲
1948m

Gouekrans to
De Hoek
12.6km

DAY 5

De Hoek to
Bothashoek
8.5km

START /
FINISH

De Hoek ⊙

⊗ 33°22'01 S
22 10'37 E

7m

▲ 849m

▲ 735m

Cango Caves ★

▲ 750m

R328

To Oudtshoorn

HIGHLIGHTS

The Swartberg Hiking Trail traverses the rugged mountains of the Swartberg Nature Reserve just north of Oudtshoorn. Hiking in these remote mountains, which reach nearly 2000m high in places, is no mean undertaking – summers can be stinking hot, winters freezing cold and the weather unpredictable at any time of year, so you might well be walking through snow even in spring or autumn. When you first get hold of a map and start researching the trail it's a bit confusing. There are various possible starting points, three huts at which you can book any number of nights, lots of day hikes that cut into the longer trail at various points, and no fixed route. Some hike into the mountains up the steep paths from trailheads on either side of the Swartberg for the day. Others do short circular routes from Ou Tol or De Hoek. Most guidebooks tell you that the Swartberg Hiking Trail is a five-day adventure – and that's certainly a popular duration. But it's really up to you, and since the huts are all linked by a Jeep track you can of course drive in and hike from one of the huts – a good option if there are non-hikers or young/old/unfit members in the group. If you don't fancy much uphill you can leave your car at Ou Tol, just over the Swartberg Pass from Oudtshoorn, and do an only moderately strenuous circuit from there.

However, my advice would be to start at De Hoek Resort, near the Cango Caves. This is a demanding option with a steep uphill on the first day (and of course, at the end of the trail, an equally steep downhill) but the mountain fynbos, the incredible views and some dramatic gorges and peaks more than compensate for the effort. The trail's one shortcoming, in my opinion, is that the overnight huts are on a Jeep track and there is no alternative but to walk along this at times. Nonetheless, this rates as one of the most spectacular marked trails in the Cape.

Interesting Fact The Swartberg Pass, built by Thomas Bain in 1888, is one of Africa's premier drives – in fact one of the most spectacular mountain passes in the world. The pass was declared a South African National Monument in its centenary year in 1988 and is a Provincial Heritage Site.

- **DISTANCE** 58km
- **DAYS** 5 DAYS. SHORTER ROUTES (2- TO 5-DAY HIKES) ARE ALSO POSSIBLE.
- **DIFFICULTY** STRENUOUS
- **MTB** ONE 24.2KM ROUTE ALONG THE JEEP TRACK OF THE RESERVE, PLUS RIDES UP SWARTBERG PASS FROM OUDTSHOORN OR PRINCE ALBERT AND INTO DIE HEL

DAY 1 De Hoek to Bothashoek
8.5km, 4 hours

The most popular circular option on the Swartberg Hiking Trail starts at the municipal resort of De Hoek, just up from the Cango Caves. Park your car near the trailhead and cross over the stile. Other than at the first river there's no water in summer so start off with full water bottles and, since the path is a bit scratchy, consider hiking in long pants, even in summer. The well-trodden trail heads up and through a turnstile gate. Most hikers take the right-hand fork from here, heading up to the

LOOKING DOWN THE SWARTBERG PASS TOWARDS PRINCE ALBERT

BOTHASHOEK HUT

Gouekrans hut for their first night. If you're only spending a couple of nights in the mountains then this is a good option, but if you're doing the full five days I'd suggest an alternative route – this way you save the best till last. Rather head along the fence line on the path that leads to the Bothashoek hut down to a river crossing. The climb out of this first valley is steep but soon the path levels out a bit and you reach a plateau where you can take a break and look back from whence you've come. From here on you're into prime hiking country: fynbos-covered slopes, great views and a real feeling of wilderness. The fynbos and the little

delicate flowers hiding under the more prominent bushes really are stunning, so take time to enjoy the walk. After 3.9km you pass the junction where the circular route from De Hoek joins the trail. You can now see where the path leads – over an obvious saddle high above you. Fortunately, though, the path is sustained and fairly steep and there's much to distract you along the way, including beautiful orange lichen-covered rocks, great purple clumps of reeds, pink erica and tiny little blue nivenia. Look to your right and you'll see a massive gash in the landscape, a great gorge carved out of the sandstone rock by a powerful river. Beyond this are the dramatic folded rocks of the high peaks while below you are small rounded hills which take on a blue-green hue in twilight or under cloudy skies, somewhat reminiscent of a Chinese watercolour painting. You keep climbing through

The Swartberg Mountains are home to a variety of mammals, including baboons, rock dassies (hyrax) and grey rhebok, and a range of cliff-nesting birds such as the Black (Verreaux's) and Booted Eagle. Caracal are occasionally sighted and if you keep your eyes peeled you'll often spot a motionless klipspringer peering down on you from a rocky perch. Rarely seen inhabitants of the range include leopard, honey badger and a termite-eating aardwolf.

There are approximately 158 species of birds in the reserve, including the endemic Cape Sugarbird and Orange-breasted Sunbird, Martial and Black (Verraux's) Eagle and Kori Bustard.

The rocky terrain is home to a number of reptiles, including a Swartberg endemic, the Swartberg African leaf-toed gecko.

LEAVING DE HOEK

DAY 1 DE HOEK TO BOTHASHOEK

The vegetation of the Swartberg Mountains is remarkably diverse, featuring renosterveld, fynbos, Karoo veld, spekboom veld (a form of succulent thicket), and numerous lilies and other geophyte species. Often you'll pass subtle carpets of pink and yellow flowering mesembs and daisies, and if, when you stop and lay down your pack, you get down on your hands and knees you'll be stunned by the density and variety of little plants by the side of the trail – delicate pink and white snakebite flowers, little kebab bushes, euphorbias, tiny haworthias that look like mini aloes and, of course, numerous lichens.

Some species will be in bloom virtually throughout the year. Most plants flower in spring, but in early autumn many flowering protea and erica species attract large numbers of sugarbirds and sunbirds. During midsummer (December to February) many of the interesting plants on the higher Swartberg peaks are in flower, including the rare *Protea venusta, Protea pruinosa* and *Protea montana.*

The Swartberg Pass area is well known for its colourful flower displays, including those of the *Nivenia binata*, a member of the iris family with stunning blue flowers, the bright pink *Erica melanthera,* the bright yellow daisy, *Othonna parviflora,* as well as showy protea species such as *Protea eximia, Protea punctata, Protea lorifolia* and *Protea repens.* Apparently at least 680 plant species are known to occur within 100m of the Swartberg Pass – so when in the vicinity don't just look at the view.

colourful erica as the path winds ever upwards. Finally you arrive at the nek, usually a windy spot. Once over the other side you can see your goal, the Bothashoek hut, in the shallow valley below. It's less than an hour down the gradually descending trail to the hut, which is pleasantly sited and has a new verandah. Bothashoek, on the Jeep track, is equipped like the other two huts on the Swartberg Trail, with bunks, mattresses, rainwater tanks and even flush toilets and a shower in the new ablution block. The hut has three rooms – of which the front-facing one is the most attractive – and a kitchen/dining room. Unless you're on the trail in the height of a dry summer, there's a natural pool (Daantjie se Gat) in which to bathe about a kilometre along the Jeep track in the direction of Ou Tol.

DAY 2 Bothashoek to Ou Tol
12.8km, 4 hours

You have a choice here as you're in the centre of a figure of eight, but if the weather is good my preferred route would be the mountain trail to Ou Tol. Walk west along the Jeep track to Daantjie se Gat where a path to the left heads uphill. If you go

TAKING A BREAK ABOVE SWARTBERG PASS

in summer the river flowing into the water hole might be dry so fill up enough for the whole day at the rainwater tanks at the hut – there is no water on the trail. It's worth starting early as there's quite a bit of up- and downhill and the path is rough underfoot. And just when you think you're almost finished for the day, there's a nasty sting in the tail – a couple of steep uphills before the final descent to the Ou Tol hut.

The path zigzags to start with then continues up in a long, fairly steep contour until you reach the ridge. You feel on top of the world up here at over 1700m above sea level. The view extends beyond the Jeep track, snaking through the valley over the second lower range of mountains towards the empty Karoo plains and Beaufort West to the north, to the road leading west down to Gamkaskloof and back towards De Hoek where you started hiking the previous day. You can see the famous gravel road to the Swartberg Pass coming up from Oudtshoorn in the south and then dropping down the other side towards Prince Albert.

The trail, though marked by cairns, is at times rocky and a bit indistinct, then roughly follows this ridgeline the whole way to the Swartberg Pass,

sometimes dipping down on the north or south side of, and occasionally going over, the highest peaks. As you wind between rugged rock formations the sweeping views change but are always spectacular. The flowers too are amazing. In summer great swathes of pink watsonia cover many of the south-facing slopes while the presence of foraging animals is evident in the number of uprooted plants and in the ant hills that have been torn apart.

RUGGED MOUNTAINS NEAR OU TOL

DAY 2 BOTHASHOEK TO OU TOL

HIKERS NEAR SWARTBERG PASS NEK

SWARTBERG HIKING TRAIL

ABOVE OU TOL

MEERKAT

FLORA EN ROUTE

Another couple of ups and downs and you're meandering through the rock maze and succulents at the top of the Swartberg Pass. The dirt road is surprisingly well used so don't be surprised to find other visitors admiring the view or getting ready to hop on their bikes and speed down to Oudtshoorn or Prince Albert. (Most will have 'cheated' and had their bikes brought up, courtesy of one of the backpackers or local adventure companies.) Once you've crossed over the pass the well-marked trail heads down to the back of the huts, a very scenic ramble through beautiful fynbos.

As you climb to the highest point on the trail (1815m) there's an impressive view of the great kloof to the north which leads down towards Prince Albert, and if you look west towards Gamkaskloof you can clearly make out the green roofs of Ou Tol in a sheltered, grassy patch at the base of a natural rock amphitheatre. You'll often hear the barking of baboons as you follow the ridge, a clear warning that you're in their territory. Dassies too are regularly sighted sunning themselves on the rocks. This high perch makes a good lunch spot, though the sight of the steep descent that you're about to make, followed by an equally steep, unrelenting climb up the other side of the ridge, is enough to put you off your food. However, fuelled and rested, you'll (hopefully) find that the zigzags aren't as bad as they looked from the high point.

Ou Tol, a spacious, well-equipped hut with a kitchen, indoor fireplace, outdoor braai and clean rooms with bunk beds and mattresses, showers and flush toilets, is in a scenic spot with some great day trails radiating out from it. But it's right next to the road so it is certainly not your typical hikers' hut. For that reason, or if you prefer to avoid the steep uphill and downhill of the first and last days from the trailhead at De Hoek, Ou Tol makes a convenient alternative start/finish and has some scenic day trails spreading out from it. If you do the hike through to Gouekrans from here,

< GOUEKRA
< DE HOEK
< KRUIN SIR
PLATBERG S
< BOTHASHO

though, you have no alternative but to hike along the Jeep track both ways between the Bothashoek and Gouekrans huts, so you miss out on the spectacular trails on the northern slopes of the range above De Hoek.

BOTHASHOEK HUT

NEAR SWARTBERG PASS NEK

DAY 3 Ou Tol to Bothashoek (via Jeep track)
13.8km, 4.5 hours

From the hut head up the road until a Jeep track heads off through a gate to your left. (The alternative is to retrace your steps over the mountain route, which isn't a bad option as it's really pretty and much more varied than the route along the 4x4 track, and, besides, you'll obviously get different vistas on the return.) Don't assume that following the Jeep track will be a walk in the park. It isn't. There are plenty of demanding sections through soft sand, uneven rocky surfaces and some steep climbs to negotiate along the way. The trail follows the softer rock band between the two ridges of resistant Table Mountain sandstone, initially descending a bit to a pleasant flat section before the first steep uphill. There's a refreshing waterfall in the Bobbejaanskloof River (that leads down to the great ravine that you could

JEEP TRACK NEAR BOTHASHOEK

see from the ridge yesterday) where you can cool off and fill your bottles. Otherwise there's very little water on the trail in summer (and the locations are not shown on the map) so, again, make sure you're carrying enough for the day before you set out. At the top of the rise the track veers right and climbs steeply to the final saddle across a scrubby flat area. Then you're in the fynbos again on the final descent towards Bothashoek.

DAY 4 Bothashoek to Gouekrans
13.4km, 4 hours

From the hut you can see the 4x4 track heading east up the valley and over a nek. After a short flat section you cross a lush valley coming down from the nek to the south that you crossed over on the first day. The protea are big and dense here and you can see the friable shale band that the road has been cut through

OU TOL HUT

SWARTBERG HIKING TRAIL

GOUEKRANS HUT

FANIE SE GAT

CHILLING AT GOUEKRANS HUT

on the steep embankment to your right. For much of the year this area is a mass of streams and even in summer water trickles down onto the road in a number of places. Once you've gained the first rise continue on for another 400m or so. The Jeep track is now just below the ridge line and if you hop up to the right there's a good tea spot on a stunning natural rock platform with great views down to the south. From here the track continues downhill, then gently climbs to a junction.

The main route continues downwards while a steep trail leads to a mast at the top of the hill. Leave your pack and hike up – it's worth the detour for the far-reaching view.

You can see the track snaking down in the distance – down, down, down. It's not good news, as you know you're going to have to regain the height again. Some big rocks on the left make a good spot for a break. Amazingly, despite the extensive views north, you can see few signs of civilization, just

the occasional green field suggesting the presence of a farm. This is one of the great selling points of the trail; the plains to the north are so barren that you really feel like you're in the middle of nowhere.

The vegetation changes again and you're now walking through rather dry, barren scrubland until the track veers to the right. Sooner than you expect, a hut comes into view, well positioned above a rocky cliff. The slopes are now much more densely vegetated, particularly with protea. The slopes below the road are in fact one of the few places you might even spot the rare *Protea venusta*. Fanie se Gat is an attractive pool at the point where the track crosses the river and begins the final 1km ascent to the hut. Though freezing cold, it's deep enough to bathe in even in midsummer and, if it's a hot day, makes a great place to lounge around before walking to the hut. Gouekrans, which takes its name from the folded cliffs off to the northeast that turn golden in the setting sun, is well camouflaged as you approach, so you suddenly stumble upon it. Fronted by a long verandah onto which the rooms open out, it has the best view of the huts on the trail, as well as interesting rooms which use the natural rock features as the back walls. There's a flush loo and a shower, and because it's also utilised by 4x4 visitors, a braai area. Note, however, that the collection of firewood is prohibited. The 4x4 track continues on down the valley and you can follow this – though it can be quite bushy and overgrown – down to the next river where there are some attractive waterfalls and pools.

DAY 5 Gouekrans to De Hoek
12.6km, 5.5 hours

It's worth rising early on your final day. Not only is the climb out of the valley steep and best done in the cool of the morning, but the pre-dawn colours are spectacular. If the weather gods are smiling, day breaks with awesome pink light over the lower hills, then as the sun comes up the high peaks are bathed in golden light. From Fanie se Gat the trail heads briefly up then crosses the river and gently climbs towards the northern flank of the mountain. Look down and you see the Jeep track that you hiked the day before and the now tiny Gouekrans hut. The path contours round and descends to a nek before traversing around on the southern side of the peaks on what initially appears to be an old road, the levelled surface of which has been achieved by the construction of a supporting wall. But it's far too narrow at times to have ever been even a 4x4 track – in fact it's a legacy of the days when there were plenty of labourers to create such a magnificent hiking path. The path then veers off down to the left before contouring around the pyramidal Perdekop. This is another area where protea are abundant. Look carefully as you walk along the stone 'road' and you'll see ground protea. Once round the peak the track descends again till you get to a junction. If you had hiked up on the circular trail you would carry on uphill from here, but your way is down. You can now see De Hoek Resort, where the trail ends, below you but you're more likely looking at a very odd feature – a great wall that cuts right across the slope below you and up the ridge on the other side of the path, presumably once used to contain animals within the area of the lower slopes. The last section is steep and soon you're back full circle, the peaks that you've just descended from appearing incredibly high and daunting from this vantage.

PROTEA

GOUEKRANS TO DE HOEK

Start/finish	De Hoek Resort outside Oudtshoorn, about five hours east of Cape Town
Group size	Minimum three, maximum 18
Difficulty	This is a strenuous but well-marked trail, which should only be attempted by fit and experienced hikers equipped with good-quality wet/cold weather gear. Do not underestimate the difficulty of the trail in poor weather when poor visibility, heavy rain, snow and slippery rocks can make the going treacherous.
Facilities	Drinking water, bunks, mattresses and toilet facilities are provided at the huts but hikers must bring all their own bedding, stoves, cooking utensils, food, etc. There is little water on the trail during the summer months. There's cellphone reception on the way up and down from De Hoek and at many of the high points on the mountain section (day two).
And the kids?	Children under 18 years of age must be accompanied by an adult, but any youngsters (or adults) attempting this trail must be fit and able to carry a relatively heavy pack.
When to go	The trail can be walked year round but the Swartberg is an area of climatic extremes. The winters are very cold, with snow on the mountain peaks, while summers can be uncomfortably hot with temperatures reaching 40°C and more. Rain occurs throughout the year, peaking in early winter and spring, and with thundershowers in the summer months. The wild flowers are at their best a few weeks after the rains, which are unpredictable, but generally August through to October or February to April are the best months to appreciate the floral splendour.
Contact	CapeNature, 021 659 3500 or visit www.capenature.co.za
Other contacts	Dennehof Guest House, 023 541 1227, ria@dennehof.co.za, www.dennehof.co.za Ecobound Tours & Travel, 044 871 4455/2274, ecobound@pixie.co.za, www.ecobound.co.za Mountain Biking Africa, 044 382 6130, arcent@mweb.co.za, www.mountainbikingafrica.co.za Swartberg 4x4 trail, 044 203 6300, sberg.cnc.karoo@pixie.co.za, www.capenature.co.za
Kit list	See general kit list, page 202
Day hikes	**Swartberg Nature Reserve** Various possibilities, open-ended. You can use the various trailheads as the start/finish for day trails on the reserve, turning around when you tire or run out of time. Ou Tol is a good starting point because you are already high in the mountains. The other popular day hike is the 12km circular route from De Hoek (four to five hours). A conservation fee is charged at the point of entry, details of which can be found on the CapeNature website. **Grootkloof, Gamkaskloof, 6km, 1.5–2 hours** This interpretive trail in Die Hel is easy but interesting. Pick up a trail leaflet at the CapeNature info centre – it details 26 stops that provide information on the natural and cultural history of the early settlers.

MTB trails	**Swartberg, 68km, 4–5 hours**

Mountain bikers can ride the 4x4 track, a 68km out-and-back trip that is moderately difficult but which can be combined with overnight stays at Bothashoek or Gouekrans huts.

Swartberg Pass

The descent of the Swartberg Pass is exhilarating and fast. Unless you really want to sweat, organise a lift to the top from one of the local backpackers then feel the wind in your hair as you speed down to Oudtshoorn or Prince Albert.

Prince Albert to Die Hel, 57km (one way), 4–6 hours

The steep, rocky ride down to Die Hel is not for the faint-hearted, but if you're into hectic gravel roads then this is a good challenge.

Competitive mountain bikers should also look at the Die Hel and back ride organized by Ecobound. There's a one-day and a two-day event in which you not only ride down to Gamkaskloof, but also back up the wickedly steep, loose track. Of course if you've got masochistic tendencies you can do it any day of the year that you fancy. Just make sure you carry plenty of water and bike spares.

Oudtshoorn to Prince Albert via Die Hel, c161km, 2 days

Mountain Biking Africa offer a two-day guided trip into Die Hel. After overnighting in the Swartberg Hotel in Oudtshoorn you ride up the Swartberg Pass (c15km) and into Die Hel for the night (50km), then the next day ride back out of Die Hel and down to Prince Albert. The ride to Die Hel is also incorporated into some of their longer mountain bike tours.

Klein Karoo Klassiek

This new three-day MTB ride, also from Ecobound, is centred around Calitzdorp and consists of a 132km ride on day one, a 95km ride through the Groenfontein Valley (the start of the Donkey Trail) on day two, with two fun rides of 45km and 15km and a 42km time trial on day three.

MOUNTAIN BIKERS ON SWARTBERG PASS

TRAIL 10

Donkey Trail

HIGHLIGHTS

One of the problems with many of the classic trails in South Africa is that you need to set aside several days to hike them. So it's always a bonus to come across trails that really get you out into the wilderness, but that you can complete in a weekend. The Donkey Trail, in the Swartberg Mountains, is one such trail – a scenic and historically fascinating journey that any moderately fit hiker will thoroughly enjoy. It falls squarely into the category of luxury slackpacking trails, but it's also a challenge. The first day's hike is basically a demanding steep uphill climb to the top of a mountain (1523m with a height gain of around 1200m) that is harder than any single day on any of the other luxury hikes on offer. Although the spectacular scenery and the ever-present spoils would be reason enough to sign up, what gives the trail its special character is the donkeys. Following in the footsteps of one of these amiable beasts of burden provides a natural rhythm and a bond between hiker and animal. There's also a sense of history, of déjà vu, taking you back to the days when there was no road to the isolated valley of Gamkaskloof, when goods were carried over the mountain passes by great trains of donkeys and their drivers.

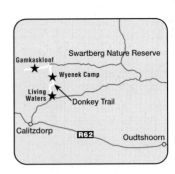

- **DISTANCE** 26km
- **DAYS** 2
- **DIFFICULTY** MODERATELY STRENUOUS

66 *Half of you are a bunch of donkeys.' Upon the demand that he retract his statement about the South African Parliament or be censured, he replied: 'I stand corrected. Half of you are not a bunch of donkeys.* 99

C.J. Langenhoven, writer, philosopher and Member of Parliament

DAY 1 Setting the scene

The trail starts at Hans and Erika Calitz's farm, Living Waters Mountain Estate, in the valley of Groenfontein, about 15km from Calitzdorp. After a welcome cup of tea or cool drink you're shown to one of the historic cottages on the farm, renovated and decorated in traditional farmhouse style with antiques and everyday items of yesteryear – old gramophone players, kettles, a foot stove to warm feet in winter, churns for cheese-making and big iron baths – but with extremely comfortable en-suite rooms, a lounge and views to die for. Then it's back to the main guest area for a swim, drinks and a detailed presentation

on the trail and how to pack. Hans still leads all the trails and is passionate about the spectacular scenery, the historical significance and potential of this new trail which opened in September 2009, a partnership between the Calitzses and CapeNature that has led to the reopening of an old trade route over the pass to Gamkaskloof.

He stresses, however, that the first day is tough; you have to get over the mountain. His photos and route maps show in detail the steep slopes you'll have to negotiate, but both he and Erika are positive that with the help of the guides they'll get you there.

Dinner that evening, prepared by Erika's mother Mimi and two local ladies,

LIVING WATERS MOUNTAIN ESTATE

FARMHOUSE AT LIVING WATERS MOUNTAIN ESTATE

If you leave your cottage make sure you close all doors and windows as the baboons are cheeky and opportunist. On our stay Mackie woke from an afternoon nap to find a baboon sitting on her bed stroking her face! Other wildlife in the kloof includes klipspringer (which you are highly likely to see on the drive out), kudu, grey rhebok, rooikat, porcupines and leopard, but unfortunately these animals seem of a shier inclination.

There are about 153 species of bird in Gamkaskloof, so keep your eyes and ears open. Sunbirds and sugarbirds flit around on the trail and in the kloof and you'll often see predators soaring ahead – and if you're lucky you might even spot or hear the distinctive cry of the African Fish Eagle.

Look out too for the remains of the old airstrip on the valley floor, where, until the 1980s when the majority of the inhabitants had left, Dr Manie Coetzee, the 'flying doctor' of Prince Albert, would land his Tiger Moth to tend his patients in case of emergency.

Cynthia, a Xhosa, and a local Groenfonteiner, Chantelle, is an absolute feast. With the attention to detail that is evident throughout the trail the menu reflects the preferences and foibles of the guests – we had non-meat eaters among us so fish and chicken were the main components of the delicious spread of salmon mousse, pickled fish, marinated chicken, fresh salads and amazing fresh bread. Then it's off to bed in anticipation of the rigours of the next day.

DAY 2 Living Waters to Wyenek camp
11km, 7–8 hours

After breakfast the donkeys are brought to the lawn in front of the main guest area and loaded up. This is one of the highlights of the trail. The friendly beasts, all previously abused animals from the Donkey Rescue Programme in De Rust, thoroughly enjoy being the centre of attention and the petting they receive as the panniers are strapped to their backs. Each hiker can send up to 5kg of personal gear – clean clothing, toiletries, books and whatever – up to the overnight camp. As the final preparations are made to the donkeys' burdens you set off along the trail carrying only a light daypack with water, extra jacket (it can get quite cold and windy on

top), camera and a pack of Donkey Trail mix – a mixture of locally produced dried fruits and nuts specially made up for the hikers. Hans points out the differences between the subtropical thicket on the west-facing slopes and the succulent Karoo vegetation, with its profusion of aloes, on the eastern slopes. The gentle beginning ends with a steep series of zigzags as you climb out of the valley. It's strenuous stuff to encounter so early in the day but if you follow the guides' advice to take it easy it's not so bad. By now the donkeys will have caught up and walking with them allows you to proceed at a pleasant pace. A plateau with some flat rocks on which to sit and have a snack provides a convenient place to stop and catch your breath and look back to the farm way down in the valley below. One big climb completed, one more to go. When you stop to catch your breath Hans points out the increasingly impressive view. You see the old school building, the olive fields of his neighbour's farm and the beautiful award-winning retreat next door, and if you cast your eyes to the sky you're likely to see a resident Black (Verreaux's) Eagle soaring overhead.

The path then contours round for a while through renosterveld before you arrive at the first of two steep river valleys. The women on the trail are invited to enjoy swimming in the pools of the first river while the men modestly retire to the second stream to bathe. This second river crossing, one of the few places on the trail where there's shade, makes a good lunch spot, at which point the guides unpack the blue lunchboxes – filled with sandwiches, vegetables, eggs or meatballs and a juice.

Once you've climbed out of this valley the scenery changes and the trail descends slightly before traversing around a spur. Look at the flowers alongside the path: pretty delicate stems of blue, pink and purple. Ahead of you are great folded mountains and as you round the spur the wide saddle of Wyenek looks a long way off. Although you're at almost 1200m it's now the heat of the day so you're expecting the climb to be tough. In fact it's a sustained, but only moderately strenuous, walk up as the path zigzags up towards the nek. There are some interesting rock formations to check out en route, including an outcrop with a big hole in the middle that resembles some prehistoric animal's head. When you stop to look back you can see not only the Groenfontein Valley but over into the next valley, to the town of Calitzdorp,

One of the things that will strike you about the Donkey Trail is the total commitment that trail developers Hans and Erika Calitz have for the area. Relatively recent migrants to the Karoo, they concede that 'we have not shaped the land, rather, in the decade we've been here, it has shaped us'. The Donkey Trail is an integral part of their work to improve the lot of the Groenfontein community, a population afflicted by high rates of unemployment and alcoholism. In setting up the trail and the Wyenek camp they sought the help of specialists – the camp developers and guide trainers from Cape Town's showcase Hoerikwaggo Trail (another community-guided project) – and the Donkey Trail guides, who trained through the Nature College, are keen and proud, eager to help you up the hills and show you their hard-earned certificates of guiding competency. At present hikes are still led by Hans, supported by a number of trainee guides that he's keen to pass the mantle to when they're ready.

The trail follows one of the many old trade routes that linked Gamkaskloof with Calitzdorp, Prince Albert, Oudtshoorn and the surrounding farms, where, in the past, donkeys were the main beasts of burden. It's hoped that opening up this old pathway will also facilitate the movement of game between the areas. Look around the dining room and you'll see evidence that the Calitzs' work is already being recognised. On the wall hangs a certificate – a Special Award from the Gouritz Biodiversity Corridor for Biodiversity Conservation. By supporting this trail you're not only having fun but supporting a community, and environment, in need.

DONKEYS AT THE WYENEK CAMP

TAKE TIME TO SMELL THE FLOWERS

It's a great excuse to catch your breath, but also to appreciate the changing flora as you hike from Living Waters in the south over to the north of the range. Succulent Karoo vegetation in the bottom of the valley on the southern side is gradually replaced by renosterveld at the lower slopes of the mountain, wet mountain fynbos on the mid- and upper slopes, and subalpine fynbos on the crest. As you lose altitude and drop into the Gamkaskloof Valley the reverse pattern occurs, with arid mountain fynbos changing into spekboom and subtropical thicket vegetation and an increasing number of succulents replacing the arid fynbos of the upper slopes. Gamkaskloof and the other river valleys are heavily vegetated with succulent thicket, Karoo acacia trees and dense stands of reeds.

Gnarly, rocky outcrops mark the final approach to the ridge – another good spot to rest, take in the view and have a snack before you leave the valley behind. It's a hard slog, but the endless patience, encouragement and water proffered by the guides (and of course the possibility of going down with the returning guides if you're really in trouble) usually keeps people going to the top. Once on the crest a magnificent scene unfolds. You're now on the north of the ridge, a gently sloping plateau full of big stands of *Protea lorifolia*. In the distance is the secluded valley of Gamkaskloof, but your route is down, through the protea and the green-sided valley towards the overnight hut. The valley narrows and you follow a tumbling river past waterfalls and rock pools. The scene is so impressive that it takes

a while before you notice the camp on a bluff above the river – the big canvas tents a spectacular sight. The camp manager greets you with a cup of tea and a warm welcome as you cross the river and sit down at the table. Once you're refreshed you're shown around. A big pool lies at the bottom of the waterfall just below camp – the perfect place to shower and bath. Not that you need to venture even that far if you don't feel like it – there's a basin, a flask of hot water, soap, shampoo, body lotion and towels in your spacious tented suite. Sleeping sheets, warm sleeping bags, pillows and comfortable mattresses on stretcher beds, lights and flowers complete the accommodation package – it's a bit like being on a luxury safari. It may have been a hard walk but you need no further proof that this is a trail where

the distinctive Red Hills, the Gamka River to the Gamka Mountain, as well as the road back from the bottom of the Swartberg Pass on which you'll return once you finish the hike. On this last section you'll probably pass some of the other guides – they went up the day before to set up camp. This is the point of no return. Any hiker who's really taking strain can elect to go back to the farm in their company.

FORMATIONS BETWEEN WYENEK & GAMKASKLOOF

all concerned do everything they can to make your life as comfortable as possible.

The wind usually gets up in the evening so make sure that you followed the advice in the briefing and brought plenty of warm clothes. If you've requested it there'll be wine and beer chilling in a rock pool and sundowners are accompanied by snacks before the main event, a warming bowl of pasta.

DAY 3 Wyenek camp to Gamkaskloof

15km, 7–8 hours

The mist usually stays till about 9am so there's no rush to get going in the morning. After cappuccinos, served in wonderful tin mugs painted with donkeys, and breakfast, the donkeys are loaded up for their return journey to the farm while you head up the hill towards Gamkaskloof. Hans points out the various mountain ranges. The Outeniqua Mountains, closest to the sea, receive plenty of rain. What's left falls here, on the Swartberg, as rain or mist, so you're basically on the edge of the arid Karoo. It's only a short walk to the top of the rise then it's downhill pretty much all the way – an easy day compared to the previous one. At the top the guides play a guessing game: there's a sea horse and a skull in the rock formations. Can you spot them?

You're now close to the top of a massive waterfall that you'll see later in the day, but you've no inkling of the precipitous cliffs below as you head right and down the steep trail to Die Hel. The views of the hidden valley just get better and better as you negotiate three steep rocky descents (with a short uphill after each) by way of zigzagging paths and descend towards the long, green swathe that is sandwiched between the barren mountains. The vegetation changes again. You leave the fynbos and the occasional colourful lilies behind and drop into bushy renosterveld. The guides note the change explaining that the leaves of the renosterveld are often used to add flavour to braai meat. They'll show you a succulent, the leaves of which can slide off the stem to form 'beads', complete with a central hole through which a string could be threaded. Apparently these were strung into necklaces by the Khoisan.

The trail levels out, rounding a final bend with great views of the aloe-covered slopes and the vegetated valley below. Keep your eyes peeled for klipspringer as you hike; the agile little buck are so well camouflaged that they're difficult to spot unless they move, but there are a good number around. You'll often

DONKEY STATUS

In *The lure of an isolated valley,* Engela Duvenage sums up the role of the donkeys in Gamkaskloof. 'To the farmer, his donkeys were a status symbol, just as 4x4s are today. They were his means of travel, his tractors, plough machine, his silent companions when he left the valley on foot. Every few months the farmer would load dried figs, raisins and animal skins onto his train of donkeys and walk a few days to the nearest town to trade these items for coffee, sugar, material and hand implements with which he worked his fields.'

CORNELIS JACOBUS LANGENHOVEN

Cornelis Jacobus Langenhoven (1873 –1932) was born at Hoeko, Ladismith, but later moved to Oudtshoorn, and is best known for writing the words for the original South African anthem, *Die Stem*, in 1918. In 1973 the South African Post Office issued a four-cent C.J. Langenhoven stamp to celebrate the centenary of his birth. Langenhoven owned an imaginary elephant named Herrie (Harry) that appeared in many of his stories. In 1929 he carved its name onto a boulder next to the N12 highway near Meiringspoort. The boulder, known as Herrie se Klip (Herrie's Stone), has been declared a South African National Monument.

Gamkaskloof was first inhabited by farmers in 1830, but the secluded, fertile valley was only accessible on foot (or donkey) so was pretty much isolated from the rest of the country for a over a century until the gravel road from the top of the Swartberg Pass was constructed in 1962. The spectacular road was named after Dr Otto du Plessis, the Administrator of the Cape at that time. Far from encouraging the inhabitants of the valley to stay and enjoy the benefits of the new link with the outside world, the road precipitated a mass exodus, leaving the beautiful clay-brick houses to decay. By the 1990s most of the valley was incorporated into the Swartberg Nature Reserve (now managed by CapeNature), and in 1999 restoration work on the traditional houses started in earnest to provide attractive, authentic tourism accommodation. Gamkaskloof was declared a National Heritage Site in 1997 and forms part of the Cape Floral Region Protected Area – a UNESCO World Heritage Site.

No one is sure where Die Hel (The Hell) comes from, but interpretive boards at the CapeNature office in Gamkaskloof suggest that a certain Piet Botha, a livestock inspector in the 1940s, had to travel to Gamka Poort every couple of months, usually gaining access by a steep footpath called 'The Ladder' – a trip he described as 'hell'. Others support the view that the name originated much earlier, when Denys Reitz and his comrades stumbled on the kloof during the Anglo-Boer War, the western end of the valley was, apparently, already known as 'The Hell'.

One of the characters you'll probably meet in the valley is a woman from Groenfontein called Mackie – usually your Donkey Trail hostess in Die Hel. When she was a young woman Mackie had a suitor – appropriately named Romeo – who lived in Die Hel. Young Romeo would hike back along the trail that you've just taken for two days to visit his beloved. If she wasn't there he'd have a cup of coffee then return to his valley. And you think you're tough.

see kudu spoor on the trail too – the animals have wisely decided that using the trail is easier than bashing through the bush! Then, almost suddenly, you're at the dirt road that cuts down steeply to the camp site. This section of road, Elandspad, which drops some 800m into the kloof, was a monumental engineering effort. According to Hans, Koos van Zyl, who with eight labourers constructed the road, decided that the only way to cut it was from the bottom, so he bravely, some might argue foolhardily, drove his bulldozer straight down the northern steep slope before starting work on the road. You can still see his original direct descent route if you look carefully. You can hitch a ride down Elandspad in one of the support vehicles, but I'd not recommend this, both for the views and the fact that travelling down in a car is quite harrowing. The narrow road is not where you want to meet oncoming vehicles. Look up to your left as you descend and you'll see the river beside which you camped last night plunging off the plateau in a dramatic precipitous waterfall.

Lunch is served in the shade of the trees at the camp site – again the familiar blue lunchboxes – before you continue to the overnight cottages. This is easy walking, largely in the shade of the trees. On the way you pass

MASSIVE ALOES NEAR "THE HELL"

through the property of Annetjie Joubert, the last remaining original resident of Gamkaskloof, where you can stop off to visit her old-world shop and have a cup of tea, a beer or cool drink or buy some home-made jams or other local produce.

If you don't fancy the walk then again there's the option to hop in a vehicle and drive down the bumpy road to your home for the night, one of the ten beautifully restored old clay houses in the valley, where the guides prepare a celebratory braai.

DAY 4 5–6km (optional)

The scheduled departure from Gamkaskloof is at 9am, so if you want to visit the CapeNature Visitor Centre at Ou Plaas or explore the kloof, get up early. The 6km easy walk along the valley floor should take no more than an hour and a half. Alternatively you can head out with a guide book on the Grootkloof interpretive trail which is roughly the same length/time. Or, of course, you can sleep in – this is a luxury trail after all! The drive out along the winding, sometimes precipitous dirt road is spectacular and the fynbos, game sightings and views keep you enthralled. Descending the Swartberg Pass is another treat, then you follow a gravel road back to Groenfontein where yet more refreshments await. After all that you've experienced, it's hard to believe that you only left the farm a couple of days ago.

SUMMARY

Start/finish	Groenfontein, 15km outside Calitzdorp.
Group size	Minimum four, maximum eight
Difficulty	Moderate to strenuous. The hike up to Wyenek is strenuous but you're only carrying a daypack and can take it very slowly if you need.
Facilities	Accommodation is in beautiful historic renovated cottages on nights one and three (on day three you'll share a bathroom). The night on the mountain is in well-equipped, spacious two-person safari tents and there's a shared portaloo. Extra water is carried by the guides, and wine and beer can be purchased in the evenings. There is cellphone reception at several points on the first day but not on the second day of the trail. However, the chief guide carries a satellite phone for use in emergency.
And the kids?	Children from 10 years up can join the trail provided that they are fit and under parental supervision at all times
When to go	The trail can be walked year round. Spring and autumn are probably the most pleasant for hiking, particularly since the temperatures are less extreme and many of the fynbos species are in flower. Winters are cold and snow is a distinct possibility on the peaks.
Contact	Erika Calitz, 083 628 9394, info@donkeytrail.com, www.donkeytrail.com
Kit list	See general kit list, page 202 **Specific** ⚐ Light slipslops for on the mountain ⚐ Insect repellent (mainly against ticks) ⚐ Cash for alcoholic beverages and curios
On your bike	There are no marked trails on the farm but the dirt road leading from Calitzdorp past Groenfontein and to the bottom of the Swartberg Pass is a great ride.

TRAILS 11 & 12

Otter and Tsitsikamma Trails

Otter and Tsitsikamma Trails

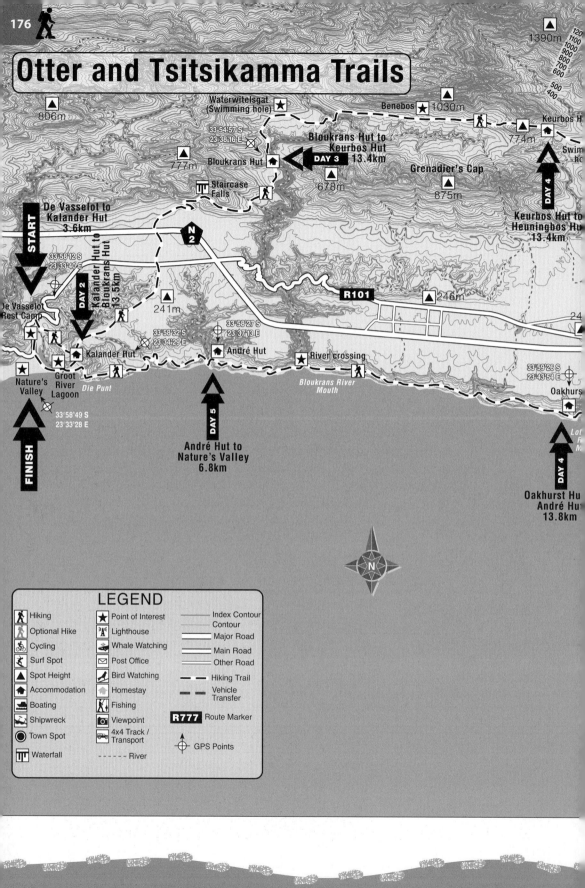

806m

1390m

120
1100
1000
900
800
700
600

500
400

Waterwitelsgat
(Swimming hole)

Benebos 1030m

Keurbos H

33°54'57 S
23°38'16 E

Bloukrans Hut to
Keurbos Hut
13.4km

774m

Swim
ho

777m   Bloukrans Hut

DAY 3

Grenadier's Cap

Staircase
Falls

678m

875m

DAY 4

Keurbos Hut to
Heuningbos Hu
13.4km

De Vasselot to
Kalander Hut
3.6km

START

N2

33°58'12 S
23°33'40 E

R101

241m

246m

24

DAY 2

Kalander Hut to
Bloukrans Hut
13.5km

33°58'27 S
23°37'13 E

De Vasselot
Rest Camp

33°58'32 S
23°34'29 E

André Hut

River crossing

Bloukrans River
Mouth

33°59'26 S
23°43'54 E

Oakhurs

Kalander Hut

Groot
River
Lagoon

Die Punt

Nature's
Valley

33°58'49 S
23°33'28 E

DAY 5

André Hut to
Nature's Valley
6.8km

FINISH

Lot
F
N

DAY 4

Oakhurst Hu
André Hut
13.8km

N

LEGEND

Hiking	Point of Interest		Index Contour
Optional Hike	Lighthouse		Contour
Cycling	Whale Watching		Major Road
Surf Spot	Post Office		Main Road
Spot Height	Bird Watching		Other Road
Accommodation	Homestay		Hiking Trail
Boating	Fishing		Vehicle Transfer
Shipwreck	Viewpoint	**R777**	Route Marker
Town Spot	4x4 Track / Transport		GPS Points
Waterfall	River		

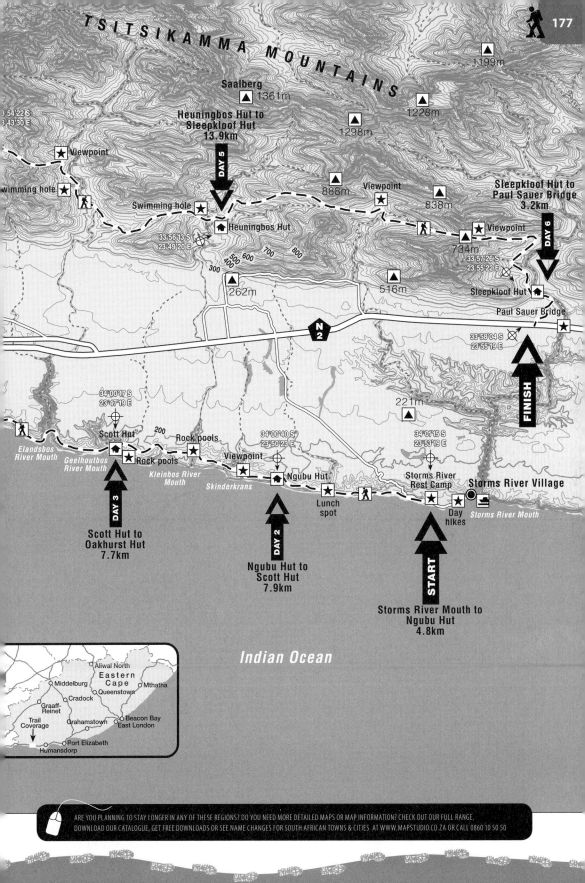

TSITSIKAMMA MOUNTAINS

▲ 1199m

Saalberg
▲ 1361m

▲ 1228m

Heuningbos Hut to
Sleepkloof Hut
13.9km

▲ 1298m

33 54 22 S
3 43 30 E

★ Viewpoint

▲ 888m Viewpoint

▲ 838m

Sleepkloof Hut to
Paul Sauer Bridge
3.2km

🏃 swimming hole ★

DAY 5

Swimming hole ★

▲ Heuningbos Hut

★ Viewpoint

33 56 13 S
23 49 20 E

33 57 26 S
23 55 22 E

▲ 734m

500 600 700 800

300 400

262m

▲ 516m

Sleepkloof Hut 🏠

Paul Sauer Bridge

N 2

33 58 04 S
23 55 19 E

FINISH

34 00 17 S
23 47 19 E

221m

200

Scott Hut

34 00 40 S
23 50 23 E

34 01 15 S
23 53 19 E

Rock pools

🏃

Elandsbos
River Mouth

Geelhoutbos
River Mouth

Rock pools

Viewpoint

Storms River
Rest Camp

Storms River Village

DAY 3

Kleinbos River
Mouth

★

Ngubu Hut 🏠

Storms River Mouth

Skinderkrans

Lunch
spot

Day
hikes

Scott Hut to
Oakhurst Hut
7.7km

DAY 2

START

Ngubu Hut to
Scott Hut
7.9km

Storms River Mouth to
Ngubu Hut
4.8km

Indian Ocean

Aliwal North

Eastern
Cape

Middelburg

Mthatha

Queenstown

Cradock

Graaff-
Reinet

Grahamstown

Beacon Bay
East London

Trail
Coverage

Port Elizabeth

Humansdorp

OTTER AND TSITSIKAMMA TRAILS

HIGHLIGHTS

Otter Trail

The Otter Trail needs little introduction. This magnificent backpacking trail through (what is now) the Tsitsikamma section of the Garden Route National Park was one of the first official trails to be opened in South Africa and is far and away the best known of the country's long-distance hikes. As a result you'll have to book well in advance (I waited three years to get a place!). But the good news is that the Otter is so spectacular that it's worth the wait. The five-day trail is only 42km long but don't underestimate it; the terrain is tough with some boulder hopping, steep sections and wide rivers to cross. But the rewards are immense. This is a truly beautiful stretch of coast, with dramatic rocks, a coastal plateau covered with magnificent fynbos, wonderful swimming spots and beautifully located overnight huts with showers, braai places and loos with views. The sunsets along the trail are awesome and you'll often see rare wildlife such as the Cape clawless otter, the Knysna Lourie, as well as more familiar birds and mammals including dolphins and whales. There are good reasons why this is a world-famous hike.

DISTANCE 42.5km

DAYS 5

DIFFICULTY MODERATELY STRENUOUS

> The fantastical setting of the Tsitsikamma National Park has lead local people to believe that mermaids live there – along with otters, dolphins and whales. While the mermaid theory may be questionable, the magical environment of Tsitsikamma is quite real and there for all to enjoy.
> SA Tourism website

DAY 1 Storms River Mouth to Ngubu hut
4.8km, 2–3 hours

Once you've registered and paid your conservation fee at the park reception you'll be shown a short, informative DVD about the trail, which, in addition to whetting your appetite for the days ahead, contains important safety tips. A map of the trail is issued – each kilometre is marked so it really is a useful reference. There's safe parking at the Storms River Rest Camp so you can head straight onto the trail, but do yourself a favour and arrive a day early to enjoy the spectacular setting – this is one of my all-time favourite camps with fabulous chalets and even more fabulous tent sites right on the water's edge. In fact, you could easily spend several days in this glorious spot enjoying the beaches, the crashing waves, the aloes, the bird life, snorkelling in the shallows, short walks in the park and the boat ride up the Storms River Gorge. There is just so much to do here. But I digress!

The trail starts at the Otter reception area close to the main rest camp gate leading down through indigenous forest to the coastline below. The first part of the trail to Ngubu hut is only 4.8km but don't underestimate it as it's largely boulder hopping – not an easy task with a full pack. After about half an hour you pass a large cave, which is worth a short stop, then, after about 3km from the start, you arrive at a perfect lunch/tea stop at the base of a spectacular waterfall fed by the Tweeriviere – the point at which day hikers have to return. If it's a warm day swimming in the pools is an absolute delight. From the waterfall the trail heads up into the indigenous forest for a short way before the final descent to a valley where, far earlier than expected, you come across the beautiful Ngubu huts. All the huts on the trail are of a similar design and are clean and airy with two sets of three bunk beds in each, a big braai with a grid and firewood, a shower (this one is in a tranquil spot in the forest) and flush loo with one-way glass. If you want another swim before dinner go to the left of the hut as you face the sea. A word of warning, you'll often see shy genet around the Ngubu huts at night so keep your eyes on your food.

DAY 2 Ngubu to Scott hut
7.9km, 4 hours

Although the second day of the trail is probably the most varied and beautiful it's a bit of a rude start to the morning, as leaving the huts you're faced with a steep climb that just seems to go on and

BLOUKRANS RIVER CROSSING

OTTER TRAIL

BLOUKRANS RIVER MOUTH

HUT

on. However, once you've reached the top (at about 120m) you're rewarded with a gentle walk through verdant forest until you emerge to see the rocky outcrop of Skilderkrans. This makes a superb photo opportunity and a great vantage point from which to scan the sea for whales and dolphins, so linger a while and enjoy the spectacular Tsitsikamma coastline. Beyond Skilderkrans the trail descends to a stream before climbing once again, then after a level stretch drops down to the Kleinbos River with its narrow gorge, lovely natural pools and waterfalls. As you cross the Kleinbos River Mouth you might notice an unusual effect – the brackish water being pushed in by the tide creates an impression of river rapids running *upriver*. Once you've cooled off in the pools follow the trail back up to the plateau and down again to the coast near Blue Bay. The crescent of sand of Blue Bay is just gorgeous and one of the few places where you can swim off the beach, but also only when the sea conditions allow (at times the waves crash in), so it's really worth it. Once you regain the path it's a steep final climb through the forest before the final descent to the Scott hut on the Geelhoutbos River Mouth – a very pretty spot where, if you're lucky, you'll enjoy a spectacular sunset over the big boulders on the shore. It's not a great bathing spot, so if you want to swim head to the pool some 400m upriver next to the waterfall, or walk a little further along the coast where there are some lovely rock pools to explore.

DAY 3 Scott to Oakhurst hut
7.7km, 5–6 hours

Day three on the trail is much more in the open than the previous day, with some steep ups and downs. You first need to cross the Geelhoutbos River next to the huts to get on the path – usually not a problem except after heavy rain when you might have a bit of a wade. The trail then follows an undulating path through the forest and along the rocky coastline until you reach the Elandsbos River, a good place for a swim and morning break. The trail continues along the shore, passing through beautiful fynbos, until you reach the Lottering River, which you can cross by using stepping stones at low tide, or wade through if you get there at high tide. From the river it's less than half an hour to the Oakhurst hut but you still have one climb left. Keep your eyes peeled for dolphins while in the vicinity of the Oakhurst hut. Bottle-nosed dolphins often come in quite close to the shore here. Before you turn in consult your tide timetable – you need to plan your start in the morning so as to reach the Bloukrans River at low tide.

DAY 4 Oakhurst to André hut
13.8km, 6 hours

Day four is the longest day of the Otter Trail but the terrain is pretty straightforward and, since the trail stays close to the coast, the views of the beautiful lichen-covered rocks and gullies are wonderful. Occasionally you climb through the forest, past tinkling streams and lily-like fungus. The only problem is that although it's one of the most scenic sections, you're inevitably distracted by the need to reach the Bloukrans River in time for low tide. It's about 10km and about four hours from the huts to the river so if at all possible rise early and leave plenty of time so that you can actually enjoy the walk. The route markings are very clear so even if you have to start out before dawn you'll have no difficulty finding your way.

Stop for a break at the top of the cliff and admire the view before you begin the steep descent to Bloukrans. There are many spots like this along the trail where you can't help but feel the privilege of being in such a magical spot – just you and a maximum of 11 other hikers.

The Bloukrans estuary is wide and quite deep on the far side so you're advised to cross the river within half an hour of low tide. Obviously the 'window' for crossing depends on how high the river is – you might have to wade in waist-deep water if you misjudge the time or, if the river is high, scramble along the cliff on the other side. Plastic survival bags come in very handy here – simply put your whole pack in the bag and, keeping the opening of the bag upright, float it across. Rest for a while before you put your shoes back on and shoulder your pack again. Although it's less than 4km to the André hut there are a couple of steep climbs to go. The path takes you past pretty shingle beaches and gullies largely following the cliff top, so you can stop often to admire the far-reaching views and catch your breath. The André hut enjoys a fantastic location in the indigenous forest next to the Klip River, but the stony beach and jagged gullies make it a poor location for swimming.

DAY 5 André hut to Nature's Valley
6.8km, 2–3 hours

You'll no doubt wake on the final day with mixed emotions – one part of you glad that you won't have to carry a pack for much longer,

There are escape routes along the trail (as indicated on the supplied Otter map) which can be used should the need arise. There are two cellphone numbers provided which are of the two rangers on standby duty and should be contacted if any emergency arises or if hikers cannot cross rivers and need to be picked up and taken around to the next hut.

If you are unable to cross the Bloukrans River for any reason, you can take the escape route labelled E6. This escape route branches to the right of the trail just before the Otter Trail descends to the Bloukrans River Mouth. The escape route climbs steeply to the top of the plateau from which you access the N2 in about two hours.

NEARING NATURE'S VALLEY

the other sad to be leaving this beautiful stretch of the world. Once you've boulder hopped across the Klip River it's a steep climb out from the huts, then the path virtually follows the clifftop all the way to Nature's Valley. You lose a bit of height dropping down to cross the Helpmekaar River, which you have to regain on the other side, but it's a pretty easy finale. After less than two hours you see the end. Enjoy the fantastic view over Nature's Valley beach and Groot River lagoon, then prepare yourself for a real knee-jarring descent. When you reach the beach and look back at the steep path down, you can pat yourself on the back before stripping off for a refreshing swim. Then continue barefoot across the sand to the Groot River camp site or to Nature's Valley.

If you're very lucky you might catch a glimpse of a Knysna Turaco hopping along a branch or a flash of red as one flies between the trees. The Knysna Turaco, *Touraco corythaix*, or as it's known in South Africa, the Knysna Lourie, lives in the mature evergreen forests of southern and eastern South Africa and is a distinctive bird with green plumage, a long tail, red feathers on the wings, a tall green crest tipped with white and a small but thick orange-red bill. The eye is brown with a white line underneath and the eye-ring is deep red. Their call is one of the most evocative sounds of the forest – a deep, croaking 'kow-kow-kow-kow'.

SUMMARY		
Start/finish	Storms River Rest Camp/Nature's Valley. Transfers back to the start can be organised through Tube and Axe Backpackers in Storms River Village, 042 281 1757, or through Hikers Haven in Nature's Valley, 044 531 6805	
Group size	Minimum two, maximum 12	
Difficulty	This is a moderately strenuous trail that demands a good level of fitness.	
Facilities	Accommodation on each night is in two log cabins with six beds (1in mattresses), so just the old sleeping bag will do. Rubbish bins, firewood, braai areas and grids are provided at each hut but there are no pots or pans. You can drink from the numerous streams along the trail; however, SANParks advise the use of purification tablets if you are not used to this water and where streams pass through communities such as Coldstream or Witels River (3.6km mark of the fourth day) and the Lottering River (7.5km mark of the fourth day). There are rainwater tanks at each overnight hut that may also be used. However, due to erratic rainfall patterns the level of these tanks may be low from time to time.	
And the kids?	Hikers must be at least 12 years old.	
When to go	Each season has its advantages. Most rain falls during April/May and October/November, so if you're a fair-weather hiker you might avoid these times.	
Contact	SANParks, 012 426 5111, bridgetb@sanparks.org, www.sanparks.org/parks/tsitsikamma/tourism/otter.php	
Other contacts	Otter Run and Southern Storm, www.magneticsouth.net/events/southern-storm/	

Kit list	See general kit list, page 202
	Specific
	☖ Survival bag
	☖ Vacuum-packed meat (for nights two and three)
	☖ Biodegradable soap, candles
Day hikes in the Tsitsikamma National Park	**Blue Duiker Trail, 4km, 3 hours** The Blue Duiker Trail winds inland through the forest. If you hike early morning or late evening you stand a chance of seeing the rare blue duiker that live there. **Lourie Trail, 1km, 0.5 hours** Named after the endemic and colourful Knysna Lourie, this short trail through the forest is a good choice for birders. **Waterfall Trail, 6km, 3–4 hours (return)** The Waterfall Trail starts at the Oceanettes at the rest camp. After following the rugged coastline and doing some boulder hopping, your reward is a swim in a clear pool under the 50m-high falls. Hikers have the option on the return trip from the waterfall of taking the Otter Trail path, just after the cave. This path is steep in places and leads through indigenous forests up to the Otter reception area close to the main rest camp gate. **Mouth and Lookout trails, 4km, 2–3 hours** The Mouth Trail starts at the park restaurant and winds for 1km along a boardwalk through the forest to the mouth of the Storms River. Continue across the suspension bridge to a wonderful pebble beach, and if you have the energy follow the trail up the steep cliff on the other side to a stunning lookout point before returning the same way. **Storms River Walks** **Ratel Nature Walk, 4.2km, 1.5 hours** This easy trail consists of three interlinked routes around the famous Tsitsikamma Big Tree; the Green Route, a 1.2km circular walk to the Big Tree; the Yellow Route, a 2.6km loop from the Big Tree past another enormous Outeniqua yellowwood; and the Red Route, a 1.6km loop branching off from the Yellow Route. **Plaatbos Nature Walk, 8km, 2.5 hours** This circular route through the indigenous forests consists of the Blue Route (830m), which starts and ends at the Storms River Bridge, and a network of three routes from the Storms River Forestry Office: the Green (5.09km), Red (7.78km) and Yellow (8.1km) routes.
Otter Run and Southern Storm Duathlon	The inaugural Otter Run and Southern Storm Duathlon will take place in September 2009. Entering the Otter Run gives trail runners the one-off chance to run the full length of South Africa's premier hiking trail (almost exactly marathon distance) in a single day. Although the Otter Run can be entered as a separate one-day event, it's also the second day of the Southern Storm, a fully serviced duathlon of trail running and mountain biking along the Garden Route from the Tsitsikamma section to the Wilderness section of the Garden Route National Park.

Tsitskamma Trail

Running parallel to the Otter Trail, the six-day Tsitsikamma Trail, which starts in Nature's Valley and ends in Storms River, is one of the finest hikes in the country. Somehow it has not achieved the worldwide renown of the Otter, perhaps because it is a more challenging hike, but that is one of its attractions – you're unlikely to struggle to get a reservation and at times you'll be the only people on the trail. But like the Otter Trail, the Tsitsikamma Trail is well marked and has superbly located mountain huts with numerous rock pools in which to swim and chill. Offered as a self-sufficient or portaged hike, it's a strenuous undertaking with steep climbs and the ever-present risk of bad weather. But your efforts are rewarded by outstanding views, pristine fynbos and the opportunity to enjoy the indigenous forests and the wonderful dells of ferns and mosses of the Tsitsikamma – the place of running water.

- **DISTANCE** 61km
- **DAYS** 6 DAYS (WITH 2- TO 5-DAY OPTIONS AVAILABLE
- **MTB** NO OFFICIAL TRAILS (MOUNTAIN BIKING IS ONLY ALLOWED ON THE ACCESS ROADS/ESCAPE ROUTES)

INDIGENOUS FORESTS FILLED WITH LUSH FERNS

66 *Those who have experienced the forest in all its moods return home enriched. They do so in the knowledge that should man destroy the last of the forests, some of his inner peace, freedom and joy will be lost forever.* 99

Dalene Matthee

TRAIL 10

DAY 1 De Vasselot to Kalander hut

3.6km, 1.5 hours

The trail starts with a short stroll along the edge of the Groot River lagoon from the De Vasselot Rest Camp in Nature's Valley to the Kalander hut, allowing you to travel that day (but my advice would be to arrive soon after lunch so you can reach camp and have time to enjoy the spectacularly beautiful beach). You initially follow a boardwalk, then a Jeep track through the tall, dry indigenous forest on the eastern bank of the Groot River lagoon. The Kalander hut, nestled in the trees at the base of Douwurmkop, is typical of the well-equipped huts on the Tsitsikamma Trail, and has four rooms with six beds each, a braai area (complete with braai grids, tongs, kettle, pan and iron pots) and covered *lapa* so that even when it rains (which it does, not infrequently) a big group can stay warm and dry. There are flush loos and bucket showers into which you can put hot water to mix with that from the piped cold water system.

DAY 2 Kalander to Bloukrans hut

13.5km, 6–7 hours

From the hut you head straight up a steep, slippery path. Detour on an obvious path leading off to the left for an awesome view from the top of the Monkey's Back (or the Pig's Head as it's sometimes shown on maps). To the east are the steep cliffs that you descend at the end of the Otter Trail, while if you look the other way you can see all the way along back over Nature's Valley. The trail keeps climbing up through the forest before easing off and giving you an inkling of

The Tsitsikamma Hiking Trail was South Africa's first officially accredited hiking trail. For more information visit www.trailinfo.co.za

TSITSIKAMMA HIKING TRAIL

LEAVE THE HUT AS YOU WOULD LIKE TO FIND IT

- Stowaway your food at night
- Plan tomorrows hike
- Leave the hut as you would like to find it

HUT ETHICS

CLOSE ALL WINDOWS AND DOORS

DON'T BE A HERO

The trail is tough, so why not make it easier for yourself and take advantage of the portage service that transports your bags from hut to hut? Not only does this allow you the freedom of hiking with only a daypack (which, believe me, you will appreciate from the first steep hill), but if you organise your food and booze into daily containers these can be refrigerated or even frozen until the night that you wish them to be delivered to your overnight spot. Cold beers, braai meat and salad – even on the last night – are quite a treat on such a hard-core trail.

BOARDWALK START NATURES VALLEY

WELCOMING ROCK POOL DAY 2

BLOUKRANS HUT

BLOUKRANS SHOWER

you may be lucky to spot a Knysna Lourie, but you'll almost certainly see white-eyes and other little canopy dwellers flitting from branch to branch. The trail climbs relentlessly through stands of yellowwoods and dense forests of ferns until you hear the welcome sound of falling water. A steep downhill and you come across dark tannin-stained pools where you can cool off and refill your water bottles.

The last section of the trail takes you through commercial plantations, much of which have been cleared so, though it's a bit scruffy, you do at least get great views. Finally you come to a dramatic gorge and the stunningly located Bloukrans hut, right on the edge of the cliffs. Just below the hut is the Tolbos River with three inviting pools, so once you've admired the view and dumped (or collected) your bags and settled in, head down for a swim before returning to the terrace of the hut for sundowners.

For such a remote mountain hut the Bloukrans hut is extremely comfortable. It consists of two bedrooms, one with 18 beds, the other with 12, an outdoor braai, a *lapa* area with an indoor fireplace, braai wood, three tables and

what lies ahead. The high peaks of the Tsitsikamma Mountains tower above you as you hike through the aromatic fynbos, so catch your breath and enjoy the view. The next few kilometres lead through afromontane forest and incredible fynbos, great clumps of pink and purple erica, bright pincushions and numerous other protea. The bird life too is incredible – keep your eyes open and

benches, frying pan, potjie pot and kettles, as well as two flushing loos and two cold water showers, one of which has the 'hoisted bucket' hot water shower option. As the sun sets you can sit out enjoying the last light on the surrounding mountains, while on a clear night the stars are incredible. Before you turn in pack your food away – a large-spotted genet pair and bushpig male are regular overnight visitors to the hut.

DAY 3 Bloukrans to Keurbos hut
13.4km, 6–7 hours

It's hard to imagine more spectacular views than those that you enjoy from the Bloukrans hut, so you're inspired to be up early to watch the sun rising over the hills to the east, bathing the hut in golden light. The trail to Keurbos drops straight down to the river – the route you would have followed if you went for a swim the night before. Cross the river and start slogging north up the hill. The path follows the ridge on the western side of the river for a while, gaining the top of the hill which is covered in really pretty tall grasses. A sign warns 'slippery and steep terrain ahead' and indeed the descent can be treacherous

when it's wet. Down you go to the Buffelsbos indigenous forest with its stunning forest tree ferns, real yellowwood, ironwood (with its telltale bleeding gum) and lepelhout trees (chewing on the lepelhout or spoonwood leaves is said to alleviate thirst). Fortunately some of the trees are labelled so you don't need to carry a tree identification guide to quickly work out what's what. A few metres into the forest there's a great spot to stop beside a stream and take a dip. The trees are incredible and some, particularly a beautiful witels and an Outeniqua yellowwood, are truly massive. A fabulous reprieve from the sweltering heat of summer, Buffelsbos is apparently where the last buffalo of the

ROCK POOL BELOW THE BLOUKRANS HUT

Look out for the tall lichen-covered cylindrical trunks of black stinkwood trees and the black, tar-like substance, which smells a little like elephant dung, which often appears on the bark of older ironwoods. Stop and stroke a forest elder – how soft and velvety the bark feels.

WATERWITELSGAT

KEURBOS HUT

ABOVE THE BUFFELSBOS FOREST

WARNING
STEEP RIVER GORGE IN PROXIMITY.
PLEASE DO NOT APPROACH THE STEEP EDGES OF THE GORGE.
PLEASE KEEP AWAY FROM SHEER CLIFF EDGES.

Tsitsikamma was shot and killed in the late 19th century.

After leaving the forest you walk along a grassy stretch for a short while before dropping down to cross the Bloukrans River at Waterwitelsgat, a massive swimming hole. Since one side of the pool offers shade it's a great place to chill, but if per chance there are other hikers there and you want a more private spot, follow the river up for two minutes and you'll find another stunning pool. From Waterwitelsgat it's a short, stiff hike up the path until it plateaus out and meanders along on the left-hand side of the valley. You'll notice remnants of old pine trees here, a bit of an eyesore but at least they offer the odd bit of shade on a hot day, and there are some small streams from which to fill your bottles. If the river is quite full you can cross it with the aid of the chains at Waterwitelsgat – but use your

common sense: if it's much above knee level rather wait for the level to drop. Detailed river safety precautions are sent to hikers booking the Tsitsikamma Trail and are on display at Bloukrans, Keurbos and Heuningbos huts.

For the rest of the day the trail traverses flatter terrain through flower-rich fynbos and relic forest until you reach Benebos, another enchanting indigenous forest of Cape beech, Outeniqua yellowwood, rooiels and spectacular tree ferns by the pretty little stream. Grab the rope as you enter – the ground can be unbelievably damp and slippery. Soon after leaving the forest you drop onto a Jeep track which offers great views of the almost 1km-high peak of Grenadier's Cap in the distance. Follow the Jeep track for a short while until the footpath diverges to cross over a saddle, rejoining the Jeep track again for the final approach to the Keurbos

KEURBOS HUT

If you're planning on taking a camera remember that you'll be in forest much of the way – and it's often overcast – so you may need to up your ISO to 200 or 400. The contrast of light and shade is often too much if it's a sunny day, so experiment with shooting in overcast weather and in early morning or late afternoon light.

hut. Just before the hut, in the Keurbos indigenous forest, is Twin Tub – small pools that resemble natural Jacuzzis in the wet season – where you can cool off. However, if you have the energy and really want to swim, dump your pack at the hut and continue for another 1.3km to the pools in the Lottering River. This is a beautiful spot with some great swimming holes 100m or so upstream from the point at which the trail crosses the river. Sit and enjoy the picturesque scene. Lovely white stones and orange watsonia frame the tannin-stained water, while the high peaks tower loftily above. The bad news of course is that you've now got to hike back up to the hut, somewhat undermining the refreshing dip. But what the hell, you can always shower at the top.

The Keurbos hut sits on the fringe of a relic patch of indigenous forest, surrounded by red and white alder, so the bird life is usually impressive (listen out for the call of the Narina Trogon as you unpack). Some say the name of the hut comes from the proximity of the Keurbooms trees – short-lived pioneer tree species

TREE FERNS DANCING

PASS THE SOAP

Cape holly, *Ilex mitis*, is a protected species in Southern Africa and has abundant beautiful red berries when in fruit. It is found growing on riverbanks in the Tsitsikamma and is a reliable indicator of a water source close by. Rinsing the leaves of the Cape holly in water produces a foam-like substance that is a substitute for soap.

WATERWITELSGAT CROSSING

STREAM BELOW KEURBOS HUT

SWIM BEFORE RUSHES PASS

FERNS NEAR KEURBOS HUT

VIEW BACK TOWARDS KEURBOS FROM RUSHES PASS

that form a natural buffer against fire, hence the name 'keur' or fire stopping. Others believe 'keur' in this context means 'choice' or 'pick' – a reference to the beautiful pink and purple flowers that this member of the pea family sports.

DAY 4 Keurbos to Heuningbos hut
13.4km, 6–7 hours

If you went for a swim last night then you're retracing your steps down to the river. But if it's wet underfoot be doubly careful on the wooden ladders that act as stepping stones to prevent you from sinking into the marsh. The path follows the right-hand bank of the river, crossing a stream, then climbing up Rushes Pass with lovely views across to Spitskop and the surrounding peaks on the left. After the rather relentless meander uphill you're rewarded, if the weather plays ball, by stunning views and a cooling breeze at the top. On a clear day you can see for miles – in the distance is Plettenberg Bay, the rugged Robberg Peninsula and the inviting blue ocean. From the saddle the path drops down into the valley through a stretch of indigenous forest and then swings right down the Elandspad River past numerous enticing swimming holes – just take your pick if

you fancy a dip. Around the 7km mark you cross the river via a wooden bridge then head up through a scraggy area of burnt pines. After a short section on the Jeep track the trail heads left and back into the bush. You're now walking through the Heuningbos indigenous forest, first ambling down to a stream and then slogging up the sustained hill on the other side. In summer you're certainly glad of the shade. You start descending again soon after emerging from the forest and get your first glimpse of the Heuningbos hut. It's just over 1km down to the hut, but as on so many of these trails there's a bit of a sting in the tail – when you reach the river you're confronted with a small ridge to cross. Rather than being tempted to cool off here, push on. It's only another 1km to go and the pools in the Kleinbos River below the hut are stunning, with lots of flat rocks to lie out on and again, in summer, they're often surrounded by striking watsonia.

DAY 5 Heuningbos to Sleepkloof hut
13.9km, 7 hours

A pool in a tranquil dell of ferns only 400m from the Heuningbos hut is a great spot for a refreshing morning swim. The trail winds through

LUITERING RIVIER
HEUNING BOS HUT
12,1 km

Tweedebos, then climbs gradually up to the Splendid Pass (named after *Mimetes splendidus*, a striking protea found on its slopes) through pristine fynbos (that has regenerated since major fires in 2005) and great swathes of colourful watsonia. All around are beautiful peaks so stop and rest a while – soon you will be out of this remote mountain wonderland so enjoy it while you can. From the top of the path you can see your next challenge – the trail heads down to a forested stream and then up again on the other side. The descent doesn't take long and soon you're down in the shade of the indigenous forest of Mostertsbos, a welcome relief from the blazing sun of the open mountain slopes. This type of isolated forest pocket is generally sparser in species composition than the larger forests of the plateau that you pass through on the second and final days of the trail, and comprises largely red alder, white alder, forest elder stinkwood and both the Outeniqua and real yellowwoods, along with beautiful ferns.

The trail continues through the forest until you reach the main watercourse, the Witteklip River, which marks the day's halfway point. The ferns here are really spectacular – great

STREAM BELOW HEUNINGBOS

towering plants that block out the light. Gleichenia, coarse ferns, maidenhair ferns and tree ferns have inhabited these relic forests since time immemorial – sacred old souls that lord over the toadstools and lichens of this damp, dark world.

Once you've cooled off, head out on the next long climb up through the dense fynbos to Nademaalsnek, the saddle between Storms River Peak and Heidekop. From the top of the pass you can see right over to the spectacular Storms River gorge and down to the Sleepkloof hut, on the slopes of a densely forested gorge. About 2.2km before the hut there are signs to a swimming hole in the indigenous forest, but unless you are really struggling in the heat it's probably worth pushing on as there are pools and a waterfall at the hut itself.

DAY 6 Sleepkloof hut to Paul Sauer Bridge
3.2km, 1 hour,
OR
Sleepkloof hut to Storms River Village
5.5km, 2 hours

You have a choice of end points, but either way the last day is short. Both routes follow the rocky track through dense forest pioneer vegetation for the first kilometre before splitting, with the route to the bridge a very easy 2km descent through forest and fynbos. The slightly longer walk to the village leads through the forest, eventually emerging on the Jeep track at the top of the old Storms River Pass. Of course, if you're really organised you will have arranged a permit and a re-supply of food and clothing and be ready to complete the circle by hiking the Otter Trail!

Start/finish	De Vasselot Rest Camp, Nature's Valley, or Paul Sauer Bridge or Storms River Village. Transfers back to the start can be organised through Tube and Axe Backpackers in Storms River Village, 042 281 1757, or through Hikers Haven in Nature's Valley, 044 531 6805.
Group size	Minimum two, maximum 24 (though only 22 people are allowed on the portaged trail)
Difficulty	This is a strenuous mountain trail that demands a good level of fitness. It should only be attempted by experienced hikers carrying good-quality warm and waterproof clothing (including a backpack cover). The map warns 'Consider turning back if there is a problem. Don't be heroic, the elements are merciless'!
Facilities	The overnight huts are all in scenic locations and are very comfortable and well equipped with pots, braai grids and firewood, etc. Bags can be driven around between huts on request. Food is kept in fridges and freezers until the day it is delivered to the appropriate overnight hut.
And the kids?	There is no minimum age, but groups wishing to include young children should contact the trail organisers beforehand for advice.
When to go	Most rain falls during April/May and October/November, so unless you fancy a slippery slide these months might well be avoided. The mountains are often misty during the winter months so if you go then, be prepared.
Contact	MTO Ecotourism, Lottering Forestry Station, 042 281 1712, gpi@mto.co.za, www.mtoecotourism.co.za
Other contacts	Buffalo Hills African Adventure Reserve, 044 535 9739, buffalohills@mweb.co.za, www.buffalohills.co.za Dolphin Trail, 042 280 3588, info@dolphintrail.co.za, www.dolphintrail.co.za Face Adrenalin, 042 281 1458, info@faceadrenalin.com, www.faceadrenalin.com Harkerville and Outeniqua Hiking Trails, 044 302 5606, cathyvrooyen@sanparks.org, www.sanparks.org Knysna Cycle Works (bike hire), 044 382 5153, freejacq@mweb.co.za, www.knysnacycles.co.za Mountain Biking Africa, 044 382 6130, arcent@mweb.co.za, www.mountainbikingafrica.co.za Tsitsikamma Canopy Tour, 042 281 1836, adventure@gardenroute.co.za, www.tsitsikammacanopytour.co.za Tsitsikamma Falls Adventure Park, 042 280 3770, tsitsikamma@lantic.net, www.tsitsikammaadventure.co.za
Kit list	See general kit list, page 202 **Specific** First-aid supplies and emergency rations in case an unforeseen emergency arises or a party becomes stranded between swollen rivers during heavy rainfall on the Bloukrans to Keurbos and Keurbos to Heuningbos sections of the trail.

On your bike	There are no marked trails but you can cycle along the escape routes/service roads that access the overnight huts. This can be coupled with portage, so mountain bikers can either overnight at a particular hut or hike sections of the trail and have their bikes transported from start to finish.
Other hikes around Knysna/ Tsitsikamma	**Overnight hikes** **Dolphin Hiking Trail** *Day 1: Storms River to Misty Mountain Reserve, 7.5km, 4 hours* *Day 2: Misty Mountain Reserve to the Fernery, 9.5km, 4 hours* Billed the 'Alternative Otter Trail', the fully catered Dolphin Trail is a guided three-night, two-day luxury hiking trail along one of South Africa's most dramatic sections of coastline. The Dolphin Trail, a partnership between the Tsitsikamma National Park and Forest Ferns and Misty Mountain Reserve, starts at Storms River Mouth in the Tsitsikamma National Park and finishes a couple of days later at the privately owned Fernery chalets and nursery, to the east. Only 17km, the trail is not unduly taxing; rather it's an opportunity to enjoy the magnificent indigenous forest, ferns, forest birds, rugged coastline and superb hospitality, and, of course, to enjoy sightings of dolphins playing in the waves. **Outeniqua Hiking Trail, 7 days, 108km, with shorter options** *Day 1: Beervlei to Windmeulnek, 16km, 5.5 hours* *Day 2: Windmeulnek to Platbos, 17km, 5.5 hours* *Day 3: Platbos to Millwood, 15.5km, 7 hours* *Day 4: Millwood to Rondebossie, 17km, 5 hours* *Day 5: Rondebossie to Diepwalle, 13km, 5 hours* *Day 6: Diepwalle to Fisantehoek, 16km, 5 hours* *Day 7: Fisantehoek to Harkerville, 12km, 4.5 hours* It seems that few hikers undertake the full seven days of the Outeniqua Trail, most preferring to break the route into weekend and three- or four-day sections. It's a strenuous hike – you walk over 15km most days carrying your pack – mostly through indigenous forest but with patches of magnificent fynbos and pine plantations. The Knysna forests comprise the largest natural forest in South Africa so it's a chance to wander in the shade of ancient yellowwoods, stinkwoods and ironwoods, to enjoy the tree ferns, the forest birds, vervet monkeys and small game. The overnight huts are well located and equipped with bunk beds, mattresses, firewood and braai grills. The Harkerville and Diepwalle huts have electricity and there's also a community tearoom at Diepwalle where you can eat during the day and, if you order in advance, even buy braai food for your evening meal.

Other hikes around Knysna/ Tsitsikamma *ctd.*	**Harkerville Hiking Trail, 27km, 2 days** Day 1 • Harkerville hut to Sinclair hut, 15km, 7 hours Day 2 • Sinclair hut to Harkerville hut 12km, 6–7 hours The coastal section of this trail is one of the most splendid hikes I have ever done, but it involves quite a bit of rock scrambling, so if it's wet and stormy, or you're not comfortable scrambling with a pack, then give it a miss. The trail starts at the Harkerville hut (where you can overnight should you wish), then meanders through the indigenous forest to the coast. This is where the trail gets interesting. After a steep descent you follow the dramatic coastline for a couple of kilometres, scrambling over the spectacular rocky headlands down onto pebble beaches or gullies filled with inviting pools. At times there is quite a drop below you, but the difficult sections are aided with chains or wooden ladders. The spacious Sinclair hut, which is equipped with bunks, mattresses, flush loos and fireplace, is on the edge of the forest so you end the day with a stiff climb up to the plateau. On the second day you hike through the fynbos on the plateau for a couple of hours before descending sharply again to the coast at the mouth of the Wit River, where you can swim in the brackish water. Again there are some quite tricky sections – and some more ladders and chains – but the views are just phenomenal and there are plenty of natural pools in which to cool off. A steep uphill climb to regain the plateau is followed by an easy final section through the forest. Take note that there is no water on the trail so fill up before leaving the hut.
Day walks	**Kranshoek Coastal Walk, 9.4km, 3.5 hours** This moderately difficult, circular trail starts at the Kranshoek picnic site and drops steeply down the Kranshoek River gorge to a rocky beach. The scenery is spectacular: jagged teeth of orange and grey rocks stand out of the blue water contrasting with the lush green of the plateau. The path follows the rugged coastline for about 3.5km to the mouth of the Crooks River then it's a steep climb up to the coastal plateau, followed by an easy walk along a gravel road back to the picnic site.
MTB trails	**Petrus-se-Brand cycle route, 24km, 3–5 hours** The route, rated moderate, begins at the Diepwalle Forest Station office (where you obtain your permit) and finishes at Garden of Eden on the N2, incorporating sections of gravel road, the contoured bed of the old narrow-gauge forest railway and some fast singletrack – in fact the best piece of singletrack in Knysna. **Harkerville cycle route** There are four circular routes in Harkerville Forest, probably the most popular and diverse cycling area on the Garden Route. All four start and finish at the Garden of Eden, on the N2, where you must get a permit. Alternatively, you can start from the forestry office, Kranshoek Road gate, or the Kranshoek picnic site.

MTB trails *ctd.*

The Yellow Route, 14km, 1.5–2 hours

This easy route is all along the well-maintained gravel service roads of the forest reserve.

The Blue Route, 12km, 1.5–2 hours

Beginners and intermediates will enjoy the more challenging Blue Route, which includes an awesome piece of singletrack along Beukespad, a forest slip-path. The trail is roughly 50% uphill, 50% downhill along the management trails in the indigenous forest and pine plantation.

The Green Route, 15km, 2 hours

The circular route follows the Grooteilandpad for several kilometres before turning eastwards into Waterpad, where there's a shady swimming hole should you need to cool off. An alternative southward loop is rewarded by a breathtaking view of the rugged Harkerville coast. The route then heads northwards along Kleineilandpad, before turning west to Perdekoppad, a delightful section of off-road track, which passes through some tall coastal forest. Once you've mastered the two wicked sections of singletrack you might be tempted to tackle the Red Route next time.

The Red Route, 24km, 3–5 hours

Often rated as the most scenically diverse mountain bike route in the country, this difficult route is much more challenging than the other Harkerville rides, with long stretches of singletrack which follow old slip paths through the forest and a scenic section of track through the coastal fynbos near the edge of the plateau.

Homtini, 19km, 3 hours

The best forest ride in the area, this moderately difficult circular route, which starts at the Krisjan-se-Nek picnic site near the Goudveld Forest Station, offers riders good views and a mix of gravel road, singletrack and a wicked 4km climb through the Homtini Forest.

Buffalo Hills, various options, c3 hours

Guided half-day mountain bike tours at Buffalo Hills African Adventure Reserve include an easy, leisurely trail for novice riders or a three-hour blast for the dirt hounds. On both you'll experience the stunning bird life and abundant game – which includes giraffe, zebra, red hartebeest and wildebeest – of the picturesque private reserve.

The Knysna Experience, 100km, 2 days

Starting in Knysna, Mountain Biking Africa's two-day guided tour follows the route of the famous Pick 'n Pay Forest Marathon through pristine indigenous forest, combining sections of gravel road, Jeep track, serious climbs and awesome descents. Day one, roughly 70km, includes about 25km of singletrack/dual track and ends, after a quick dip in a forest pool, at Drifters Forest Inn. On day two you are transferred to the Harkerville Forest to ride the famous Harkeville Red Route, rated as one of the best MTB trails in South Africa. It's an exhilarating 30km singletrack loop incorporating forest riding, clifftop sea views, a few challenging climbs and awesome singletrack descents. Also on offer is a three-day, two-night tour of around 200km.

MTB trails *ctd.*	**Storms River MTB route, 22km, 2–3 hours (return)** This circular route from Storms River Village follows the old national road through the Tsitsikamma National Park and along the Storms River Pass. After a steep 5km descent to the Storms River you cross the low-water bridge (a good spot for a swim) before climbing steeply up the other side of the pass. The gradient eases off after a couple of kilometres and once you reach the top of the plateau it's a fairly easy ride through the pine plantations before the trail markers lead you back to the pass and another steep descent and climb back to the village.
Southern Storm	September 2009 will see an MTB/trail-running duathlon from the Storms River Rest Camp to Wilderness. Day one of the five-day event is a marathon trail run along the Otter Trail, with the remaining days consisting of both trail running and MTB sections. The Otter Run can also be entered as a separate, one-day trail run. Running the whole trail in one day, how cool is that?
Bungee	At 216m, Face Adrenalin's bungee jump off the Bloukrans Bridge holds the *Guinness Book of Records'* honour as the highest in the world. If you're in the area, it simply has to be done.
Treetop Canopy Tours	The Tsitsikamma Treetop Canopy Tour was the first of its kind – a magical journey on a series of slides between raised platforms in indigenous forest near Storms River Village listening to, and if you're lucky sighting, birds and other forest dwellers. At the nearby Tsitsikamma Falls Adventure Park you're in more open countryside whizzing from platform to platform over spectacular gorges.
Other activities	George, Knysna and Plettenberg Bay Tourism can supply information on the numerous other hiking/MTB/4x4/paddling adventures on the Garden Route. Other good contacts include SANParks and CapeNature who manage several of the trails.

GREEN FLAG ACCREDITATION

(For details see www.trailinfo.co.za)

The principle behind *Green Flag accreditation* is not to distinguish subjectively between "good" and "bad" trails but to give recognition to trail owners who adhere to the concept of responsible management: delivering a product that is "*value for money*" to the hiker and which is responsible towards the environment.

Correct information

Responsibility towards the hiker is ensured by relaying the correct information concerning the type   of accommodation and environment (so that the prospective hiker can make an *informed choice*) and ensuring a *safe* hiking experience.

Accommodation is classified as being either "excellent", "standard" or "rustic" according to the type of facilities (such as pit toilets *vs* flush) and not the quality thereof such as in hotels (e.g. TV channel list).

The type of environment is classified as either being "pristine", "natural", or rural". It is portrayed with a symbol of 1, 2 or 3 trees. ("Pristine" would typically be wilderness areas, "natural" areas might be forestry/plantation areas, "rural" is a farming environment. ("Semi-urban" landscapes, representing Urban Green Belts are also identified).

The difficulty ratings are calculated in terms of the energy (kCal) required to hike the trail - each day is given separately. These figures are "translated" onto a scale of 1 to 10+; representing "easy", "moderate", "difficult" and "extremely difficult" categories. The rating is done in terms of reasonably fit hikers who hike at least several times per year.

Safety

Safety (and facilities) on the trail is measured in terms of items such as car parking, accommodation, *en route* walking (mugging, bridges and ladders, medical and evacuation procedures, cell phone access, etc.).

Environment responsibility

This is done by evaluating the ecological conditions on the footpath as well as the overnight hut environment. Issues such as erosion, pollution, vandalism are investigated. A trail where negligence is shown in this regard will be removed from the system.

Credibility
The Green Flag Accreditation System (GFT) is run under the auspices of HOSA (Hiking Organization of Southern Africa) and is underwritten by SAHTOA (SA Hiking Trail Owners' Assn). GFT is a member of SATSA and is being implemented by all major trail owners in South Africa (such as SANParks, Cape Nature, KLF (Komatiland Forest), MTO, KZN Wildlife, regional and provincial authorities and major municipalities such as Johannesburg and Pretoria. This is the only national (and international) accreditation system for hiking trails.

M L Hugo MA, ML, D.Phil Ecological and Tourism Planner cell:+27(0) 82 578 3023 email: leonhugo@vodamail.co.za

Dolphin HIKING TRAIL

Classification

A two day fully catered luxury trail

Environment: - pristine

Accommodation: - excellent

Difficulty Rating: - moderate

GREEN FLAG TRAILS
ACCREDITED HIKING TRAIL
www.trailinfo.co.za

Accreditation underwritten by:
South African Hiking Trail Owners Association (SAHTOA),
Hiking Organization of Southern Africa (HOSA),
Southern Africa Tourism Services Association (SATSA).

Accommodation Facilities

The Fernery Chalets (Sleeps 12)
Tsitsikamma N.P. (Sleeps 12)

types:
(A) excellent
(B) standard
(C) rustic

Misty Mountain (Sleeps 12)

Accommodation: (A) Good quality hut/lux.tent/cottage/house-with several sleeping rooms OR
(B) Basic hut or tent(s) provided OR
(C) Shelter against elements for sleeping/tent site

Toilet: (A) Flush toilet inside hut (1-6 people) OR
(B) Separate toilet building, flush facilities outside hut
(C) Pit toilet (max 50 m min 20 m from hut) or alternative hygienic system

Drinking water: (A) Clean drinking water INSIDE hut, OR
(B) Clean drinking water on site, or nearby stream/pool/tank (20 m max), easily accessible OR
(C) Stream/fountain or no water

Beds: (A) Single / double beds only OR
(B) Bunk beds OR
(C) No beds provided

Mattresses: (A) Thick (10 cm) high density foam or spring. OR
(B) Thin OR
(C) None

Washing: (A) Shower &/or bath (hot & cold with geyser or "donkey" pre-lit by attendant) OR
(B) Shower and/or bath (hot and cold with "donkey") OR
(C) Shower (cold) or nearby stream/dam

Barbeque area: (A) Under cover barbeque, with windshield, lapa (1:10 people) OR
(B) Barbeque area, covered only with grate. OR
(C) Barbeque (open) area with grate only or no fires allowed or possible

Fire wood provided: (A) Ample chopped wood (also for campfire) OR
(B) One only bundle for braai OR
(C) Dry tree/logs with saw/axe provided or no fires allowed/possible (Cape H. no fires allowed)

Kitchenware: (A) Fridge/cooler and cutlery/crockery: provided OR
(B) Fridge/cooler or cutlery/crockery: provided OR
(C) Fridge/cooler and cutlery/crockery: NOT provided

Kitchen: (A) Separate "kitchen"/common room with basin/tap inside hut OR
(B) Dish washing / cooking place near or adjacent to hut (with table/surface) OR
(C) No separate facilities provided. Water available nearby stream/dam/fountain

Lighting: (A) Electric/gas/solar OR
(B) Candles/paraffin lamps or similar OR
(C) None of these provided

Sheets: (A) and pillow AND mirror(s) provided OR
(B) One sheet or mirror(s) provided OR
(C) None of these

Heating: (A) Air conditioning OR
(B) Interior heating/cool /wood stove OR (2 houses)
(C) None of these

Cooking facilities: (A) Hot plate/Burner and kettle, pots & pans (restaurant facilities) OR
(B) Stove/Hot plate/Burner or kettle, pots & pans OR
(C) None of these

Difficulty Grading

1	1.5	2	2.5	3	3.5	4	4.5	5	5.5	6	6.5	7	7.5	8	8.5	9	9.5	10	10.5	
EASY				MODERATE							DIFFICULT							EXTREME		
0	375	750		1125		1500		1875		2250		2625		3000		3375		3750		

→ Day 2
→ Day 1

ENERGY USE (kcal)

Basic Trail Description

The Dolphin trail runs for 17 km along the spectacular Tsitsikamma coastline – a narrow coastal strip between the Indian Ocean and the interior plateau bordering the Tsitsikamma Mountains. The trail is fully catered and all baggage is transported. The accommodation is fully luxurious and the scenery is pristine; crossing coastal fynbos, indigenous rainforest, rugged coastal rocks along the splashing waves and ending at the Sandrift River. The chances of spotting whales, dolphins and perhaps otter, are good. En route many birds including the gorgeous Knysna Loerie (turaco) can be heard and spotted while walking at leisure through the forest. Tree ferns and majestic Yellowwood trees give character to this experience. Along the coast the endangered Oyster catcher is to be seen. Swimming and snorkelling in the rock pools is possible at the discretion of the guides.

Environmental Character: Definitions

A PRISTINE environment depicts an area where nature still exists in its more-or-less pure form: clean drinking water in streams, indigenous vegetation and animal life with no trace of human constructions, activities or sounds nearby.

In a NATURAL environment one could expect to see and hear human activities to a limited extent; such as e.g. associated with farming and forestry. Exotic plants (e.g. pine plantations) might be prevalent; as well as cattle, fences and constructions such as earth dams.

To hike through a RURAL environment would imply close contact with rural development and its associated noise, crossing of public roads, hiking on forestry/farm roads, visual contact with agricultural fields, cement dams, domesticated animals, etc.

Generalized Classification

Day 1	Day 2	Day 3 transported by vehicle to start
Pristine	Pristine	Natural

© Leon Hugo

Trail Facilities and Safety

Facilities:

Booking Facilities & Info: Internet, telephone, fax

Reception office: Office on site

Road signs: Clear road signs to start of hike: public & private roads

Access road: Tarred

Parking: Open

Trail Format: Open ended with transport back to vehicles

Map: Colour with contour lines and additional information.
Available on website. All groups are guided

Brochure: Guided Trail

Markers: Guided

Environmental education: Trained guide

Safety:

Accommodation: Safe

Warning signs: Well managed

Crossings: Effective

Telephone: At start of trail. Field guide radio contact

Medical Aid: First aid kit, guide with first aid training

Hikers' safety en route: Safe

Water: Available

Parking: In Tsitsikamma National Park

Contact /Booking Information

The Fernery
Dolphin Trail Reservations

Tel: +27 (0)42 280 3588
Fax: +27 (0)41 394 5114
Website: www.dolphintrail.co.za
e-mail: info@dolphintrail.co.za

Swellendam Hiking Trail

Classification

A self-guided, self-catering circular
5 to 6 day hiking trail with shorter loops
Environment: *pristine*
Accommodation: *various types*
Difficulty Rating: *moderate to difficult*
Facilities and safety: *acceptable*

CapeNature

www.trailinfo.co.za

Accreditation underwritten by:
South African Hiking Trail Owners Association (SAHTOA),
Hiking Organization of Southern Africa (HOSA),
Southern Africa Tourism Services Association (SATSA).

Basic Trail Description

The Swellendam Hiking Trail, a magnificent five- or six day trail, is situated in the Langeberg (Long Mountain) immediately North of Swellendam, in the Marloth Nature Reserve. Managed by the Cape Nature Conservation, the trail covers mainly fynbos area, although there are some pine plantations near the beginning and end of the hike. Some sections are very difficult. Shorter options and day walks are available.

The footpath is well established and is marked with distance indications from the starting point at 500 m intervals. Although wild game is seldom seen, birds are plentiful, and the shear beauty of the fynbos vegetation and clear natural water steams make up for this. Drinking water and swimming in streams are available. Carry-in carry-out principle is applied at three of the six overnight cabins.

Beautiful views reward the hiker in the mountain, while the silence and open sky at night is something to experience. The hiking accommodation caters for parties between 16 and 22 persons.

Trail Facilities & Safety

Facilities:

Booking facilities and information: Internet, postal, telephone & fax
Reception office: On site
Road signs: Clear road signs to start
Access road: Last section graded gravel
Parking: Some shade trees
Trail Format: Circular
Map: Good colour with contour lines,
Brochure: General basic information on trail and environment
Markers: Distance indication on map/trail. Trail markers
Environmental education: None

Safety:

Accommodation: Safe
Warning signs: Dangerous places marked
Crossings: Safe and effective river/road crossing
Telephone: At start and end of trail
Medical Aid: Basic aid near start and end of trail
Hikers' safety *en route*: Safe
Water: Each day, rainy season only
Parking: Relative safe from public areas/veld fires, fenced enclosure

Accommodation Facilities

types:
(A) excellent
(B) standard
(C) rustic

Glenstrom
Boskloof, Goedgeloof & Proteavallei
Wolfkloof
Nooitgedacht

Accommodation: **(A)** Good quality hut/lux tenthouse with several sleeping rooms
(B) Basic hut or tent(s) provided
(C) Shelter against elements for sleeping or tent site only
Toilet: **(A)** Flush toilet inside hut (16 people) and toilet paper
(B) Separate toilet building, flush facilities outside hut (toilet paper provided)
(C) Pit toilet (max 50 m min 20 m from hut) or alt. hygienic system (toilet paper)
(C) None
Beds: **(A)** Single / double beds only
(B) Bunk beds OR
(C) No beds provided
Mattresses: **(A)** Thick (10 cm) high density foam or spring
(B) Thin
(C) None
Washing: **(A)** Shower and/or bath: with geyser or "donkey" pre-lit by attendant
(B) Shower and/or bath (hot and cold with "donkey"
(C) Shower (cold) or natural place to bath
Braai area: **(A)** Under cover barbecue, with windshield, lapa (1:10 people)
(B) Barbeque area, covered only, with grate.
(C) Barbeque (open) area with grate only or no fires allowed or possible
Fire wood provided: **(A)** Ample chopped wood (also for campfire)
(B) One only bundle for braai
(C) Dry treelogs with saw/axe provided or no fires allowed/possible (delete one)
Kitchenware: **(A)** Fridge/cooler and cutlery/crockery: provided
(B) Fridge/cooler or cutlery/crockery: provided (delete one)
(C) NOT provided
Kitchen: **(A)** Separate "kitchen"/common room with basin and tap inside hut
(B) Dish washing / cooking place near or adjacent to hut: (with table/surface)
(C) No separate facilities provided
Lighting: **(A)** Electric/gas/solar
(B) Candles/paraffin lamps or similar
(C) None of these provided
Heating: **(A)** Air conditioning or stoves in all rooms
(B) Heating by means of fire place; coal/wood stove in common room
(C) None of these
Cooking facilities: **(A)** Stove/hot plate/burner and kettle, pots & pans
(B) Stove/Hot plate/burner or kettle, pots & pans
(C) None of these

© Leon Hugo

Environmental Character: Definitions

A PRISTINE environment depicts an area where nature still exists in its more-or-less pure form: clean drinking water in streams, indigenous vegetation and animal life with no trace of human constructions, activities or sounds nearby.

In a NATURAL environment one could expect to see and hear human activities to a limited extent; such as e.g. associated with farming and forestry; Exotic plants (e.g. pine plantations) might be prevalent; as well as cattle, fences and constructions such as earth dams.

To hike through a RURAL environment would imply close contact with rural development and its associated noise, crossing of public roads, hiking on forestry / farm roads, visual contact with agricultural fields, cement dams, domesticated animals, etc.

A SEMI-URBAN environment will be typically an urban green belt or city park or similar where the built environment is adjacent to the trail and where the noise of vehicles and associated aspects of pollution will often be prominent.

Generalized Classification

Glenstrom to Boskloof	Boskloof to Goedgeloof	Goedgeloof to Proteavallei	Proteavallei to Nooitgedacht	Nooitgedacht to Wolfkloof	Wolfkloof to Glenstroom
67% Pristine	75% Pristine	83% Pristine	75% Pristine	83% Pristine	67% Pristine

Contact / Booking Information

Bookings/Reservations:

Tel: 0861 CAPENATURE/021 659 3500
e-mail: bookings@capenature.co.za
or visit
www.capenature.co.za

Difficulty Grading

1	1.5	2	2.5	3	3.5	4	4.5	5	5.5	6	6.5	7	7.5	8	8.5	9	9.5	10	10.5

EASY | MODERATE | DIFFICULT | EXTREME

← Start-Glenstroom

Wolfkloof - End
← Proteavallei- Wolfkloof via Vensterbank
Goedgeloof-Proteavallei

← Boskloof-Goedgeloof

Nooitgedagt-Wolfkloof Glenstroom-Boskloof
← Proteavallei- Wolfkloof via Kruispad
← Proteavallei- Nooitgedagt

Tsitsikamma Hiking Trail

Classification

A self-guided, self-catering open ended 6 day hiking trail with shorter loops

Environment: *pristine*
Accommodation: *standard*
Difficulty Rating: *easy to extremely difficult*
Facilities and safety: *very good*

GREEN FLAG TRAILS
ACCREDITED HIKING TRAIL
www.trailinfo.co.za

Accreditation underwritten by:
South African Hiking Trail Owners Association (SAHTOA),
Hiking Organization of Southern Africa (HOSA),
Southern Africa Tourism Services Association (SATSA).

Basic Trail Description

The Tsitsikamma hiking trail is a southern Cape hiking paradise, running through indigenous afromontane forests and mountain fynbos alternatively, creating a continuously varying landscape. Deep gorges and valley with streams of clear mountain water and beautiful swimming pools are alternated with distant views of the landscape of the interior mountains. Some of the best specimens of South Africa's national tree, the Outeniqua yellowwood, abound. Animal life includes baboons, vervet monkey, genet, bushpig and bushbuck. It is a haven for many lesser known bird species such as rameron pigeon, narina trogon, somber bulbul, forest buzzard, sunbirds and flycatchers.

Beginning at Natures Valley and ending 60-km further at either the Storms River Bridge or Village, this six day, one-directional (open-ended) trail takes hikers through the heart of the Tsitsikamma mountains. Shorter variations (2, 3, 4 or 5 days) are possible as everyone of the huts can be reached by means of vehicular tracks.

Optional equipment porterage (slack-packing) provides hikers with the chance of carrying only their day packs.

The Tsitsikamma has been the first trail in SA to be accredited and has recently been allocated the Green Flag certificate for a trail under excellent management.

Trail Facilities & Safety

Facilities:

Booking facilities and information: Internet, postal, telephone & fax
Reception office: On site
Road signs: Clear road signs to start
Access road: Tarred
Parking: Shade trees
Trail Format: Open ended with transport to be arranged
Brochure: Excellent
Markers: Effective trail markers
Environmental education: None

Safety:

Accommodation: Safe
Warning signs: Good
Crossings: Safe and effective river/road crossing, can be dangerous during flooding
Telephone: Partial cellphone reception
Medical Aid: Emergency numbers in huts
Hikers' safety en route: Safe
Water: Ample for drinking whole year
Parking: Relative safe from public areas/veld fires

Accommodation Facilities

types:
(A) excellent
(B) standard
(C) rustic

Kalander
Bloukrantz
Heuningbos
Keurbos
Sleepkloof

Accommodation: (A) Good quality hut/lux.tenthouse with several sleeping rooms
(B) Basic hut or tent(s) provided
(C) Shelter against elements for sleeping or tent site only
Toilet: (A) Flush toilet inside hut (1:6 people) and toilet paper
(B) Separate toilet building, flush facilities outside hut (toilet paper provided)
(C) Pit toilet (max 50 m min 20 m from hut) or alt. hygienic system (toilet paper)
Beds: (A) Single / double beds only
(B) Bunk beds OR
(C) No beds provided
Mattresses: (A) Thick (10 cm) high density foam or spring
(B) Thin
(C) None
Washing: (A) Shower and/or bath: with geyser or "donkey" pre-lit by attendant
(B) Shower and/or bath (hot and cold with "donkey")
(C) Shower (cold) or natural place to bath
Braai area: (A) Under cover barbecue, with windshield, lapa (1:10 people)
(B) Barbeque area, covered only, with grate,
(C) Barbeque (open) area with grate only or no fires allowed or possible
Fire wood provided: (A) Ample chopped wood (also for campfire)
(B) One only bundle for braai
(C) Dry tree/logs with saw/axe provided or no fires allowed/possible (delete one)
Kitchenware: (A) Fridge/cooler and cutlery/crockery: provided
(B) Fridge/cooler or cutlery/crockery: provided (delete one)
(C) NOT provided
Kitchen: (A) Separate "kitchen"/common room with basin and tap inside hut
(B) Dish washing / cooking place near or adjacent to hut (with table/surface)
(C) No separate facilities provided
Lighting: (A) Electric/gas/solar
(B) Candles/paraffin lamps or similar
(C) None of these provided
Heating: (A) Air conditioning or stoves in all rooms
(B) Heating by means of fire place, coal/wood stove in common room
(C) None of these
Cooking facilities: (A) Stove/hot plate/burner and kettle, pots & pans
(B) Stove/hot plate/burner or kettle, pots & pans
(C) None of these

Environmental Character

A PRISTINE environment depicts an area where nature still exists in its more-or-less pure form: clean drinking water in streams, indigenous vegetation and animal life with no trace of human constructions, activities or sounds nearby.

In a NATURAL environment one could expect to see and hear human activities to a limited extent; such as e.g. associated with farming and forestry. Exotic plants (e.g. pine plantations) might be prevalent; as well as cattle, fences and constructions such as earth dams.

To hike through a RURAL environment would imply close contact with rural development and its associated noise, crossing of public roads, hiking on forestry/ farm roads, visual contact with agricultural fields, cement dams, domesticated animals, etc.

A SEMI-URBAN environment will be typically an urban green belt or city park or similar where the built environment is adjacent to the trail and where the noise of vehicles and associated aspects of pollution will often be prominent.

	DAY 1	DAY 2	DAY 3	DAY 4	DAY 5	DAY 6
	25% Rural	42% Rural	83% Pristine	83% Rural	83% Pristine	50% Natural

Difficulty Grading

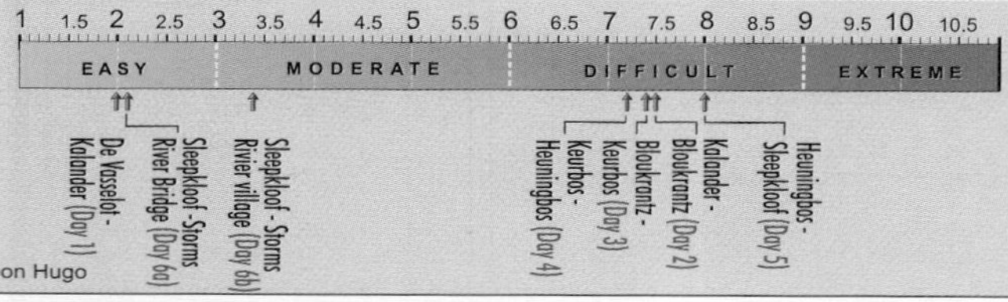

EASY		MODERATE		DIFFICULT		EXTREME
1 1.5 2	2.5 3 3.5 4	4.5 5 5.5	6 6.5 7	7.5 8 8.5	9 9.5 10 10.5	

De Vasselot - Kalander (Day 1)
Sleepkloof - Storms River Bridge (Day 6a)
Sleepkloof - Storms Rivier village (Day 6b)
Keurbos - Heuningbos (Day 4)
Keurbos - Heuningbos (Day 3)
Bloukrantz - Keurbos (Day 3)
Kalander - Bloukrantz (Day 2)
Heuningbos - Sleepkloof (Day 5)

© Leon Hugo

Contact / Booking Information

Bookings:
MTO Ecotourism
Nadia   (042) 2811712
Fax: (042) 2811778
E-mail: ivy@cyberperk.co.za
gpi@mto.co.za
Website: www.mtoecotourism.co.za

Whale
Hiking Trail

Classification

A self-guided, self-catering open ended
5 day hiking trail. Transport back to start available
Environment: *pristine*
Accommodation: *excellent*
Difficulty Rating: *moderate to difficult,*
varies between 3.4 & 7.5
Facilities and safety: *Excellent*

 CapeNature

Accreditation underwritten by:
South African Hiking Trail Owners Association (SAHTOA),
Hiking Organization of Southern Africa (HOSA),
Southern Africa Tourism Services Association (SATSA).

Basic Trail Description

The Whale Trail is named after the more than hundred southern right whales that return every year to the marine protected area at De Hoop to calve and mate.

The 54 km route stretches from Potberg to Koppie Alleen and includes five overnight stops. The trail offers unsurpassed natural diversity of the De Hoop Nature Reserve, where the fragrance of fynbos on the Potberg Mountains and the limestone fynbos plains, intermingle with the salty sea air of the Indian Ocean. Along the way, hikers can marvel at the abundance of indigenous plants and sightings of the last remaining Cape vulture colony in the Western Cape, numerous other birds and small antelope.

Unique habitats and natural contrasts make the Whale Trail of special ecological interest and an exceptional hiking experience.

Trail Facilities & Safety

Facilities:
Booking facilities and information: Yes
Reception office: Yes
Road signs: Adequate
Access road: Gravel
Parking: Shaded parking area
Trail Format: Open ended
Map: Good (full colour)
Brochure: Not supplied
Markers: No markers but distances frequently shown
Environmental education: Excellent. Poster in huts

Safety:
Accommodation: Safe
Warning signs: Needed at certain spots on coastline
Crossings: Safe
Telephone: Cellphone reception at stone cairns spots
Medical Aid: None along trail. Contact office
Hikers' safety *en route*: Good
Water: None on trail
Parking: Safe

Accommodation Facilities

types:
(A) ▢ *excellent*
(B) ▢ *standard*
(C) ▢ *rustic*

Potberg
Cupidoskraal
Hamerkop
Vaalkrans

✓✓✓✓	Accommodation: (A) Good quality hut/lux.tent/house with several sleeping rooms
✓✓	(B) Basic hut or tent(s) provided
	(C) Shelter against elements for sleeping or tent site only
✓✓✓✓	Toilet: (A) Flush toilet inside hut (1:6 people) and toilet paper
✓✓	(B) Separate toilet building, flush facilities outside hut (toilet paper provided)
	(C) Pit toilet (max 50 m min 20 m from hut or alt. hygienic system (toilet paper)
✓✓✓✓	Beds: (A) Single / double beds only
	(B) Bunk beds OR
	(C) No beds provided
✓✓✓✓	Mattresses: (A) Thick (10 cm) high density foam or spring
	(B) Thin
	(C) None
✓✓ ✓	Washing: (A) Shower and/or bath: with geyser or "donkey" pre-lit by attendant
✓✓	(B) Shower and/or bath (hot and cold with "donkey")
✓	(C)Shower (cold) or natural place to bath
✓✓ ✓	Braai area: (A) Under cover barbecue, with windshield, lapa (1:10 people)
✓✓	(B) Barbeque area, covered only, with grate,
✓	(C) Barbeque (open) area with grate only or no fires allowed or possible
✓✓✓✓	Fire wood provided: (A) Ample chopped wood (also for campfire)
	(B) One only bundle for braai
	(C) Dry treelogs with saw/axe provided or no fires allowed/possible (delete one)
✓✓✓✓	Kitchenware: (A) Fridge/cooler and cutlery/crockery: provided
	(B) Fridge/cooler or cutlery/crockery: provided (delete one)
	(C) NOT provided
✓✓✓✓	Kitchen: (A) Separate "kitchen"/common room with basin and tap inside hut
✓✓	(B) Dish washing / cooking place near or adjacent to hut. (with table/surface)
	(C) No separate facilities provided
✓✓✓✓	Lighting: (A) Electric/gas/solar
	(B) Candles/paraffin lamps or similar
	(C) None of these provided
✓✓✓✓	Heating: (A) Air conditioning or stoves in all rooms
✓✓	(B) Heating by means of fire place; coal/wood stove in common room
	(C) None of these
✓✓✓✓	Cooking facilities: (A) Stove/hot plate/burner and kettle, pots & pans
	(B) Stove/Hot plate/burner or kettle, pots & pans
	(C) None of these

Environmental Character

A PRISTINE environment depicts an area where nature still exists in its more-or-less pure form: clean drinking water in streams, indigenous vegetation and animal life with no trace o' human constructions, activities or sounds nearby.

In a NATURAL environment one could expect to see and hear human activities to a limited extent; such as e.g. associated with farming and forestry; Exotic plants (e.g. pine plantations) might be prevalent; as well as cattle, fences and constructions such as earth dams.

To hike through a RURAL environment would imply close contact with rural development and its associated noise, crossing of public roads, hiking on forestry/ farm roads, visual contactwith agricultural fields, cement dams, domesticated animals, etc.

A SEMI-URBAN environment will be typically an urban green belt or city park or similar where the built environment is adjacent to the trail and where the noise of vehicles and associated aspects of pollution will often be prominent.

DAY 1	DAY 2	DAY 3	DAY 4	DAY 5
75% Pristine	*75% Pristine*	*92% Pristine*	*92% Pristine*	*88% Pristine*

Difficulty Grading

EASY	MODERATE	DIFFICULT	EXTREME
1 1.5 2 2.5 3	3.5 4 4.5 5 5.5	6 6.5 7 7.5 8	8.5 9 9.5 10 10.5

↑ Day 1
↑ Day 2
↑ Day 3
↑ Day 4
↑ Day 5

Contact/Booking Information

Bookings/Reservations:
Tel: 0861 CAPENATURE(227 3628873)/
021 659 3500
e-mail: bookings@capenature.co.za
or visit
www.capenature.co.za

© Leon Hugo

General kit list

- ❏ Comfortable walking boots / shoes
- ❏ Daypack (for carrying water, camera, sun block and packed lunch on the walks)
- ❏ Long trousers (two pairs) and long-sleeved shirts (two) (for evenings and also sun protection)
- ❏ Zipped trousers that convert into shorts are great in the summer months. Lightweight, breathable fabrics that can be layered to add warmth are ideal.
- ❏ Waterproof jacket (particularly in the winter when waterproof pants are also useful)
- ❏ Shorts
- ❏ Comfortable change of clothes for the evening, including change of shoes (lightweight running shoes, Crocs, sandals or even spa-style slippers)
- ❏ Bathing costume and small towel (if travelling between October and March)
- ❏ Bath towel
- ❏ Camera, preferably small (spare film, batteries, memory card) and small binoculars
- ❏ Glasses / lenses (spare)
- ❏ Wide-brimmed sun hat (or warm hat in winter months)
- ❏ Insect repellent
- ❏ Personal toiletries
- ❏ Pyjamas / underwear
- ❏ Small torch
- ❏ Snacks – dried fruit, nuts, biltong, energy bars, biscuits and sweets
- ❏ Sun protection – sunglasses, high-factor sunscreen and lip protection
- ❏ Sweater and/or jacket
- ❏ Water bottle – at least one litre per person
- ❏ Thermos for tea / coffee if desired

Hiking trail for a day
- ❏ Shoes / boots
- ❏ Wide-brimmed hat
- ❏ Costume / fast drying shorts
- ❏ Daypack / backpack
- ❏ Water bottle
- ❏ Sunglasses
- ❏ Camera
- ❏ Binoculars
- ❏ Hiking pole / walking stick
- ❏ Sunblock
- ❏ Toilet paper
- ❏ Food

Hiking trail 3 days, 2 nights
- ❏ Sandals
- ❏ Warm jacket
- ❏ Beanie / warm hat
- ❏ Pyjamas
- ❏ Gloves / mittens
- ❏ Nylon stocking (over socks)
- ❏ Scarf
- ❏ Poncho
- ❏ Backpack
- ❏ Headlamp / torch
- ❏ Map
- ❏ Small garden shovel (toilet or coals)
- ❏ Mobile phone in a bag
- ❏ Refuse bags
- ❏ Duct tape
- ❏ Needle / thread / floss
- ❏ Emergency 'space' blanket
- ❏ Toothbrush & toothpaste
- ❏ Lip balm
- ❏ Glycerine soap
- ❏ Sunblock
- ❏ Insect repellent

- ❏ Body lotion
- ❏ Stove and gas
- ❏ Matches / lighter
- ❏ Mug / cutlery
- ❏ Small cooking pot
- ❏ Leatherman™ tool / knife
- ❏ Dishwashing liquid and sponge
- ❏ Pot scrubber
- ❏ Sleeping bag
- ❏ Sleeping bag inner sheet
- ❏ First aid (see list below)
- ❏ Food (see list below)

Hiking trail over 2 nights

- ❏ 2 or more shirts
- ❏ Long / short trousers (zip-offs)
- ❏ Rain jacket / poncho
- ❏ Cycle shorts (lycra)
- ❏ Gaiters
- ❏ Extra laces
- ❏ Backpack raincover
- ❏ Candles
- ❏ Water bladder / water bottles
- ❏ Nylon cord
- ❏ GPS / compass
- ❏ Straps (to repair backpack)
- ❏ Water purifying tablets
- ❏ Whistle
- ❏ Pen & paper
- ❏ Firelighters
- ❏ Wetwipes™
- ❏ Ziplock™ bags
- ❏ Mattress
- ❏ Tent
- ❏ Groundsheet
- ❏ First Aid (see list below)
- ❏ Food (see list below)

Food

- ❏ Stove
- ❏ Pots / pot-grabber
- ❏ Spare gas / fuel / waterproof matches
- ❏ Cup
- ❏ Can-opener
- ❏ Rubbish bag
- ❏ Knife / fork / spoon
- ❏ Fresh food
- ❏ Dried food
- ❏ Emergency rations
- ❏ A treat like chocolate / whiskey sachets etc.
- ❏ Tea / coffee / isotonic powder

First Aid

- ❏ Snake-bite kit
- ❏ Matches / flint
- ❏ Whistle
- ❏ Compass
- ❏ Candle
- ❏ Safety pins
- ❏ Rubber bands
- ❏ Bootlaces
- ❏ Torch
- ❏ Bandages / wound dressing
- ❏ Cotton wool
- ❏ Gauze dressing
- ❏ Adhesive first-aid tape
- ❏ Scissors
- ❏ Painkillers
- ❏ Antiseptic
- ❏ Anti-diarrhoea pills
- ❏ Water purifying tablets
- ❏ Tweezers
- ❏ Needle / thread
- ❏ Knee and ankle guards
- ❏ Disposable hot & cold packs

Outdoor gear retailers

Cape Town and surrounds

Seven Summits/Mountain Mail Order

www.mountainmailorder.co.za

Specialise in rock climbing, backpacking, mountaineering and expedition equipment

29 Vineyard Road, Claremont
021 683 6026

The Cairn/ Mammoth Outdoor

www.thecairn.co.za/www.mammothoutdoor. co.za

The Cairn specialise in outdoor clothing and equipment for mountaineers, climbers, hikers and trekkers. Mammoth Outdoor also features paddling, cycling and travel gear and apparel.

Cnr Natal and Calcutta Street,
Calcutta St Entrance (next to Inkwell Signs),
Paarden Eiland
021 671 4385

Outdoor Warehouse

www.outdoorwarehouse.co.za

Suppliers of hiking, backpacking, camping, 4x4, water sports and travel gear

Willowbridge Shopping Centre
Shop 1
Cronje Avenue
Tyger Valley
021 914 1358

Somerset West
The Interchange, 5 Dynagel Street
021 851 2304

Due South

www.duesouth.co.za

Suppliers of a wide range of adventure and outdoor products including hiking, backpacking, mountaineering, camping and mtb gear

Tygervalley Centre
Shop 544, Upper Level
Cnr Willie van Schoor Ave
021 917 8426/5

Canal Walk
Shop 514, Upper Level
Century Boulevard
021 529 3141

Somerset Mall
Shop 228
Intersection N2 & R44
Somerset West
021 850 1972

Paarl Mall
Shop 41
Cecilia Street
Paarl
021 863 5542

CAPESTORM

www.capestorm.co.za

Specialise in trekking, running, cycling, climbing, aquatic sports, ski, golf and travel gear

Canal Walk
Shop 104
Century City
021 555 0655

Cavendish Square
Shop CF43
Cavendish Street
Claremont
021 671 1626

Clock Tower
Shop 114
Clock Tower Precinct
V&A Waterfront
021 421 1149

Kloof Street
Shop 4
8 Kloof Street
Gardens
021 424 4583

Somerset Mall
Shop 63
Intersection N2 & R44
Somerset West
021 850 0188

Wynberg
45 Lester Road
Wynberg
021 761 2098

V&A Waterfront
Shop 123 Victoria Wharf
021 419 8882

Cape Union Mart

www.capeunionmart.co.za

Specialists in hiking, camping, trail running, mountaineering and travel gear

Quay 4
V&A Waterfront
021 425 4559

Blue Route Mall
Shop 51
Tokai Road
Tokai
021 715 8470

Canal Walk
Shop 152
Sable Road
Century City
021 555 2846

Cape Gate Shopping Centre
Shop u90
Okavango Road Interchange
Brackenfell
021 982 2000

Cavendish Square
Shop 9
Vineyard Road
Claremont
021 674 2148

Constantia Village
Shop 7
Main Road
Constantia
021 794 0632

Gardens Centre
Shop 54
Mill Street
Gardens
021 461 9678

Cape Union Mart Paarl
Shop 58
Paarl Mall
021 863 4138

Somerset Mall
Shop 82
R44 Somerset West
Cape Town
021 852 7120

Bayside Centre
Shop e3
Otto du Plessis Drive
Table View
021 556 3861/75

Tygervalley Centre
Shop 500
Durban Road
Bellville
021 914 1441

Mountain Shopping Centre
Shop 25
Worcester
023 347 1484

Zevenwacht Mall
Shop 014
Jan van Riebeek Road
Kuils River
021 903 0865

Travel & Safari Victoria Wharf
Specialises in travel and safari apparel and gear
Shop 142
Victoria Wharf
V&A Waterfront
021 419 0019

CUM Outlet Store
Shop B35
Access Park
Chichester Road
Kenilworth
021 674 6398/9

West Coast

Cape Union Mart West Coast
Shop L28
West Coast Mall
Saldanha Road
Vredenburg
022 713 4113/4114

Stellenbosch

Outdoor Escape
www.outdoorescape.co.za
*Specialises in hiking, camping, climbing, diving,
    fishing and kayaking*

12 Simonsrust Centre
Stellenbosch
7600
021 883 2444
orders@outdoorescape.co.za

Garden Route

Cape Union Mart Garden Route
Shop 110
Garden Route Mall
Knysna Road
George
044 887 0048/9

Cape Union Mart Knysna

Shop 6

34 Main Street

Knysna

044 382 4653/2

Cape Union Mart Mossel Bay

Shop 35

Langeberg Mall

Mossel Bay

044 695 2486/1841

Cape Union Mart Plettenberg Bay

Shop DL36/38

The Market Square

Plettenberg Bay

044 533 4030

Due South

Garden Route Mall

Shop 109

Knysna Road

George

044 803 8061/2

Tons Sport Cycles

Cycling and general sports shop

Shop 10

Queen's Sq.

Queen's Lane

Oudtshoorn

044 279 2423

Published by MapStudio™

Fiona McIntosh Author
Shaen Adey Photographer
Robin Taylor Designer
John Loubser Production Manager
Elaine Fick Project Manager
Carla Zietsman Editor
Braam Smit Senior Cartographer
Denielle Lategan Researcher
Myrna Collins Production Manager
Thea Grobbelaar Proofreader

Special Thanks

Base material for hiking maps (contours) kindly supplied by The Chief Directorate Surveys and Mapping, Mowbray and The Surveyor-General. Reproduced under Government Printer's Copyright Authority. For more information contact, Chief Directorate: Surveys and Mapping, 021 658 4300 www.w3sli.wcape.gov.za

Copyright Information

About the author

A freelance writer, photojournalist and the editor of OutThere Adventure and OutThere Travel magazines, Cape Town based Fiona McIntosh spends most of her time hiking, climbing and diving – all in the name of work. Recent book titles include The Table Mountain Activity Guide, Southbound Pocket Guide to the Cape Floral Region Protected Areas and Slackpacking – a guide to South Africa's Top Leisure Trails.

About the photographer

Shaen Adey has the enviable life of a photojournalist who calls the fun she has shooting in the outdoors 'work'. When she is not testing the latest camera gear, running extreme marathons, hanging off crags, scuba diving or training for her 2nd Dan in karate, she manages to fit in a bit of studio and book work. She has several titles tucked under her belt including a few international ones. Her favourite assignment was a two year stint with New Holland Publishers exploring Australia from rainforests, across deserts and into the outback alone. Currently she is a Gallo/Getty photographer living in Cape Town.

About the publisher

We are delighted to present our Hiking Atlas of the Western Cape. Map Studio™ always aims to have a multitude of versatile products to suit your needs. These products are accurate and constantly updated. We are proud to be the supplier of choice for maps and map-related products of Africa and the World.

We publish a range of Street Guides, Concise Streetfinders, Street Maps, Pocket Maps, Street by Street Navigators, Road Maps, Visitor's Guides, Road Atlases, Regional Wall Maps, Street Level Wall Maps, Provincial Wall Maps, South African Wall Maps, African Wall Maps, World Wall Maps, Educational Wall Maps, Custom Maps, National Geographic Adventure Maps, Atlases and many more.

If you find that our product offering does not suit your requirements and you require a customised map tailored to your individual requirements, let us know as we have a special department dedicated to this.

There seems to be no end to what we can do, but if you can think of anything we don't already do, please let us know by sending your suggestions to research@mapstudio.co.za

www.mapstudio.co.za

TALK TO THE PUBLISHER JOHNL@MAPSTUDIO.CO.ZA
SEE MORE MAPSTUDIO™ PRODUCTS AT WWW.MAPSTUDIO.CO.ZA OR CALL 0860 10 50 50